We Come From The Sea

# By Hans Hass

DIVING TO ADVENTURE

UNDER THE RED SEA

MEN AND SHARKS

I PHOTOGRAPHED UNDER
THE SEVEN SEAS

# HANS HASS

# We Come From
# The Sea

Translated from the German by
ALAN HOUGHTON BRODRICK

GARDEN CITY, NEW YORK

Doubleday & Company, Inc.

1959

Published in Germany under the title

*Wir kommen aus dem Meer*

To

MY DEAR BRAVE WIFE

# Contents

The phottgraphs in this book were taken by Jim Beudecker (1), Irenaeus Eibl von Eibesfeldt (7), Lotte Hass (12), Kurt Hirschel (9), Jimmy Hodges (3), Leo Rohrer (2), Gerry Weidler (1), and the author (52). The colour photograph of *Xarifa* was taken by Kurt Hirschel and the rest by the author.

For the underwater photographs were utilized the *Unterwasser-Leica*, system Hans Hass (cover by *Akustische-und Kinogeräte-GmbH*, Vienna) and the *Rolleimarin Hans Hass* (by Francke und Heidecke, Brunswick). All the underwater colour pictures were taken with the *Rolleimarin* with addition of flashbulbs (Philips and Sylvania) as well as, in some instances, with close-up lenses 1 and 2.

# Illustrations

## (*Black and White*)

## (Maps)

## (Color)

# ACKNOWLEDGEMENTS

For the assistance and support we received on our Red Sea expedition, we should like to thank the Austrian Ministry of Education for the subvention allowed us; the *Sascha-Filmverleih GmbH* and its director Anton Schuchmann; the Austrian National Bank; the *Akustische und Kinogeräte-GmbH;* the *Philips-GmbH;* the *Semperit AG* and engineer Hans Hornicek (all in Vienna), District Commissioner William Clark and Mr. Georges Serabis in Port Sudan; Hassan Effendi in Suakin.

Our thanks for assistance on our Australian expedition must go to Dr. Jerome Schweitzer and Mr. Paul Cherney (in New York): Dr. Gilbert P. Whitley, Dr. Frank A. MacNeill and Miss Elizabeth Pope all of the Australia Museum in Sydney: Dr. V. Coppleson, Dr. Tom Marshall and Mr. Ralph R. Doyle of the R.K.O. film distributors, also in Sydney: Dr. H. Flecker and Mr. MacDonald in Cairns.

We should also like to mention those whose excellent work and assistance were of such value to us in the reconditioning of *Xarifa* in Hamburg. Shipyard Work: *Norderwerft* and its proprietor Johann Köser, Messrs. M. Breuhs and P. Päpke as well as all the builders and shipyard workers; Masts, Rigging, Sails and Keel: E. Krassmann, *Stahlbau-Eggers GmbH,* Fritz Stein, Salzmann & Co. (Kassel); Hans Hinsch (Glückstadt) and the Huge Peters Shipyard (Wewelsfleth); Installation of Machinery: Klöckner-Humboldt-Deutz AG (Cologne-Deutz); *Reintjes Eisenwerke* (Hameln), *FMA-Pokorny Maschinenbau AG* (Frankfort on the Main) and *Ruhrpumpen GmbH* (Witten). Electrical Installation: *Siemens-Schuckert AG* (Erlangen), *Atlas-Werke* (Bremen), *Hagenuk* (Kiel), *Conz-Electricitäts-GmbH* and *Johann Hedemann* (Bremen); Ship's Installation and Supplies: Dr. Kurt Herberts (Wuppertal-Barmen), *Linde Eismaschinen AG, AFA-Accumlatorenfabrik AG,* Bernhard Schmeding, A. M. Niemayer, H. Hommel (Mannheim), M. Fehrmann, M. Noske Successors, *Triton Belco AG, Grünzweig und Hartmann AG,* M. Fienemann, *Armaturenwerk Niederscheld GmbH* (Dillenburg), John Pehrs, Theodor Zeise,

*Teppich-Schwabe, Minimax AG, Hartmann und Braun AG* (Frankfort on the Main), *Miele-Werke, J. H. Peters und Bey,* Georg Ott (Ulm), *E. B. Lattorff und Valan-Werke GmbH* (Bissingen).

For advice we thank: Admiral Bernhard Rogge, Vice-Admiral Leopold Siemens, Count Felix von Luckner and Consul Heinrich R. Wahlen as well as the German Hydrographical Institute, the German Lloyd, the Veritas Bureau, Engineer Paul Lembke, Captain Erich Kühn, Herr C. H. Greve and Herr W. Norling. For other valuable services we would thank Carl Prior, Th. Lexau, M. V. Joost, Georg P. Möller and the Federal German Office for Maritime Surveying.

We would also like to mention the following for their help and aid during the preparation for and the realization of the *Xarifa* expedition: *Herzog-Filmverleih* and our supporter Herr Herbert Tischendorf, *Drägerwerk* (Lübeck), *Francke und Heidecke* (Brunswick), *Arnold & Richter* (Munich), *Kabelwerk-Rheydt AG* (Rheydt), Mole & Richardson (London), Vinten Ltd. (London), *AGFA* (Leverkusen), *Deutsche Philips-GmbH, Anorgana* (Gendorf), *Barakuda-Gesellschaft* (Hamburg), *F. Gossen & Co. GmbH* (Erlangen), *Hartmann und Braun AG* (Frankfort on the Main), Hartley Cooper & Co. Ltd. (London), *Albingia Versicherungs AG* (Hamburg), *Norddeutscher Regatta-Verein, Deutscher Amateurradio-Club* and its chairman Rudolf Rapcke.

All other firms and persons, staff and assistants who aided us in the fitting out of the ship and the preparation of the expedition who cannot be named here please accept our most heartfelt thanks.

For assistance during the expedition we must express our gratitude to M. Max Gumpel (London) and Mr. George Tremain (Cornwall) in England; Messrs. Cymbron Borges de Sousa and the crews of the whalers, in the Azores; the members of the Austrian and German Legations in Venezuela; Lieutenant-Governor W. de Hazeth and Herr Gerharts in Bonaire; the Royal Dutch-Shell and Captain Lenderingk in Curaçao; Mr. Nelson Magner in Cristobal; the resident Ecaudorian officials in the Galapagos; the Ministry of the Interior in Costa Rica, the Yacht Club Italiano in Genoa.

For information and corrections I would thank Dr. Otto Schindler and Dr. Th. Haltenorth of the Bavarian State Zoological Collection in Munich, Dr. S. Dijkgraaf in Utrecht; Dr. Wolfgang Klausewitz of the Senkenberg Museum in Frankfort on the Main; Dr. Irenaeus Eibl von Eibesfeldt of the Max Planck Institute in Buldern and Dr. George Scheer of the Hesse Provincial Museum in Darmstadt. My thanks go to the

*Ullstein-Verlag* in Berlin for the obliging way in which they co-operated in the production of this book. With special deference I must thank Professor Dr. W. E. Ankel, director of the Zoological Institute of the Justus Liebig University in Giessen, for his many valuable suggestions.

# We Come from the Sea

IT WAS a dull, rather windy morning and I was sitting nearly sixty feet below the level of the sea at the entrance to a coral grotto on the Great Barrier Reef of Australia. I had explored the cavern and I was wondering whether, if some sudden danger threatened, I could hurry back into the deep, dark, tortuous passages like a snail withdrawing into its shell.

I was sitting on the outermost rampart and below me the wall of the coral reef dropped perpendicularly into the abyss. I could make out the cliff far down until it faded and then disappeared. Before me, seen as from a seat in a theatre, was the immense stage of gloomy, hostile waters in which innumerable fish would glide in from every side, swim towards me, eye me and then lose themselves in the distance. There were also two sharks among the fish.

Although the water was clear enough I could not perceive anything above forty metres or say a hundred and twenty feet away from me. But had some wizard endowed me with the ability to pierce through the waters then I would have been able to look down into a chasm greater far and more mighty than the Grand Canyon of Arizona. I could have gazed over a plain of deep-sea mud nearly two miles under the surface of the ocean, a plain that stretched as far as the towering bastion of New Guinea.

Rather more to my right I would have looked past the

Solomon Islands, between the doorway formed by the Phoenix and Gilbert Islands, and through the whole mighty expanse of the Pacific Ocean as far as the American shores, though, of course, my vision would have had to follow a curve since the seas cover the convex surface of the globe.

As I sat there with my little diving-gear at the entrance to the coral cave I watched the fishes through my diving-mask and they looked at me. All at once the feeling came over me that their eyes were the eyes of the sea itself, the eyes of a great, good-natured giant who may, from the outside, seem sometimes a little angry if the winds bother him, but who in his wide depths lies just as still and calm as the spirit of an old man purged of all the torments of life.

As in a flash, I imagined the whole sum of the seas as one immense, vibrating being which, as it were, lies prone and embraces the whole world, a being whose many arms, tentacles and fingers reach out towards the continents and caress them with the kindly, regular motions of the tides.

I realized how the sea, rising in clouds of mist into the air, showers rains and spreads its blessings upon the thirsty soil, how the waters may tarry saltless in remote lakes or come bubbling, splashing, streaming, rushing back again to the sea from which they had arisen.

Down here in the sea once upon a time had been lighted the mysterious spark which produced a marvellous evolution upon our lifeless planet once it had cooled down. Here, indeed, in the sea occurred the greatest of all mysterious happenings, the appearance of life itself. Here in the sea were formed the first sensitive creatures which, ever evolving, ever climbing higher up the ladder of organic development, eventually colonized the dry land and lastly culminated in Man whose spirit is capable of perceiving, of taking count of himself.

Were the waters, were the seas really but a great bath, a gigantic reservoir in which all this happened? Was this moving, whirling thing in which carbon, nitrogen and oxygen were dissolved as well as chalk and silicic acid, iron, aluminum, radium and gold, was it not an essential part of what we call life? Is not all life but a sort of pattern of development as exemplified in the blossoming of a bud—a result of the concentration and the arrangement, under the action of the sun's rays, of some peculiar properties possessed in the very substance of the seas?

There came into my mind those arid words in which, at the university, we were taught the lesson of the fossils, when we learned how the first algae, countless ages ago, ventured out onto the dry, naked rocks and there, after millions of years, developed into ferns and flowering plants. How the sea-worms crept onto the land and there became centipedes, spiders and glittering butterflies, how some fish, in shallow waters, staggered about on their fins and used them clumsily as legs. How these fish, from a modification in the form of their gullets, developed the first lungs and how gradually salamanders and frogs evolved from such fishes. How again some of these creatures developed a skin thick enough to protect them from evaporation and how thus lizards and snakes arose—how lizards became birds while other reptiles developed hairs and suckled their young ones. And, finally, how from amid the mammals, Man, the most highly developed of all living beings, Man endowed with reasoning powers, appeared.

Down on a lonely seat in the middle of the sea, I saw in my mind's eye the whole succession of land animals and land plants against the background of their original home. I saw them as marine beings in exile. While they pushed forwards, as pioneers, far from their native sea and in exposure to the air, while they perfected themselves, they must still always take great care never to lose their own supply of water, their most precious possession which must on no account be abandoned and must, indeed, continually be renewed.

Tradition induces us to believe that God created us just as we are today. Nevertheless, the evidence of many branches of natural science makes it certain that all the phenomena of life on this globe of ours—a world that was once fiery and fluid—yes, all the phenomena of life, ourselves included, are but the products of an astounding evolutionary process which first became manifest—possibly about one and a half thousand million years ago—in the seas which were then beginning to cool. Still, when we come to think of it, is such a method of creation really less flattering to our self-esteem, less wonderful, less divine? All the evolutionary possibilities of life must have been hidden and foreordained in the first primeval nucleus. There must have been in that nucleus all the stupendous evolutionary possibilities which led from the first piece of living matter right up to Man with his immense potentialities of spiritual development. This marvel, greater far than would be a single creation of all the different sorts of living organisms, took place somewhere in the womb of the ocean. I am never free from such thoughts and they have led me to regard with redoubled reverence and curiosity what I have seen and experienced in the seas.

# Riding on a Shark

THE sea does not willingly reveal its secrets. We are often
asked how it is that when diving we are able to avoid the great
creatures that inhabit the waters. However, to tell the truth, it
has always been much easier to avoid them than to find them.
For some of such animals we have searched for years in the different seas of this globe. We have dived in places where the natives seemed full of fear, and in spots where they prophesied for
us a sure and sudden death. But nothing happened. We had to
hunt through vast expanses of water before we met with one or
another of the fabulous monsters. But sometimes we were lucky
and such was the case on a memorable day in 1950.

It was 7th May and at the beginning of my second expedition
to the Red Sea. We had left Suakin in the morning. The flat,
desolate, desert coast, dotted here and there with the lonely
outlines of ancient ruined cities, dissolved into the air behind
us. We kept out about eight miles off-shore. The sea was like a
looking-glass and merged into the sky with almost no trace of a
horizon. The sun was still low and shimmered through the
vapour-laden air like a lantern seen through a pane of opaline
glass.

There were five of us in the boat: Wawrowetz the engineer,
Gerry Weidler, Mahmud, Lotte and I. We were all rather
drowsy. The men had not shaved and we yawned as we waited

for the moment when we might see, ripping through the waters, the sickle-shaped fin-tips of a great manta ray.

On my first trip to this region I had been lucky enough to swim quite close to one of these animals and to photograph it under-water. My photographs were published in illustrated magazines throughout the world and this time mantas were to be among the star performers in the film we were making. Lotte stood next to me on the bow with her camera prepared to shoot. Behind us, ready for use, there lay neatly arranged, masks, harpoons, diving-gear and under-water cameras.

The sea was dead calm. We could see far down into the clear waters but not one fish could we find. Only small ptero-pods drifted by. I pulled out some of them. In the hollow of my hand they fluttered about still very lively and flapped their wings like small butterflies.

'Not a bad sign,' I said to Lotte. 'It was just like this the last time. It seems that mantas relish these little creatures as titbits.'

Not long afterwards we saw in the distance a stream of foam above which a great number of birds were hovering or ruffling about. We drew nearer. Under the churning water we could get a glimpse of a great black shadow. The stream of foam moved steadily and slowly forwards. All at once the birds seemed to take fright. They broke up. The foam smoothed out and when we got to where it had been nothing more was to be seen.

All the same we moved crisscross back and forth over the spot and peered down into the abysmal depth of the pellucid water. But nothing save pteropods was to be seen. The birds, also, got over their alarm and gathered together again but a little farther ahead than before. We made for them. Then, after about five minutes, Mahmud, in a state of great excite-ment, grabbed my shoulder.

We looked behind us. Some way off, almost where we had been sailing to and fro, there stood up from the surface a tall, black triangle. It looked like the dorsal fin of a shark, only much larger. It might, indeed, have been a piece of wood but where had it come from? The sea was here two hundred and

(ABOVE) A manta with unusual pigmentation. The large white areas on either side of the head reach back as far as the eyes. (BELOW) A manta ray, devil fish, or eagle fish (*Manta birostris*), fifteen feet across. The pilot fish actually swim inside its wide-open mouth.

fifty fathoms deep, and then, again, the triangle was moving slowly along the water.

We put about and made our way back. We slowly came to the conclusion that some animal or other was swimming along, but it must be an animal of most unusual size. Through the clear, calm water we could make out distinctly enough a shadow that appeared to have no end. I cut off the motor about a hundred yards from the object and put on my flippers.

Mahmud rolled his eyes and started an excited pantomime. He bent down as though he was going to catch hold of a heavy burden, and place it on his shoulders, straightened up as though he had been Atlas bearing all the weight of the earth and then he let the burden slip down sideways and rolled his eyes. This procedure he repeated several times. He was much put out that I could not understand what he meant.

'Shall we row after you?' Gerry asked.

'Yes, but very carefully and gently.'

'It's got some sort of spots or stripes,' added Wawrowetz. I hung the under-water camera round my neck and slipped into the sea. The harpoon rope was fastened with a loop to my shoulder. Thus I had my hands free for swimming and taking photographs but I could also grab my spear if I needed it. The water was pleasantly warm. Below me yawned an immense abyss. I swam away from the boat and in the direction of the fin. It was moving very slowly along the surface and its rear edge was jagged.

The nearer I got the more difficult it was for me to control my nerves. In spite of myself I could not help thinking of the tales about men who had suddenly disappeared from the sea's surface and had never been seen again. Maybe a cry might be heard or a spot of blood seen, and then, again, they might vanish silently without leaving a trace.

No known danger can be so terrifying as the unknown menace, the invisible horror which our imagination inevitably exaggerates with all sorts of horrible details. Above water the mysterious fin was so near that I almost thought I could grasp it, but under-water I could see nothing, only empty,

The first under-water photograph of a whale shark (*Rhincodon typus*). This rare animal may reach a length of sixty feet and feeds on plankton.

blue, bottomless sea. My sole guide was the shaft of silvery arrows darted by the sunlight. They spread out in vibrating rays wide into the depths and met again, far, far below where my own shadow fell.

At last, however, I perceived some blurred outlines. The veil lifted and I was able to see quite clearly. What I beheld was so extraordinary that I hung motionless in the water. Ahead of me was gliding along a shark fully twenty-five feet long. His whole gigantic body was flecked with hundreds of white spots.

He kept at an almost even depth just under the surface and the immense, crescentric tail-fin swung very slowly from side to side. Towards the beast's foreparts the spots were small and very numerous, farther back they became larger and merged into lines. Between the lines were protruding ridges, the most marked of which ended in the root of the tail.

But the most extraordinary thing about the monster was his mouth, for this was placed, not as in all other sharks somewhat back, under the point of the nose and towards the belly, but quite far forwards and at the very end of the head. Moreover he held his mouth slightly open and I could see that it had what may be called lips. Despite his terrifying appearance and gigantic size, the animal seemed good-tempered and harmless. I remember thinking that he was rather like a great garden plot, decked with ox-eye daisies, floating along under the surface of the water.

From pictures in scientific works as well as from a stuffed specimen I had seen in the London Natural History Museum, I recognized the shark at once. It was a specimen of the largest of all the shark tribe, a whale shark, or *Rhincodon typus*. Since one of these had been first described by a South African zoologist in 1849, such sharks had not been sighted, from ships, more than a hundred times. This shark lives in tropical seas, the Indian Ocean, the waters near the Philippines and off Southern California. Some of the specimens sighted are reported to have been of the almost incredible length of twenty metres or over sixty feet and to have weighed up to ten tons. Mostly the animals

were swimming calmly and slowly alone just under the surface
and they seemed to be harmless.

They feed, as do the giant rays, the mantas, on plankton
which they filter from the water with their fimbriated gills.
William Beebé encountered, on his Zaca Expedition, a whale
shark twelve metres long which one of his men harpooned
from the boat. The shark at once dived but surfaced again a
quarter of an hour later. When Beebe's men tried to harpoon
him again, his skin appeared to have stiffened, indeed to have
changed into armour against which the steel harpoon-points
crumpled up. From close quarters Beebe fired two revolver
bullets into the creature's head but the giant swam quite peacefully on his way. The cable of the first harpoon was fastened
to the expedition's ship but the tension became too great and
the point came off. With regular tailstrokes, as if nothing had
happened, the monster disappeared slowly into the distance.

Williamson, when he was in his 'submersible boat', came upon
a whale shark too, and filmed the spotted skin of the animal
through the glass, but never, to my knowledge, had a swimmer
observed a whale shark under the water.

My shark in the meantime had noticed me. He hung, as
though pendant from his dorsal fin, just under the surface and
squinted across with his little eyes towards me. It did not seem
to bother him in any way when I swam nearer towards him.

I was so excited that, at first, I snapped a number of quite
useless pictures. I had forgotten to focus properly and to allow
for the parallax of the viewfinder. None of these shots turned
out to be of any value. Moreover, I was constantly beset by the
thought that the beast might get frightened at my intrusion and
suddenly plunge right down into the depths. But the monster did
not get alarmed and did not dive away. With admirable com-
posure he just went swimming along.

Each time I surfaced I could hear excited cries from the boat
—they all wanted to know what I had seen. Gerry, with flourishing harpoon, was up in the bow and kept on shouting to me and
asking whether he should come to my aid. I yelled back that the

Gerry alongside the shark which let us come quite close. We were even able to catch hold of his fins and ride him.

shark was perfectly harmless but that Gerry should come all the same.

Now I was not two yards from the monster's body. It was astounding that my presence did not seem to disturb the creature in the slightest. I swam right up to him and even touched his skin. It was rough like fairly coarse sandpaper and the white blobs looked as though they had been dabbed on with a thick brush. Between the dots there ran, moreover, narrow white wavy lines which, as they merged into a confused pattern, might have been reflections of sunlight. Slowly the body glided past me and the great tail-fin swung in my direction. That made me feel very daring and I grabbed hold, with my two hands, to the upper end of the fin. At once I was shoved, quietly but with entirely irresistible strength, off away. The tail took me six feet to the left, then six feet to the right. But the movements became more rapid. Obviously the beast was vexed.

I let go fast enough. Perhaps I had frightened him away. However, to my relief his progress soon got slow again, and the good-natured fellow swam on as unconcernedly as before.

Gerry was now a little way off just beneath the surface. He was an excellent swimmer and had joined up with us just out of lust for adventure. Hardly, however, had he imagined that in the third week out he would be swimming in the bottomless sea after a shark twenty-five feet long. I motioned to him to come closer and we approached the shark amidships so to speak. Thus I could take photographs which showed the animal's size in comparison with that of a man. I was quite myself again and able to concentrate on my work. Methodically I photographed the shark from all angles. When, later on, we studied the pictures, we realized that no one had really had a correct idea of the shape of the creature's head. In most drawings this is shown as though it had a raised forehead. Apparently these pictures were made from dead specimens which had been hauled on land. In these the head, from its own weight, had sunk downwards towards the ground. Anyway, my shark showed no signs of such an intellectual forehead. The line of the back ran quite straight as far as the upper lip while the belly swelled out to a thick 'throat' that reached the under lip. Therefore, the mouth lay just under the surface of the water, a very convenient position since it is there that the most plankton is to be found.

By this time the whale shark had also spotted the boat and made a broad swirling curve to approach it. Our cockleshell pitched and tossed while Lotte and Wawrowetz scrambled over the benches and changed films and lenses. Of their first photographs too, none, as we later found out, was of any use.

I swam towards the boat and grabbed my cine-camera.

'What about me?' Lotte looked excitedly with wide-open eyes at me. 'Shall I come too?'

'A bit later on.'

I bawled out to Gerry to dive near the shark, to swim near him but not to touch the animal.

'In front of him or sideways?'

'Diagonally from behind.'

We went quickly under the water. I held my breath for I had the viewfinder filled with what looked as though it would be the finest picture I had ever taken. There was the shark, like a submarine, and little, tiny men swimming about it.

The camera mechanism hummed away, then, suddenly, it stopped. I turned the crank, shook the case, but nothing happened. I banged on the thing with my fist but the camera had gone dead. The film-spool must have jammed. There was nothing for it. The case had to be opened and the film pulled along a bit. Cursing and swearing to myself I made for the boat and pushed the camera into Wawrowetz's hands.

'Take the other in the meantime,' suggested Lotte and held out our second cine-camera. I grabbed hold of it and hurried back to the shark.

The situation was really grotesque. The second camera was provided with a telephoto lens which we used for close-ups when we wanted detailed pictures of small fishes. Now, here was this unique creature in remarkably clear water with streaming sunshine, and I had in my hands a camera which, with the best of good luck, could take in only a third of the monster. Even when I moved off to the maximum range, I had only half the body in the picture. It was just as though I had gone giraffe-hunting armed with a butterfly-net. All the same I was able to film a few interesting close-ups.

By now the whale shark had settled down at about ten feet below the surface and the first thing I did was to examine one of his eyes. It was small and very mobile. It reminded me of the eye of an elephant. In the one beast as in the other there is a small peep-hole in a thick hide, a tiny aperture through which the animal's self observes the world. The expression of the shark's eye seemed to be one of cleverness, even of intelligence. While I swam towards the shark and, at the same time, focussed my camera, the beast regarded me with interest. I stopped and let the shark glide by past me. I could see how his eyes remained fixed upon the camera and how he turned his eye far backwards. I thought it was like that of a passenger in a submarine who was watching me with careful curiosity.

Quickly I wound up the spring of the camera again, and swam on a little ahead of the shark. My next shot I started from in front of his head. This time I set a fixed focus of a metre and a half and swam directly over the back towards the farthest tip of the tail, so that even if I managed, with this camera, to get in only a part of the animal, still the film would give an idea of the expanse and the size of the giant. Again I wound up and swam again along the shark towards his head. Although he was swimming slowly it was no easy job to over-take him. From time to time, I had, like a dolphin needing air, to rise up to the surface.

Now the time had come to photograph the mouth. Before the shark's half-opened jaws there were scurrying about a dozen small pilot fish swimming in and out of the black cavern as though it were the simplest and most ordinary thing in the world. Some of them pushed out a little into the open water but as soon as my purring camera and I drew near they took refuge inside the jaws. There is a widely held belief that these fish guide sharks to their booty—hence the name 'pilot fish'. We were, however, never able to observe any such manœuvres

Pilot fish in front of the shark's slightly open mouth.

which, in this case, anyway, would have been practically speaking impossible, for pilot fish certainly cannot steer sharks towards plankton.

What then are the pilot fish after, what do they look for in the huge gullets? I came to the conclusion that here was something similar to what I had observed with mantas in whose wide-open jaws I had also seen pilot fish which there feed upon small, parasitical Crustacea. There is a real symbiosis, a community of interest which is of mutual advantage. The pilot fish clean the jaws of mantas and whale sharks, cleanse them from clinging parasites, and in return the giants allow the fish to live in their mouths and do not gulp them down. This is an admirable arrangement for the pilot fish since, in this way, they find plenty of food and are effectively protected from fish of prey.

I dived under the shark's belly and filmed some slender sucker fish that were swimming close to his skin. One of them suddenly broke away and darted off to snatch at a small fish.

This apparently trivial incident gave the answer to a question that had long puzzled us. Up to this time it had been assumed that sucker fish attach themselves with the sucking-disc they have on the tops of their heads onto the bodies of sharks and other great marine creatures to enjoy a free ride and to feed on the crumbs that drop from the repasts of their hosts. But, as against this theory, we had been surprised to note that these fish, at least during the daytime, make absolutely no use of their sucking-disc. They do, indeed, swim very close to the skin of their hosts, but we seldom saw any of these fish actually attached to it. I had, in fact, been able to check off this observation on my own body. Small sucker fish had come swimming up to me as though they had imagined that I was a shark. They kept under my belly and if I disturbed them they switched over and took up a position between my legs. In this way they would accompany me for considerable distances, but never had one of them as much as touched me with its sucking-disc.

The sucker fish obviously use the great marine animals as a means of protection and as hiding-places. By swimming close to the bodies of their hosts they are able to get, unperceived, close up to small fish. We have always noted that these never show any fear in the presence of a large marine animal. Obviously their instinct tells them that they are altogether too small fry to be worthy of the sea-giants' attention. For the big carnivorous sharks these fish are not large enough to count as potential prey, for the great plankton eaters they are of too great size and they swim too fast. Therefore they let the monsters swim through their shoals and are neither frightened nor disturbed. And for this reason also the sucker fish hides against the bodies of the giants.

'The camera's all right now,' I heard Wawrowetz call out as I surfaced, so I swam quickly to the boat and grabbed what he held out in his hands. I had lost all feeling for space or time. It was as though through a cloud that I saw Wawrowetz lean over, take one camera away and hang another round my neck. Although I had been exerting myself to the utmost I did not want to take even a minute's rest. If you have waited years

Two sucker fish (*Echeneis naucrates*) close to the whale shark's body. Sometimes small sucker fish would swim with us as though we were sharks.

for something, and then it finally does happen, your body responds to a quite new scale of demands upon it.

Gerry had by now disappeared and I had to wait until he came up again.

'We're going to carry on,' I yelled.

'What . . .' came back the answer.

'Dive, swim close to him but don't touch him.'

'O.K.'

Once again I felt exhilarated at the unique spectacle.

The camera ran for two or three seconds and then the buzzing sound became noticeably higher. I was ready to cry with rage and disappointment. All the strain counted for nothing against my helpless despair. This time the film perforation was torn and the catch went churning uselessly on. This was the reason for the sudden increase in speed and also for the higher hum. The camera would have to be opened and the film put in place anew.

It needed all the self-control I could command to keep my head. I swam to the boat and clambered in. I dried my hair and hands with Lotte's towel and then opened up the camera to get it to work again. Meanwhile the shark came quite close to the boat; maybe he wanted to see what was the matter with me. But, no, what he really was looking for was something else. He shoved his head right under our keel and then began to rub his body against it.

Mahmud skipped excitedly from side to side and I then realized what he had meant by the queer pantomime he had gone through earlier. In order, apparently, to rid themselves of troublesome parasites, the whale sharks display a tendency to swim towards fishing-boats, against which they scratch themselves. If it happens that the shark is exceptionally large, and if he performs his toilet rather more vigorously than usual, it may be that he lifts up a whole boat and topples it over. Thor Heyerdahl told me once he had the gravest misgivings when in the Pacific a huge whale shark swam under the *Kon-Tiki* raft and rubbed his back against the rudder.

This performance shows a remarkable likeness to the behaviour of mantas which also scratch themselves and for this reason are hated by fishermen. In the case of the mantas, however, the parasites attach themselves firmly to the inner side of the horn-like lobes of the head. In order to work these parasites loose the manta uses for preference the anchor-chain of a moored fishing-smack. He takes the chain between his horns and whizzes along it, so that he may rip the anchor loose and even carry along the whole boat with him. It is true that in the case of both shark and manta their behaviour stems just from very comprehensible hygienic preoccupations, but they may be calamitous for fishermen.

When the camera was open I laid the film carefully in place. Then the perforation tore again. I put in another spool. Then a cry rang over the water. Gerry, who was swimming a little way off, was beside himself with excitement.

'Another one, another one!' he roared.

So I put the wretched thing on one side, seized the other camera into which Wawrowetz had already slipped a new roll of film, and at once leapt into the water.

There really was another whale shark swimming along. He was rather smaller than the first and was approaching unconcernedly as though he was going to pay a visit to his friend under the boat. At a distance of about ten yards, however, he swerved off calmly to another direction. I followed him, but he was evidently shy for he speeded up a little. Although I did my best to entice him back I had to give up the attempt after about two hundred yards. He had become visibly alarmed and disappeared into the distance.

Possibly the two beasts belonged to one another. Sharks effect a real copulation during which the male twists himself in a ring round the female. It is difficult to imagine these even-tempered giants in a state of excitement, but apparently when they are in a state of heat they rush through the vast expanses of the sea in pursuit of each other while all other inhabitants of the waters look on in fearful wonder at the spectacle.

It is thought that whale sharks bring forth their young alive. Nevertheless, some American ichthyologists have mentioned an ancient story from Ceylon in which there is explicit mention of eggs discovered inside the body of a female shark of this species.[1] Still, it is not likely that they lay eggs since they could hardly attach themselves suitably on the sea bottom. Most probably the young sharks develop in eggs but then are actually born alive.

Nothing is known about the age to which whale sharks may live. In the case of fishes you can make a reckoning from the rings of the scales and from the layers of their otoliths, but with sharks there are no such pointers. In general, the monsters of the animal kingdom reach an advanced age—simply because they need decades to develop their huge bodies. Giant tortoises may live as long as three hundred years and large whales have also been credited with a life of more than a century. Since the whale shark, as a plankton eater, does not find in the tropics an over-rich supply of foodstuffs, there must elapse a considerable space of time before it reaches the size of sexual maturity.

I swam back again. The first shark was now hovering about a yard from the side of the boat—and on his back sat Gerry as comfortably as though he had been lolling on a sofa. Moreover, I noticed on the beast's body several rust-red lines or stripes which had certainly not been there before. They ran diagonally all over his flanks. When Gerry caught sight of me he slid down from off the shark and brandished his harpoon in triumph. Its iron shaft—which had been quite rusty—now shone as though it had been polished. Gerry had been rubbing it on the emery-paper-like hide of the shark. So the rust-red lines were further proof of the beast's marvellous patience.

Mahmud was beside himself with delight. He hopped about and did a sort of St. Vitus's dance as the two of us now clambered up onto the shark's back. We held on fast by the stiff leathery dorsal fin—and we rode the shark. Everything I had experienced under water during the preceding fourteen years paled into insignificance before this incredible reality.

An old Hawaiian legend tells of two shipwrecked men who,

[1]Gudger 1952, *vide* Bibliography.

at night, held on fast to the dorsal fin of a shark and were dragged along by the animal for several hours until they reached an island. From what we did that day I am inclined to say that such an adventure appears not to be at all impossible. It may well be that a huge whale shark carried the men near to shore.

'That's enough,' I said to Gerry, 'now you swim over his head and when you hear me filming give him one on the snout.'

'O.K.'

I swam forward a little and then with my film running made straight for the shark's mouth. I waved up to Gerry who was using the flat of his hand to hit the beast on the snout. The kindly old fellow opened his jaws wide and I finished off my reel with a shot of the inside of his white-fleshed throat.

The film critic of the *New York Times* remarked, later on— in an article which was indeed a very favourable report—that this photograph must have been taken with a camera lowered down into the water. I should like to assure Mr. Bosley Crowther, however, that his supposition was not correct. The whole scene was shot just as I have described above.

I should also like to refute the suggestion of a German ichthyologist who asserted that we had first of all stunned the shark with dynamite. That we had not done so can be easily proved. If we really had used an explosive then we should hardly have been able to photograph the pilot fish in front of the shark's mouth and the sucker fish under his belly. If there had been any explosion then these fish would of course have been all killed off.

I knew from experience with other sharks that they can be frightened by a cry emitted under the water. I tried this out with our whale shark but he did not react in any way at all. Then we held out one of the small oxygen flasks from our diving apparatus and let the gas drive with a force of a hundred and fifty atmospheres against his head. The whale shark turned a little to one side and that was all. For a plankton eater delicate senses are hardly necessary, especially for a colossus of this size who could have hardly any enemies and who, moreover, is protected effectively by an armoured hide.

Lotte, Gerry and I slipped on our diving-gear so as to be able to observe the animal more quietly, but we arrived only just in time to witness his departure. The whole great mass of his body came slowly into movement. His visit was at an end. Some invisible alarm-clock had warned him that it was time for him to take his leave. He swerved round and swam obliquely downwards into the depths.

It was with a feeling almost of reverence that we gazed after the gigantic beast for there was something majestic and solemn in the gradual disappearance of the giant. In the vast expanse of the yawning abyss he grew smaller and smaller. He seemed to shrink together, to become paler in colour and blurred in outline. At the last we could see only the rhythmical swish of his tail far down below us in the deep blue chasm of the sea. Then this last vision faded into space and the expanse of waters was as empty as before.

We were once more sitting in our boat. We were munching sardines and the rather sour local bread. It was only very gradually that we recovered from our experience. As I gazed out over the sparkling surface of the sea my thoughts went back to the past. I was remembering my former colleagues Jörg Böhler and Alfred von Wurzian and that day eleven years before when we had beheld, in the Caribbean, our first great shark swimming towards us. Then we experienced the poignant feeling that comes over you when, for the first time, you confront some entirely unknown enemy.

In those days too, in our imagination, sharks were the weird and uncanny creatures depicted in grisly tales told by seamen or recounted in adventure stories. But, despite our misgivings, we had dived in shark-ridden waters. In some way or another we had to come to terms with the sharks if we would achieve our goal which was the careful exploration of the wonders found at the bottom of tropical seas.

In 1937 I had, off the shores of the French Riviera, begun my career as a submarine hunter. Then in Vienna I had trained a group of diving enthusiasts. In 1938 we shot the first under-

The promenade deck of a sunken ship. When the wood has rotted away, the metal becomes overgrown with a rich variety of coral, among which many pearl oysters (*Meleagrina margaritifera*) open their sharp serrated shells.

water photographs off the Dalmatian shores and in the next year, 1939, we undertook an expedition lasting eight months to the West Indian coral reefs where we dived and took photographs. Four thousand under-water photographs, both monochrome and in colour, in addition to the first submarine film, were the harvest of this expedition. With these we hoped to be able to demonstrate that we were not only devoting ourselves to a 'crazy sport' but were also putting a new method of research at the disposal of scientific workers.

Up to that time the bottom of the sea had been known only from samples and specimens brought up by drag-net and grab from the depths. A few explorers had, indeed, gone down below water but they were clad in unwieldy helmets and diving suits. In free diving, however, it was possible to transform oneself into an amphibious creature and swim about with the creatures of the sea. In this way could be learned not only a great deal more about their modes of life but also about their reactions, their behaviour, the function of their senses and their intelligence.

Once I was convinced of these things I felt that my course was clear. I began to study zoology and I devoted my efforts to the perfecting of a breathing-apparatus which should be light in weight. First of all we experimented with compressed air but the noise of extruded air frightened the fish. We then consulted Herr Selzner, the chief engineer of the Draeger Works in Lübeck, who was an eminent expert in all connected with diving. At our request he adapted a U-boat surfacing apparatus for our needs. In this apparatus you breathed in pure oxygen and the expelled carbon dioxide was absorbed in chemicals. Thus breathing took place in a closed circuit and no bubbles were formed—and we could observe the animals in conditions of complete tranquillity.

In 1942, on an expedition to Greece, this apparatus proved excellent. We were able to push down into deep submarine grottoes and there to discover new kinds of sponge- and coral-fauna. I specialized in research work on the laws of growth in colony-forming Bryozoa and was able, through the assistance of the *Kaiser-Wilhelm-Gesellschaft,* to carry out further studies at the Zoological Station at Naples. In some scientific publications I stressed the utility of our methods for various special branches of marine research.[1]

In those days there was one vision ever before my eyes— that of my own research ship—for only with such a vessel could we hope to carry on intensive and fruitful research work in far-off parts, especially in the tropical coral seas. The ship must have laboratories, a workshop, a scientific library, a darkroom, storage space for specimens and all that was necessary for our diving operations. But where was the money to come from?

I wrote some books. I gave a number of lectures. We even founded an institute. By 1943 we had by our own exertions achieved our goal. I was able to buy for the institute a one-hundred-and-fifty-ton sailing-yacht with an auxiliary motor. She was *Seeteufel* and had served Count Luckner for his last voyage round the world. She was just what we wanted.

However, we were never destined to make an expedition with *Seeteufel.* At the end of the late war, the ship was seized, taken away by the Russian troops of occupation and we never got any further news of her. Of our institute there remained nothing but a few sheets of paper with a nicely embossed heading. Our little research group was scattered to the four winds.

The last of a dream? Well, no. I was quite determined to start all over again from scratch, as millions of other men had to do in those days. I still had a diving-apparatus and after a long period of waiting I obtained what was even more important—a visa. All alone I set off in the autumn of 1949 bound for Port Sudan on the Red Sea. After an absence of eight weeks I was able to bring home the first black and white photographs ever to be taken under-water in those waters.[2]

A film company got interested in the preparation of a larger expedition. Three months later everything was ready. I had

[1] Hass 1948.

[2] Hass 1952.

got back from my solitary voyage in January. In April there were six of us who turned up in Port Sudan.

All our future then depended upon our being able to make a good film. If we were lucky enough to do just that, then my dream of having my own research ship might be realized.

At first we had our troubles. Our professional camera-man could not stand the great heat. During some trial shots made in the shallow water of Port Sudan swimming-pool, he suddenly fainted. Then he developed symptoms of mental derangement. Obviously he had to be sent back home. We left him in Port Sudan—he was to take the next ship—and went off to Suakin.

That had been a few weeks ago.

Then came the news his condition had got worse and that the shipping company refused to let him on board. So I had to send Alfons Hochhauser, my right-hand man—we always called him Xenophon—back to Port Sudan to arrange airplane transportation for the camera-man.

So it came about that I had to take the film by myself. Since our expedition had been financed by advances from the film company, this meant that I was saddled with a very heavy responsibility. In his last lucid moments the unfortunate man had given me some explanations about how to handle and operate the big cine-camera. Today, at the most decisive moment, the most important underwater camera had come out of commission. . . .

The vision of my own ship faded away ever farther into the distance. We sat in a rowing boat barely eighteen feet long. Before me lay an empty sardine-box. Illusion and Reality seemed very, very far from merging into one.

Three days later Lotte and I dived near the entrance to Suakin harbour. It was a Sunday. We had been setting out each morning well before sunrise and had been prospecting interminable reaches of sea in a search for whale sharks. Today each one of us was to do what he liked. Wawrowetz and Gerry had got hold of camels and wanted to ride out into the desert. Xenophon, back from Port Sudan, wished to set to work and sort out our much jumbled-up gear. Lotte and I had gone off with Mahmud. I had an idea that I would like to show her how you kill a fish by the old, half-forgotten method of a hand-spear.

Near the reef where we had anchored there were fish enough, but all the same I had no luck at all. I was out of training, my arm was stiff and the fish evaded me every time. Every time when I dived down, they warned each other, by fin-strokes, of approaching danger.

Lotte watched me for a while, then she swam into shallow water and began to hunt about with a light underwater gun. I still persevered obstinately in my attempt. Near a tall clump of coral standing out directly on the rim of the old navigation channel I spotted the tail-fin of a motionless snapper half hidden behind a rock. I dived to the bottom at some distance from the fish and slowly made my way towards the coral. Then the tail-fin disappeared and in its place there was a slim brown shark.

All my pent-up fury went into a blow that did not miss its mark. The next second I was behind the shark. He was unusually small—only about as long as myself—but he was full of energy. The harpoon had worked loose and was tangled up in his tail though one of the barbs stuck in his skin. The point might at any moment pull out. I did not waste much time in making up my mind. I pulled myself nearer by means of the line and grabbed hold of the shark's tail. As sharks normally cannot turn their heads round far enough to reach their tails, I thought I was in a safe position. My shark, however, was the exception to the rule. Owing to his slimness he curved round, and at the same moment I felt a sharp smarting pain in my right forearm. As quickly as I could I struggled up to the surface.

I held up my hand but the shark had still got me. When he did let go, my arm looked as though it had been through a mincing-machine. The muscles were severed right to the bone and a great pool of blood was spreading around me.

I yelled to the boat that was bobbing about some three hundred yards away. Mahmud had let down the anchor and was

A black-tipped shark (*Carcharinus*) charging Lotte. She repulses him by shouting. Most sharks hate noise and let themselves be chased off by it.

sleeping peacefully. Moreover, as the wind was against us, he could not have heard me anyway.

'What's the matter?' Lotte called out as she came swimming quickly towards me.

'Stop where you are,' I yelled back, for I was afraid the blood would attract larger sharks. Then I managed to swim into shallow water, still pulling the shark after me.

Lotte gave a terrified look when she saw my arm. She swam with me and we both shouted as loudly as we could. Luckily my wrist had protected the artery, otherwise I should have been drained of all my blood. It was only when we got quite near that Mahmud heard us. He jumped up, pulled in the anchor and rowed in our direction.

Why I did not let go of the harpoon I do not know. I handed over the shark to Mahmud. He hauled it up and battered its head in with a cudgel. Lotte and I clambered up into the other end of the boat. She gave me her thick Turkish towel and I bound it tightly round the wound, but not a minute later the towel itself was soaked in blood. Then Mahmud took the cord from the outboard motor and used it as a tourniquet.

But now we had no cord to start up the motor and it was only after much excited fussing and manœuvring that we finally got under way. About twenty minutes later we were nearing the Suakin rest-house that is right on the quay and is one of the few buildings still standing in the ruined town. We saw three unfamiliar figures making signs to us from the terrace.

After all my bad luck, things now took an extraordinarily favourable turn. The people were the pastor of Port Sudan, his wife and a friend of hers who had made a Sunday outing to Suakin. One of the ladies was an experienced hospital nurse. The three at once put me into their car and drove off to the ambulance field-hospital in the nearest locality. Since it was there judged that my wound was serious they took me on directly to Port Sudan hospital.

Since you can never tell what a shark has eaten before he bites you, a shark-bite may always mean a case of septic poisoning. My shark, luckily, had given me a clean bite. I was sewn

The whale shark watching me as I film his eye in close-up. The expression of the small brown shark that nearly killed me is less friendly.

up and the following day with my arm swathed in a thick layer of dressings I was allowed to leave. However, I was warned not to go into the water for three weeks.

Another piece of bad luck for our expedition! With my left hand I typed out a first article for an illustrated magazine with which we had a contract. I must confess that what I related did not seem very credible. Within the space of four days I had held two sharks by the tail. The first one, twenty-five feet long, had shaken me off although we did manage to ride on his back. The second shark—exactly five feet four inches long and thirty-seven and a half pounds—had nearly killed me.

# The White Death

OUR first and foremost preoccupation on all our expeditions was with sharks and other marine creatures that are ready
to attack. This was a matter vital for ourselves as well as for
other scientists to whom we wanted to recommend our diving
methods as useful for research. If, up to now, tropical waters
have been closed to men that is because in these waters dangers
are always lurking.

To anticipate a little, I may say that we never did meet with
the fabled giant octopuses. No doubt there are some of these
creatures that grow to an immense size and are armed with
eight or ten tentacles. Huge specimens have been found in the
bellies of sperm-whales; still such monstrous cuttle-fish live in
great depths and are only very rarely to be met with in waters
accessible to divers. Most of the stories about life-and-death
struggles with devil fish must be relegated to the limbo of divers'
yarns—I mean gigantic octopuses as are often shown in American films—such beasts are made of rubber and worked by machinery.

As far as our experience goes much the most dangerous denizen of the seas is the shark. Although their offensive proclivities
have been much exaggerated, still these beasts have caused all
too many dreadful wounds and fatal accidents. A shark's jaw
is the most appalling instrument for murder in all the animal

world. A twelve-foot shark can chew a man's arm or leg clean off. An eighteen-foot shark can bite a man's body in two.

The shark's dentition is what is sometimes called a 'revolver' one. Just as in a revolver the bullets are automatically replaced as and when used, so are a shark's teeth renewed. They are set in several rows one behind the other. When one row is worn out then its place is taken by the next row.

It is possible to see in the embryos of many sharks just how these teeth originate. Ordinary scales grow in from above and below over the edge of the jaw and into the mouth where they develop into stronger points than those on the outside of the body. Both layers of skin take part in the formation of the teeth. The inner dermis pushes the dentine forward and the epidermis coats it over with the exceedingly hard enamel. The teeth are arranged in rows just as the body scales are arranged in rows. Moreover, since the shark possesses the property of being able continuously to change scale material into fully developed teeth, so he is able to renew continuously his teeth.

The modern scientific view is that from the sharks' teeth stem those of bony fishes, amphibians, reptiles, mammals and thus those of ourselves. In the long series of our direct and indirect ancestors there must have been animals of the shark family which were the first to 'invent' teeth. From sharks, teeth have been inherited by all the higher vertebrates which have adapted them to the various demands of their special and peculiar ways of life. So, then, at long last, even the great tusks of the elephant are derived from the placoid scales of sharks.

The idea that proud man must admit the ugly and horrid shark into our pedigree may shock many of us. But there is further evidence that shows clearly such relationship. Many animals reproduce or recapitulate in their embryonic development the characteristics of their remote ancestors. In Man also there are traces of remote antiquity. Thus the human embryo, in the fourth week of its development, presents four gillapertures which, later on, are transformed into other organs. The modern diver who manages to swim into the depths by means of a heavy and cumbersome breathing-apparatus may well regret this loss of gills. A man with gills in his throat would seem to us a monstrous product of the infernal Powers. But if we really had them we would probably find them just as normal as our pointed noses and the peculiar shells of our ears. We might, indeed, admire the beautiful gills in a pretty girl and the cosmeticians and fashion-designers would have yet another task before them.

The condemnatory word 'ugly' must be considered, when used in connection with nature, as in the highest degree subjective. In its way, every living creature is marvellously adapted to its surroundings and its needs. No animals can be called really 'ugly', not even worms or spiders or woodlice and, above all, not such a magnificent beast as a shark. At the lectures I used to give early on in my career I often aroused—unintentionally—a good deal of laughter when I described sharks as royal, majestic and beautiful. However, since those days other spear fishermen and sport divers have got the same impression as ourselves. The view of a shark as he sweeps onwards, in sovereign control of gravitation and the resistance of the water, through the expanses of the ocean, is a sight so fascinating that you cannot resist it. If then sharklike creatures do figure in our genealogy, why, there is no need at all for us to be ashamed of our origins.

Teeth—the astonishing link between us and the sharks—form also the best pointer for distinguishing between the different species. The white shark—the most dangerous of all and sometimes called 'The White Death'—has large, triangular teeth with sharply indented edges like those of a saw. The almost equally dreaded tiger shark possesses teeth that are bent and assymetrical. In the Australian grey nurse shark each tooth develops into a long, two-edged dagger.

Since sharks have no bones—their 'skeleton' consisting of highly perishable cartilage—the teeth are the only parts that survive for any time after the animal's death. In deep-sea mud such teeth are found in great numbers and they comprise specimens both from long extinct as well as from extant genera. Some of the teeth are of terrifying size. In the Cretaceous—about a hundred and thirty million years ago—there lived an ancestor of the present-day white shark which, judging from the size of its teeth, must have reached a length of from ninety to a hundred and twenty feet. Such monsters could gobble up at one gulp a beast as big as a full-sized ox.

It is, of course, just possible that such forbears may still exist. The researches of the *Challenger* expedition proved that the huge creatures still flourished at a period that, in terms of the world's history, is not really so long ago. We may remember that the 'primeval' Coelacanth, which was thought to have become extinct sixty million years since, turned up unexpectedly in 1938, when a living specimen was hauled up from a depth of thirty fathoms off the South African coast. The well-known English sport fisherman, Mitchell Hedges, tells in one of his books how once, off the coast of Cuba, some unknown animal ripped right through his thick manila rope as though it had been a piece of string.

In my writings I have, indeed, presented sharks as less dangerous than is generally thought. They are, in fact, not so dangerous provided you behave in a suitable fashion. All the same, and above all in tropical waters, you must be very careful. Even today we know really very little about animals of the depths. You must be everywhere, and at all times, prepared for surprises.

In those days of our second Red Sea expedition we were not so very prudent; now that I come to think back, I blame myself a good deal.

When my arm had healed up, we dived down onto a sunken ship near Ata. I had already partially explored it during my first trip to these waters. About sixty years ago she had, during a storm, struck a reef and had sunk to a depth of from about twelve to twenty fathoms. The bows were completely smashed to bits but the midship and stern remained in fairly good condition. What had been the deck lay almost horizontal and had, in the course of years, been transformed into a wonderful coral garden.

I examined the different species of coral which were more or less developed according to the rate of growth of each kind. I also filmed the fish that darted about amid the ruins. Here, just as in a normal coral reef, each kind of fish seemed to have quite definite homes which suited its living-habits. Lotte helped me with the camera while Gerry kept watch and held his harpoon ready to ward off any unwelcome intruders. All three of us were equipped with light oxygen apparatus with which we could hold out for as long as an hour in depth up to about ten fathoms.

When I had finished filming I made a sign to Lotte and Gerry and then swam to the surface where Xenophon changed the spool. However, when I got back down again I found Lotte alone; she was crouched upon a large sheet of iron and seemed rather benumbed. As soon as she noticed me, she signalled that she wanted to surface at once. I swam up with her. At the boat we had to help her to get her gear off, then, with a sigh of relief, she climbed in.

'What's happened?' I asked. 'Where's Gerry?'

'Don't worry, he'll turn up soon. He saw a grouper and swam after it.'

'Well, what about you, eh?'

'Oh, nothing much. I'm much better already, but at the moment I was so frightened that I could hardly move. When I saw Gerry disappear, my first thought was—what if a shark came along now? Then I turned round and there he was. I'd say that he must have been about nine feet long and he had dreadfully wicked eyes. He came right above me, veered to the left so as to stare at me with the right eye, then he swerved to my right and looked at me with his left eye. I couldn't have moved to save my life, I was sort of all congealed inside, but maybe he didn't want to do anything except give me the once-over——'

'Well,' I said, partly to cheer her up and partly to laugh off my own carelessness, 'now you've had your baptism of fire.'

'Yes,' and she smiled a little now, 'but it was a pretty cold one.'

I thought of Lotte's parents who had confided her to my care and I, too, felt a shudder run down me. Three years before, Lotte had passed her matriculation, and then, as she was interested in biology, had joined up as an assistant at our institute.

I had no idea then that she was preparing herself in secret to take part in an expedition. She studied photography and trained in swimming and diving—finally I had consented to take her with me to the Red Sea. Now that she was plunged right into the raw reality of an expedition she had astonished us all by her courage and her endurance. When we had got to Port Sudan I had said to her: 'Now, don't forget that for the future, you're a man.' She had quite understood and behaved accordingly.

After sharks, what gave us the most trouble were venomous animals. You must always be very careful before you touch anything on the bottom of tropical seas. There are poisonous corals which can give you a nasty burn—the so-called 'fire corals', which belong to the *Hydrozoa*. Then there are sea-urchins and starfish with very cruel spikes. And there are, further, many fish which have developed poisonous stings at their tail, on the gill cover, or on the dorsal fins.

If we harpooned a fish and it slipped off into a hole in the coral we were careful not to clamber into the hole without first making a close inspection. If you are unlucky there may well be a moray eel lurking inside. In the tropics these snakelike fish may attain a length of as much as six feet. They have poisonous teeth and if you disturb them they may attack.

Compared with such animals we found the notorious barracudas were, in nearly all cases, harmless. Breder, in his book *Marine Fishes of the Atlantic Coast,* gives it as his opinion that these large pike-like creatures have been the cause of many accidents which have been attributed to sharks, but we were not able to confirm this either in the Caribbean or in the Red Sea. Giant barracudas swimming alone did, indeed, sometimes come towards us in a threatening manner, but at a distance of four or five yards they always turned round and then followed us for a while—just like faithful dogs. Often they would split open their sharp-toothed jaws—but that was all. Only on one single occasion did I encounter a whole swarm of half-grown barracudas which seriously seemed to consider an attack. I showed no signs of alarm and kept still. After a while and quite of their own accord, they all swam away again. However, it is quite

An unusual shot: a brown shark (*Carcharinus milberti*) and a five-foot barracuda face to face.

possible that barracudas do not behave in the same way at all the different coasts.

I was very anxious to film a scene showing the harmlessness of these fish. I got an opportunity when, in a passage between two reefs, I came across a shoal of from forty to fifty barracudas stiff and motionless in the water. They looked well fed, though, here and there, they were snapping up a few morsels as dessert. When they caught sight of me they stared in their typically menacing way, then, one after another, they began to move and soon the whole swarm was making for me. They eyed me with curiosity. I hurried up to the boat and fetched Lotte. I asked her to scare them off with her hands. Since Lotte had just been an hour under water her own apparatus was not ready, so Xenophon gave her one of the spare ones.

'It's a bit big for you,' he said, 'but it'll do all right.'

She hitched it on quickly and we both plunged in. The barracudas were just where they had been when I left them. I guided Lotte to a coral where she could sit down and hurried some little distance away from where I thought I would get a good picture. The barracudas were kind enough to oblige and went through the same manœuvres as before. One after another, like fighter-pilots, they got together in close formation and streamed to-wards Lotte. I could see her in the viewfinder. She kept on look-ing from me to the barracudas and then upwards . . . suddenly she dashed with thrashing flippers up towards the surface.

I managed to catch her before she surfaced and grab her by one leg. I towed her back to the coral and made signs for her to sit there quietly. When the barracudas got close she should scare them off with her arms, just that. As, up to then, Lotte had always shown rather too much than too little courage I could not understand her unexpected panic. The barracudas were just inquisitive. That was all.

Lotte seemed to want to explain something to me but there was no time for conversation. The barracudas were back again. I pushed her down on the coral, made off, wound up the spring and then turned round. What did I see but Lotte with her flippers thrashing the water. She was on her way up again.

When we got to the boat it turned out that her behaviour had had nothing to do with barracudas at all. In his haste Xenophon had forgotten to tighten the screw on the breathing-tube.

Our diving-apparatus was so devised that the exhaled carbon dioxide was absorbed by chemicals contained in a bag on our backs. In former days divers used caustic soda but this proved to be dangerous if there was any infiltration of water. We adopted, therefore, a special sort of chalk prepared by the firm of Draeger. This compound was quite harmless but still had a rather bitter taste. Lotte's breathing-bag had been half full of water. She spat as she shook herself:

'Oh, heavens, that filthy, horrible taste! I began to notice it as soon as I dived but I didn't want to spoil the show so I put up with swallowing water. But then it became awfully bitter. And when you pulled me down again I thought I could not swallow. My God, what muck! . . .'

About this time Leo Rohrer came out to join us. I had cabled to him when our camera-man had got sick. Rohrer was an ex-cellent diver and could help me a good deal with underwater photography. He made his appearance in Suakin a week before we expected him. The sun had burned him dark brown and he seemed in the best of spirits . . . what had happened was that he had been so afraid my cable was due to some misunderstanding he had not waited for his tickets but had cleared out at once, trusting to luck. In Alexandria his money ran out, so he dived in the harbour, harpooned fish and then sold them until he found a ship that would take him on board—so there he was.

The five of us explored the reefs in the neighbourhood of Suakin and ventured, in fact, into some quite dangerous areas. I made all the observations I could on the growth of coral reefs while we watched and filmed the fishes and sharks which lived in those waters. We paid especial attention to the behaviour of the sharks.

Captain Cousteau, who a year after us also made an expedition to the Red Sea, has given it as his opinion that sharks' conduct cannot be predicted. I would not, right off-hand, quite agree to this judgement. It is true enough that in different areas sharks do not all behave in the same fashion—and this is true especially of Australia where we were to experience some surprises. However, all in all, the comportment of each genus seems pretty fixed and constant.

Since we dived often, and for some considerable time, on a given reef we got to know well enough the ways of the grey, brown and black-finned sharks which had their home there. Just as in the Caribbean, the sharks in the Red Sea have their definite headquarters where they can be met with again and again. Some of the animals indeed, which had clearly marked characteristics, we could easily recognize when we saw them again. Most of them put in an appearance as soon as we set to work. They would watch us for a while and then disappear for the rest of the day. If we wanted to film them we had to take our shots during the first half hour after our arrival. Sharks are what may be called the police of the sea. Their sense-organs are so delicate that they can hear, from a long way off, sounds such as the noise of an anchor being let down or of men diving into the water. Then they come along very swiftly to see what is going on. It often happens that the smaller grey and brown

Lotte with 'Dopey' a hundred and twenty feet down. This grouper
or rock cod (*Epinephelus striatus*) followed us around like a pet dog.

sharks suddenly shoot near to a diver and circle around him at close distance. Anyone who experiences this for the first time may, of course, think that he is being attacked, but, in reality, the young creatures are just giving vent to their play-instinct. In such a way a young shark tries out his strength. And then, of course, he does take a pleasure in frightening other animals. I have seen sharks dash about among swarms of fish or turtles though surely not with any offensive design but just to enjoy the reactions aroused.

Really big sharks, I mean ones of twelve feet long and more, are not often to be met with in the reefs and in any case generally swim past quietly on their way. If you come up against these large sharks the best thing to do is to remain quite still, then, in most cases, the creatures keep steadily on their course. In Australian waters the pearl-divers behave in this way. One of them told me that once he was almost asphyxiated from lack of air, but that, all the same, he clung fast onto a coral and remained there motionless until a big shark that was cruising nearby had quite vanished.

If you are spotted and if a shark comes heading for you and seems obviously bent on attack, then you should on no account show fear. If you swim off hastily, you will the more attract his attention and arouse his predatory instincts. It is the same with carnivorous land animals. We had found out, as far back as 1939, during our first encounters with sharks in the Caribbean, that even large sharks can be frightened off if you swim towards them without hesitation. The shark, of course, is accustomed to see all other creatures flee before him. If such a strange being as a man thrusts towards him and displays all the signs of offensive intent, then there is aroused in the shark a flight-reaction to which he tends to yield.

Furthermore, we often had occasion to notice that approaching sharks can be frightened off if a loud cry is let out near them under the water. No doubt many will laugh at this, but, all the same, underwater hunters have used this subterfuge successfully in various parts of the world. In 1943, by employing this means, three survivors of a German U-boat managed to save their lives off the West Coast of Africa. When they were attacked and even bitten by sharks they remembered, in their last extremity, what they had heard, and they were able, by holding their heads under water and by shouting, to chase the sharks away. Also, in an official report of the American Air Force—'Airmen Against the Sea'—it was recommended that flying-men shot down in the sea should shout under water as the most effective means of defence against sharks.

All the same, we must say that we have noted some exceptions to the rule. Some sharks, such as a species we were to meet with off the Azores, show absolutely no reaction to noise, and there are other regions in which the sharks seem to be impervious to shouts and cries—for instance, in the waters around the Greek islands, where, as we noticed in 1942, since the fishermen use dynamite charges, the senses of the sharks are, apparently, dulled by the explosions. The same must hold good for sharks which hover about in the neighbourhood of public bathing-beaches and thus get accustomed to the human voice, as also for sharks that follow ships and become used to the noise of the propellers.

All sharks, however, change their behaviour as soon as there is blood in the water. When a shark smells blood then his usual indecision, and indeed, cowardice, leave him and he becomes visibly restless and turbulent. His movements get nervous and twice as rapid as usual. His reactions can no longer be foretold. Still, all the same, some sharks in such circumstances can be very slow in attacking as is proved by the reports of shipwrecked men and of aviators who have been shot down in the sea and who, in some cases for hours or even days, have been able to keep on their way although followed by sharks. An American officer, whose ship was sunk off Guadalcanal, has told how sharks nipped little pieces off his body, one after the other. The beasts were around him all the time yet there elapsed intervals of from ten to fifteen minutes between the attacks.

Even more astonishing is the report of an Ecuadorian airman who carried on for thirty-one hours in the sea although both of his companions had died at his side and had been eaten by sharks. For the length of a whole day he had the sharks so close to him that he frequently kicked them with his feet; all the same, he was not bitten once.[1]

We have no opinion to offer concerning the preparation (copper acetate) developed by the American Air Force as a means for warding off sharks, for we have never used it any more than we have used iron cages. The chemical may afford some protection to those shipwrecked, but for under-water divers, especially when they are holding a wriggling fish in their hands—and that is when they are most likely to be attacked—the preparation would seem to be of very problematical value, for in these circumstances the sharks come up so swiftly that no substance with a repulsive smell could be released in the water rapidly enough to keep off the marauders.

Since, nowadays, there are more and more sporting divers who venture into the seas off tropical coasts, the whole problem of the shark assumes a great importance for a wide public. In the case of many shark stories it is hardly possible to determine exactly to just what sort of shark reference is made. Out of over a hundred different kinds of shark, eight or nine only are dangerous for human beings. In the 'under-water struggles' we see depicted in so many films, it is mostly the Atlantic *Ginglymostoma cirratum* which is shown. It is a quite harmless beast and although it looks like a real predatory shark, it has a small mouth and has never been known to attack a man.

It is entirely untrue that any damage can be done with a knife or dagger—however sharp it may be—to a really dangerous shark. The time-honoured old yarns about natives who slit open the bellies of attacking sharks are no more to be credited than the fable that ostriches stick their heads in the sand.

When a murderous shark is near enough for anyone to use a knife on him, then the chances of doing him any harm are slender indeed. The larger sharks have uncommonly tough, hard skins and their comparatively small hearts lie protected by layers of cartilage. In my opinion it would be quite impossible to cling fast to a shark as is often described. Moreover, even if

[1]Llano, *Airmen Against the Sea,* p. 67.

anyone did manage by some means to inflict a serious wound on a shark, the struggle would be far from over. First of all, the thrashing, the violent movements and the blood of the animal would attract other sharks and, secondly, a shark's hold on life is quite astounding.

There is a reliable report of a blue shark which was mortally wounded with a blubber-knife while a whale was being flensed. Nevertheless, the shark went on eating greedily until it was overcome by death and sank motionless down into the depths.

Far the best weapon of defence against sharks is a spear or a stick provided with an iron point. This, in case of need, can be held out in front of one between oneself and the shark. Cousteau, also, and the members of the Italian expedition—under the leadership of Vailati—which followed him a year later to the Red Sea, found such sticks very useful. If you have not to deal, simultaneously, with more than one shark, such an instrument provides an almost certain defence.

Professional divers have for long observed that a shark is by no means obliged to turn over on his back in order to make a bite. It is also a dangerously fallacious belief that sharks are harmless in shallow waters. On tropical coasts and especially towards the evening quite large sharks may come close to the beaches. There are many fully authenticated stories of children and dogs attacked in shallow water.

It is, of course, a fable that sharks follow a ship with a corpse on board. Sharks do follow ships but not because there may be a body laid out in a cabin, but in order to snap up the bits and pieces the cooks chuck overboard. When there is a burial at sea, the corpse is sewn into a shroud of tough sailcloth and provided with heavy weights before it is lowered into the sea. That a shark can do anything to such an object which sinks so rapidly into the depths can hardly be conceived.

On the other hand, it is very dangerous to dive off a ship into waters where there are sharks about for these animals are accustomed to gobble up offal and discarded food thrown away into the sea. A South Sea islander named Treackle dived in this way right into the gaping jaws of a hammerhead. Luckily the shark could not manage to bite the man's head off and Treackle, with great presence of mind, felt for the creature's eyes and pushed them in. The shark let go and Treackle was saved. For a modest fee he is quite prepared to show his dreadful scars.

I had a very dangerous experience with a shark when we had moved our headquarters from Suakin to Port Sudan and were exploring the reefs near the latter place. On that particular morning we set out for the Sanganeb atoll some eleven miles off-shore. Bill Clark, the Commissioner of Port Sudan, was with us. He was an ardent fisherman and liked to accompany us whenever his official duties allowed him. By about nine o'clock when we got to Sanganeb we already had several large fish in the boat.

We tied up to the long wooden jetty that leads from the precipitous face of the reef to the lighthouse on the flat surface of the atoll. While the rest of us climbed up to the top of the lighthouse in order to shoot some films, Bill and Xenophon went off to the northern edge of the atoll where we could see them busily fishing. They came back shouting and laughing. In just one and a half hours Bill had caught fully twenty-three fish which weighed altogether some two hundred and sixty pounds. I asked him for some of the larger ones, split them and threw the bits into the sea from the end of the jetty. The lighthouse keeper had told us about two hammerheads which often came up when offal was thrown into the sea. To film hammerhead sharks had, for years, been one of my dearest wishes and now, with the smell of fresh blood, I hoped to lure them on. Of course, I realized well enough that, in such circumstances, it was a pretty dangerous thing to go diving.

It was agreed that no one should follow me when half an hour later, equipped with diving-gear and armed with my underwater cine-camera, I went in; I floated down, keeping close to the precipitous wall of the atoll. Plenty of eyes were fixed on me as I moved about. Right above me, on the upper edge of the wall which there reached up as far as the surface of the sea, Lotte and Leo lay prone in the shallow water and peered down at me. A little to one side and close to the black outline of the projecting jetty I could see the shadow of our boat bobbing and swaying about; nearby was a light-coloured circle with a black spot on it—that was Xenophon staring down through the lens of the spy-glass.

Just below the jetty there was, swimming some six fathoms down, a black-finned shark. He was fully nine feet long. He was snapping and snatching at bits of meat which had got caught in the corals. Below me the wall of the atoll dropped sheer down to abysmal depths. But there were no hammer-heads anywhere. I picked out a coral block that jutted out into a sort of prow about forty feet down and seated myself astride it.

The shark soon spotted me and came along, obviously rather upset, to eye me over. However, when he had got to within three yards, he swerved round and swam off. He described a large circle, came back, then, once again, at a distance of three yards, he veered away. This performance he repeated four or five times more. From the filming point of view the shark was ideal. He always came head on towards the camera and when he swam off I had to get my reel going again.

I sat slewed rather sideways on my bit of coral and concentrated all my attention on the shark. Then, all of a sudden, I felt a peculiar sensation in my back and turned round.

There right behind me was a shark, but a huge one this time. He had come swimming up, keeping close to the wall, and from the other side, until he was close to me. From his shape and colour I saw at once what sort of a shark this one was.

He was a White Shark. The White Death.

Generally speaking, these creatures live in the open sea and only very seldom visit the coasts. For a moment that seemed like eternity, I watched the great, broad head moving towards me. His mouth was stretched into an evil outline. Thoughts chased each other swift as lightning through my brain. My spear was floating over my shoulder but it was too late to think of attacking him. It was six feet long and the shark was now within four or five feet of me. I let out a yell and made motions with my hands and feet against the aggressor, but calmly and inexorably

The research ship *Xarifa* under sail in the Pacific Ocean.

Shy and hard to photograph: the yellow-marked angel fish.

One of the most beautiful of the coral fish in the Red Sea: the peacock fish.

the cruel mouth drew near. The creature obviously intended to take a bite out of me. Perhaps he thought I was a piece of meat anyway. Clearly the shark had eaten not long before and had the taste of blood in his mouth.

Among all the thoughts that jostled through my mind there was one that jarred me as though I had received an electric shock. All I had to defend myself were my naked hands.

I must at all costs avoid hitting the shark on his nose for then he would just snap his jaws together and my arm would be caught between his teeth. So, when his snout was almost touching me, I drove a blow with my right hand behind his mouth and against his gills. The impact certainly did not hurt the animal but the unexpected stroke did frighten him. I felt the water surge against me. The shark had turned round and was swimming away.

He did swim away but he swam in a circle and returned to me. This time I grasped my harpoon and shoved it against his head. The point hardly grazed his skin but he swirled off again. Then I realized that another shark—the one I had been filming —was also preparing to attack.

With all the strength I could muster I drove the spear round sideways and hit him. Then I pulled my weapon in again and shot out a hit at the other shark. Still, it was clear I could not ward off attacks from both sides at once. The shaft of my spear was so long and offered so much resistance to the water that I could not turn it fast enough from one side to the other. There was only one thing left—the most dangerous of all. Flight.

As fast as my flippers would carry me I shot upwards—close against the wall of coral. The sharks hesitated for a moment and then, with their tails thrashing, they darted after me. I managed with my harpoon to keep them off me but since, as I rose, I had to keep my eyes downwards I scraped myself badly once or twice on both back and shoulders against the projecting teeth of the coral. Then I got to the surface, quite close to Lotte and Leo. I took them with me and plunged into shallow water. The sharks were still there. They kept quite close in, stopped from time to time and then swam excitedly to and fro along the edge of the reef.

We held our spears out in front of us and awaited the attack, but the sharks did no more than glare threateningly at us. Then finally they calmed down. The white shark made one final turn before he glided downwards. The other shark swam away in the opposite direction.

Our knees were a little wobbly as we clambered up onto the small jetty. If the level of the water had been rather higher then the adventure might well have had a sad ending. We had struck a shark that meant business. The first one had come for me probably because he grudged the other the meal. It was like two dogs when one of them finds a bone. In this case I very nearly was the bone.

Since that day I have never again met with a large white shark. I have read a number of reports by divers who have told of encounters with such creatures but I am not convinced that, in all cases, these really were white sharks. Anyway, if all of them behave as did my specimen then you must really be on guard against these beasts.

My experience had also shown us that our spears must not be so long. One metre twenty centimetres, or four feet, is the most useful length.

Well, are sharks dangerous or are they not? The case I have just described really forms an exception among over a thousand encounters I have had with large sharks, but the story does show that you must never feel too safe and that it is very imprudent to dive anywhere if there is a smell of blood about. You must be prepared, always and everywhere, for any sort of surprise.

# Fish Talk

MANY things in nature that we take for granted turn out, when we get to closer grips with them, to be very puzzling. There is, for instance, the question of how fishes find their way about. Since they have eyes, it is pretty obvious that they can observe their surroundings. That there is a problem, however, is at once evident if we put on a diving-mask and go down under the turbid waters of a large river such as the Danube or the Mississippi.

You can barely see four inches in front of you, yet fishes live in such conditions. They swim about, they seek their food, they chase after other fish, are themselves hunted, they get together in shoals and remain together, they seek out their mates, they have a hole in which they live and to which, despite the current, they always find their way back. They do all this, although they can hardly see anything and they never collide with a stone or rock. How do they manage it?

Then, again, what happens at night? It is well known that many carnivorous fish hunt for preference at night-time. Sharks swim at night through inky blackness, steer their course with incomparable skill through coral reefs, track down their prey, chase after it—and never bump into anything.

I got a hint of a possible solution to the puzzle during my very first attempts at diving off the coast of the French Riviera. I took my harpoon with me and swam in clear water illuminated with brilliant sunshine. But the fish did not seem so much to see me with their eyes as to feel my movements. If I made a clumsy plunge and smacked about on the surface, then every fish in the neighbourhood had got a warning. If, when I was stalking one, I made too brusque a movement, then at once he would dart off. When, however, I swam silently and easily then I could get so close to many fish that I was within striking distance of them—although their eyes were turned right in my direction.

Once I was swimming close beside a steep wall of rock against which fairly large waves were breaking when I saw, a good way off and about six fathoms below the surface, the tail of a large grouper sticking out from behind a stone. The creature was almost hidden and only the slowly and gently moving tail was visible. Still looking downwards I extricated myself from a cloud of foam and plashed up to the surface. There was the fish whirling round and round. Its head appeared and the creature stared up at me. There was no doubt at all that he had noticed my presence. Despite the thundering impact of the waves, he had heard the slight noise I had made by my clumsy movements.

We may be sitting at a concert. A thousand notes and sounds fill the air around us. Then a door creaks and despite the waves of music we hear that creak. Obviously we hear it with our ears, but we record the noise with our brains. So it may have been with that grouper. The pounding of the surf was something he was accustomed to, but the noise of my movements was for him like the creaking of a door.

It is true that fish have no external auditory meatus, but such an opening is not necessary in the water as the tissues themselves are admirable conductors of sound. Also, it would appear that the swim-bladder plays a part in picking up sounds. Fish can be trained to recognize certain notes, one for food, another for a blow with a glass stick, and they soon learn to distinguish between the sounds. Then, the notes will be struck at closer intervals. In this way it has been found out that carp, for instance, possess an acuity of hearing comparable with that of human beings, so that sounds differing from one another by a quarter of a note can be recognized.

Now we come to the problem as to whether musical sounds

can be compared with those made by a swimmer in the water, that is to say whether fishes really do 'hear' with their ears such vibrations through the water.

Fishes possess, in a number of regions of their body, small buds which occur in especial profusion along the sides of the animal. These sensitive protuberances are in connection with a canal filled with mucus and which through numerous openings is in contact with the surrounding water. From each sensitive bud there extends a diminutive hair-like sense-organ into the canal. Sharks have, in addition, peculiar sense-cavities in their heads, the so-called ampullae of Lorenzini. All these organs have been known for a long time, but no one has been very sure as to what their function is. Generally speaking, they have been ignored or explained away quite vaguely as organs for the perception of water currents. Since, however, the nerves from the sense-buds lead to certain well-developed areas in the fish brain, it must be assumed that the organs have some more important significance for the animal.

In a few books I have found the suggestion advanced that the 'lateral lines' provide fish with a tactile sense that operates at a distance, just as is the case with bats which move about in the dark without ever colliding with anything. This peculiarity of bats' flight was a lasting puzzle until two researchers discovered that bats, when flying, emit rapid squeaks which are inaudible to the human ear. These cries are echoed back from surrounding objects (just like the rays from a pocket-torch when we flash them onto anything in the dark) and the echo is picked up by the extraordinarily sensitive ears of the bat. Thus they find their way about and perceive their surroundings as though they were provided with radar. They recognize obstacles although they cannot see them with their eyes.

Maybe it is more or less the same with fish. The movements they make in swimming send out vibrations into the water and these vibrations may be returned to them from rocks and other objects, vibrations which may be perceived by the 'lateral lines' of the fish. Thus the creatures may be able to 'see' what lies around them even in quite turbid or dark waters, and 'see' not by means of rays of light but by the aid of the impact of vibrations which, sooner or later, reach the individual's sensitive observation-buds on the body and enable the animal to conceive in its brain a spatial, three-dimensional image of its environment.

All this sounds pretty complicated I know, but perhaps only because we cannot easily imagine something that lies outside the sphere of our own senses. We are like opaque sacks pierced with a few holes. Through such holes—our senses—we see and perceive the world round us. But there are plenty of animals which have other 'holes' than ours, other senses, so that they perceive and judge the world in a way quite different from ourselves.

For instance, whereas for us sight is the principal sense, a dog 'sees' mainly with his nose. His picture of the world is in all probability not even conceivable for us. Still more remarkable is the case of many insects which possess some sense functions which are quite incomprehensible for us. The same may be true of fish and sharks. Since, in dark and turbid water, their eyes are only of limited use to them, such creatures may construct their image of the world, first and foremost, from the impressions which are communicated to them through the vibrations in the water.

Thus would be explained why fish and sharks, when they perceive a man, always put themselves sideways. This would be not so much to turn their eyes to a lateral position as to place their bodies so that the sensitive areas may receive the impressions conveyed by vibration through the water. The wider apart these sensitive areas lie from each other, so much the stronger would be the plastic image received by the animal—just as we use a stereo-telescope to increase the focal length of our eyes and so obtain a better perspective of distant objects. We may then come to the interesting conclusion that the bigger a fish or a shark (and thus the greater the area sensitive to vibrations) the better is its range of perception and its conception of space.

I had got to as far as this in my theory when, in 1939, we made some very interesting and, I think, remarkable observations off the coast of the West Indian island of Curaçao.

On the stormy northern coast where there are many sharks, these always put in an appearance when we harpooned a large fish; indeed, there would not elapse more than from ten to twenty seconds before the creatures could be seen, although just before there was no sign of them in all the wide expanse of the sea. Had the smell of blood attracted them? Hardly. Since visibility under water was as much as forty yards, the sharks must have been at least fifty and possibly a hundred yards away. It was impossible that a smell of blood could spread so rapidly. So what? We came to the conclusion it must have been the frightened struggling and flapping about of the harpooned fish that they heard, or, to use the term we have just been employing, that they 'saw'.

Again, if we missed a fish and the creature in fright swirled around vigorously, then, at once, up came a shark. In this case there could be no question of the marauder being attracted by the smell of blood. At the first opportunity I dived, at the same spot, right down to the sea-bottom and flapped about as hard as I could with my flippers. We waited. No shark came. A little bit later on we shot a fish and several sharks appeared at once.

Either my theory was false and it was not the noise of struggling that attracted the sharks (though maybe the fish emit a cry that is inaudible to us) or sharks can distinguish between the splashing and floundering about of a desperate grouper and the noise made by my flippers. For the sharks there were two different sorts of vibrations.

This second possibility gave me some food for thought. Since the various sorts of fish are very different in shape and possess also very distinctively formed fins, it might be that each sort of fish emits into the water vibrations which are characteristic of and peculiar to it. Fish even of the same kind and species have different movements according to their state at any given moment. A healthy fish does not behave as does a sick fish, a hungry fish has a different comportment from a fish at mating-time. Might it not be possible that sharks—and fishes too—could perceive such differences? Could it be that, in this way, they might be able to recognize each other even in turbid waters and in the dark?

I remembered some fish we had seen swimming quite close past the snout of a shark without anything happening. Maybe they knew from the shark's movements that he was full up and not inclined for hunting.

Then there are fish in love play. We had noticed how, in many species, the partners swam round and round one another while rapidly vibrating their fins. Was such comportment just the expression of their excitement or was it just the opposite? It might be that fish by trilling their fins get themselves into a state for copulation. Maybe it is with their fins that they make their declarations of love, exactly as birds do with mating-calls.

In the depths of the oceans there are many fish provided with luminous organs which may serve them to distinguish between the other fish they may meet. Still, it is not very probable that a hunted fish will light the way for its pursuer! In the depths there are robber fish which have to face many difficulties in tracking down and recognizing their prey. Maybe these creatures are guided by the melody of fins.

If these suppositions of mine are valid, then the silent world of the sea must be full of noise even if it is a noise made up of countless 'voices' just as imperceptible to our ears as are the cries emitted by bats in their flight. Even the black, terrifying abyss of the ocean would be quite 'light' and 'welcoming' though it is not illuminated by the sun's rays but 'lighted' by vibrations that zigzag and crisscross through the moving waters.

These considerations put the problem of living bait in a new perspective. I think that the custom of using a live fish impaled on a hook is a cruel one. The hook is skilfully fastened through the back of the fish so that it may remain alive as long as possible. Certainly you catch more this way than by using dead bait. Why? Because carnivorous fish like best the taste of living prey? Could it not be that flesh-eating denizens of the sea—such as sharks especially—are attracted by the wriggling of live bait? It may well be that the cry of pain of the tortured animal is transmitted by vibrations through the expanse of the water.

William Beebe on his Zaca Expedition made a very interesting observation. In his report he relates how he had caught fish
on the line and then through an observation box watched the
behaviour of two sharks and a sea perch. Every time that he
jerked the line and the fish began to wriggle about, the maraud-
ing fish came near 'like dogs ready to bite'. If, however, he let
the line alone and the impaled fish swam in a natural manner,
then at once the sharks and the sea perch lost all interest. Only
the wriggling, squirming, injured fish attracted them. Beebe
thinks it is a law of nature that abnormal conduct urges carnivorous animals on to accomplish their work of destruction.

We now had the possibility of checking off my observations.
If fish and sharks really did have a 'language', a special means
for obtaining information and for recognizing each other, maybe
we could capture some of these vibratory melodies with an
under-water microphone and through an under-water loudspeaker emit similar sounds which would deceive fish of the
same or other species.

Take for instance the case of fish that swarm together in
shoals: how do they manage to find each other in dark or turbid
water? According to my theory a fish 'hears' the music emitted
by the school and is attracted by it. Perhaps it might be possible
by broadcasting the fish theme-song to induce a swarm to form
up! Then there was the problem of certain carnivorous fish
which follow the shoals. Apparently these marauders locate the
swarms by vibrations they give out. Could not such killers be
attracted by a noise like that of a shoal of fish? Moreover, take
marine animals in the mating season: there again, we might be
able to deceive the sexual partners by imitating the calls or
vibrations they give out through the water.

I published my observations in two books. First of all in 1939
in *Jagd unter Wasser* and then three years later in *Unter Korallen und Haien*. After the end of the Second World War I took
out for my scheme a patent valid in all countries. It seemed to me
that the most suitable subjects for a first experiment would be
sharks. All we needed was the recording of a wriggling fish. If
we were successful in picking up its vibrations, and furthermore

in broadcasting them, we should have achieved something of great significance for commercial fishing. Shark-fishing is profitable only on a small scale, simply because not enough sharks can be found. If, however, it were possible to lure them near then it would be very much easier to catch them with nets or hooks or by means of newly-devised electrical apparatus. A 'sharker' ship could cruise along the coasts, process liver-oil, prepare leather and convert the rest of the animals into fertilizers. In addition, my scheme could also be utilized to clear shark-infested beaches —such as those of Australia—from ever-present dangers.

I therefore addressed myself in Vienna to the *Akustische und Kinogeräte-Gesellschaft* and was able to persuade the firm to devise for us an under-water transmitter and an under-water microphone. The Magnetophone installation was very kindly placed at our disposal by the Philips company. Wawrowetz was one of the engineers of the Vienna company to whom the firm had given leave for the duration of our expedition so that he might look after the under-water appliances. We had taken batteries with us so that we could generate electricity and in Port Sudan we managed to discover a large but portable dynamo.

.We conducted our first experiments in the muddy lagoon of Suakin, but what we needed was a ship to take us and our apparatus to places where we could harpoon larger fish in front of the microphone and where there were also sharks—so that we could try out how the emissions worked. No very difficult problem, you might think; still, as a matter of fact, we nearly lost our lives in our attempt.

We looked about for a ship with a motor but could find none for hire. We were advised to search among the old sailing cutters in Flamingo Bay. These had been once the proud monarchs of the Red Sea but now lay, half-decayed wrecks enveloped in swarms of flies. We did not have to get very near before we smelled the stench. The few still seaworthy sailing vessels were employed in pearl-oyster and *Trochus* shell fishing which rather evil-smelling wares were auctioned off in Flamingo Bay.

Emaciated, sickly-looking figures were squatting under plank shanties for all the world resembling dog-kennels. Masses of flies clustered round the eyes of the apathetic children wandering about. We were told that the owner of the best ships was a rich Arab by the name of Tachlowe. After we had inspected what seemed to be the most presentable of these craft, I sent the owner an invitation to visit us in the house we had rented.

A large car glided up to our door and out of the car an uncommonly fat man extricated himself. He was followed by an interpreter. I accompanied both of them to the terrace and invited Mr. Tachlowe to take a seat on our strongest chair while Gerry brought orange juice and water. I mixed a drink and we clinked glasses to good fellowship and a satisfactory conclusion to our business negotiations.

The next moment I realized that all was not well. The first gulp of the liquid stuck in my throat. My God, I thought, the wretched Gerry has made an awful mistake; he has grabbed out of the ice-box a bottle of film developer instead of the water jug. But I did not, I hope, give any signs of panic. I just swallowed the appalling stuff. It was not poisonous anyway and in no case must our guest find out that we had welcomed him with a glass of photographic chemicals.

'An Austrian national drink,' I remarked casually.

The interpreter interpreted. Mr. Tachlowe, who had looked at his glass with some surprise, then nodded in acquiescence—and took another swig at the liquid, which appeared to assuage his thirst.

We struck a bargain. For a hundred pounds a week we could have the ship with a crew of ten men—all Arabs. Mr. Tachlowe also stated that he would have *El Chadra* cleaned up specially for us. Over the open hull two boards were to be laid down. The somewhat raised deck aft was sheltered by an awning measuring twelve feet by fifteen and this was to serve us as living-, sleeping- and work-room. The crew kept to the fore deck.

Two weeks later we were pitching and tossing about like sea travellers of a hundred years ago, while *El Chadra,* with her tall, picturesque sail, was moving slowly along the coast. The large dynamo was down in the hold with the Magnetophone equipment packed in water-tight cases. Our life was as primitive

*El Chadra* carrying our sound equipment.

as can be imagined. Bill Clark had rigged up for Lotte a portable camp-bed. The rest of us slept in a circle on rubber mattresses.

We were all enthusiastic enough. We put up with the heat, the stench of mussels, the tiny flies that would crawl into our nostrils, and the huge cockroaches that grew fat on the insecticide powder we scattered about us. Lotte's raised couch was airy but it had the disadvantage of being directly under the main boom on which the cockroaches took their evening walks. When a cry of alarm aroused us from our slumbers then we knew that one of the insects had dropped onto Lotte's face.

When we awoke in the early morning we could see the crew, clad only in loin-cloths, kneeling on the planks and bowing and raising the upper parts of the bodies as they prayed in the direction of the rising sun. They were all willing and friendly though the helmsman had wild eyes. Mahmud told us that sometimes he chucked fits. On these occasions he became quite stiff though when incense was burned under his nose he would come to once more. The captain was calm and composed. Not so long ago I learned that three years after our trip, *El Chadra* foundered in a storm and the whole crew was drowned.

However, I was soon in open conflict with the captain because he would not anchor in any of the places suitable for our experiment. He wanted to spend each night in one of the muddy bays on the coast. But what we required was clear waters with big fish and such exist only in the open sea and near a coral reef. When we had been three days out I took over the command myself and we moored just over the wreck of *Ata*.

It had been agreed that Bill should follow after us by car on land, so I sent off both of my assistants in the launch to bring him to the ship. The launch had been out of sight for about half an hour when we saw making towards us from the shore a broad glistening streak of water. A few minutes later we were struck by the first blows of a terrific storm which burst with incredible savagery. Although it was only five in the afternoon, it was dark as night. The flood-waters of the sky descended and a deluge enveloped us.

*El Chadra* tossed about like a cockleshell in the ever-increasing fury of the waves. Through the wall of rain we could make out the excited crew letting down two more anchors, but the hawsers snapped one after the other. Shouting and gesticulating the men dragged out from the hold still another and very special sort of anchor. It was attached to a very strong cable and was a standby to be used only in cases of direst necessity. They got the anchor overboard just at the moment the last of the others snapped away. If the special anchor should fail us then we were certain to get our passport to eternity.

It was pitch dark. Drenched through and packed tightly one against the other, we crouched on the deck. I had plenty of time to reflect on the captain's arguments. He had talked about sudden storms while I had thought of fish and micro-

phones. I had waved his storms away with a gesture. In order
to divert her attention from the frightful rumbling around us I
bawled some nonsense into Lotte's ear. We had by now shifted
so much that we lay not more than forty yards from the reef
over which the storm breakers were crashing with a terrifying
roar. The storm, in fact, was driving us towards the reef. The
launch was near to the coast and in any case would have been of
no use. For six miles all around us the sea was thick-set with coral
reefs. Whether we were on *El Chadra,* in the launch or swimming, we should be crushed between the upper and nether
millstones of the reefs and the breakers.

Now in our imaginations we saw with other eyes the wreck
that lay beneath us. On its deck, now a beautiful coral garden,
there had crouched once, no doubt, just such woeful figures as
ours. Maybe that *Ata's* company too had put their trust in
some special, reserve anchor.

Slowly, very slowly, the night hours crept by. The storm
howled about us. We were buffeted by what seemed interminable assaults. Only very gradually did the tempest abate. The
lashing rain slackened. In the first pale glimmer of dawn we
stared at each other and at the battlefield of the deck. The
dirty, grey sea, smoothed by the rain, rose into a heavy swell that
swept back and forth over the reef. The sailors slept, sprawled
out like dead men down in the hold. The whole night long they
had hung onto the anchor rope and counterbalanced its movements so that it did not tear off in an especially violent gust of
wind. Groaning and sighing, *El Chadra* wallowed about. She
was a hundred years old and spoke in no uncertain voice of her
dissatisfaction with me and my ideas.

About ten o'clock Bill came up with the launch. He had
caught three fish. The three men had spent the night partly in
and partly under the car. At the captain's request we dived for
the lost anchors and after some trouble managed to tie up the
broken cables again. By midday we had set sail and were making back for Port Sudan.

I chose as our next goal the island of Makawa lying sixty
miles to the north. We could there moor in the lee of the island.

The water was clear and apparently there were plenty of fish. Once more we jolted up and down along the coast. When we had got about half-way our complacency was rudely disturbed.

A shrill cry rang out from the hold. The crew, who had been sitting about drinking coffee, changed at once into a shrieking mob in the middle of which O Sheikh, the interpreter, was thrashing about like a madman. His lips were flecked with foam. But he was overcome and tied up. We watched the captain picking up a knife from the flooring.

Mahmud explained with rolling eyes that O Sheikh had swallowed some intoxicant and had wanted to kill me with the knife. Why just me and no one else was not clear. Anyway, O Sheikh was a nice young fellow and we all liked him. He was witty, intelligent and had been with us since our stay at Suakin. It was not until later we learned that many of the young 'Fuzzy-Wuzzies' are addicted to intoxicants. According to Mahmud's graphic gestures O Sheikh kept the stuff under his tongue.

What was to be done? If we obeyed maritime law, then we ought to take him to the nearest port and hand him over to the police. That meant Port Sudan. We decided to sail *El Chadra* into one of the *shabs* and anchor there while Xenophon and Mahmud took the young fellow back in our launch to Flamingo Bay. Since the trip, using the outboard motor, would take a good ten hours, it would be the second day before we could expect the boat back again.

When it finally came, the motor was at its last gasp and we had to send it from Mohammed Ghul in a truck back to Port Sudan. So we lost not only two days' time, but our interpreter and our motor-boat. We now had only a rowing-boat for our experiments at Makawa.

We wanted to carry out our researches at the extremity of a reef lying on the south side of the island. Our crew had to work their hands to the bone before they were able, with all their skill, to steer *El Chadra* against the wind to the place we had chosen. I had to promise the captain that we would tie up for the night in some quiet creek or inlet of the mainland.

Finally about noon we lay at the chosen spot. While Waw-

Wawrowetz at the tape recorder.

rowetz busied himself with the apparatus on deck, we took the microphone and the loudspeaker to the sea bed. Gerry was to harpoon the fish while I was to try to hold the microphone before it. Leo carried the cine-camera and Lotte the still camera. We left the loudspeaker six fathoms down on the bottom and swam through a gently sloping valley where there were plenty of large fish.

Unfortunately not one of them would allow himself to be harpooned for scientific purposes. Our procession aroused obvious mistrust. What seemed to frighten the fish most of all was the microphone's long curved cable. We had noticed much the same sort of thing if we swam with a harpoon attached by a rope to a boat. Certain South Sea islanders say that when they are swimming they must hold a cord rolled up and let it out in the water when sharks make their appearance. The sharks would swim away since they think that if any animal has so long a tail it must be very big itself. Whether this is right or not I cannot say, but other fish exhibit much the same sort of reaction.

When we saw we were not getting anywhere we hid the cable between the corals, and I took up my position against a wall about three feet high behind which the reef broke down into a steep declivity. Before registering I was to scratch with my nail on the microphone—then Wawrowetz was to switch on the tape-recorder. When we were finished I was to shout into it and he would switch off. Each one of us stood waiting at his post among the corals. Plenty of fish were swimming to and fro but, alas, they all shunned the microphone. I made a sign to Gerry and he swam over the barrier into deep water there to harpoon a fish; for our object, indeed, we needed something more. The animal must be harpooned right in front of the microphone, but I hoped that Gerry's wriggling catch might attract others which were not so shy.

We heard a clattering noise and saw something squirming about. Six seconds later we spotted the first shark. Another followed. Gerry swam back in haste and pulled the harpooned mackerel off the barb. From other directions came two more sharks. Not forty seconds had elapsed before there were altogether six sharks moving up and down behind the barrier. Here was certainly some confirmation of my theory, but we were not any nearer to achieving our aim.

Very calmly and deliberately there slid out from beneath the coral block on which I stood a moray eel that was a good four and a half feet long. He grabbed the mackerel Gerry had thrown away. A moray was about the only sort of fish unsuited for our experiment, since as it has no fins it can hardly emit perceptible vibrations. Lotte and Leo swam nearer, filming and photographing while the moray slunk off again into his hole. Then each of us took up his look-out post once more. Three of the sharks were still moving about up and down the barrier, but the fish were as shy as ever.

Suddenly we heard music. The whole sea was filled with it. Wawrowetz had got bored with waiting and was trying out a record of modern concert-music through our loudspeaker. It is a great mistake to imagine that the sounds of music come distorted through water. The notes reached us as clear and free from interference as though on land. It was an incredible experience to watch the submarine world swaying as though to the accompaniment of musical rhythm. To all appearances the fish took not the slightest notice of the sounds.

As it was no use waiting any longer I put the microphone down and swam to the loudspeaker, around which some fish were nibbling. At one very loud movement I saw some slight reaction in them. The record had come to an end. But a Viennese waltz followed.

This, too, made no impression on the fish, but while I was watching them the water near me suddenly darkened and I was the witness to an astonishing occurrence. No fewer than three hundred large, gleaming, silvery jacks came up in close formation and began to circle around me and the microphone. They kept at a distance of about nine feet and swam as though in the mazes of a close round dance. Very likely the music of the waltz—it was Johann Strauss's 'Rosen aus dem Süden'— had nothing to do with the show, but it was curiosity and the sounds which had attracted the fish. However, the impression conveyed that the fish were really waltzing was so striking that later on I reproduced in our film this scene just as I had witnessed it.

I did not suspect that this waltz would secure for me some rather dubious publicity. When afterwards, in Hollywood, an American version of our film was prepared, the editor made the waltz an essential feature of the film. Our experiments in trying to capture inaudible vibrations did not impress him very much, so he altered the make-up and showed us sending out all sorts of remarkable noises into the sea. Since cow-bells, revolver shots, children's yells and the like had had no effect upon the fish, the splendid idea occurred to me (in this American version) of trying out a Viennese waltz. Then the fish took their partners (the editor used photographs we had taken of fish in love-play) and all began to sway to the strains of the music. Although we had the right to reject any alterations introduced while the film was being made, we got our first view just before the première in New York when everything was finished and settled. There was nothing more we could do except to mention the error in interviews—and to accept congratulations for our having proved that fish are musical.

During further attempts we noticed that the movements of the cable seemed to produce crackling noises, so we left it, as much as possible, untouched, especially as there were other disturbing sounds we could not suppress. The recording tape, owing to the heat, disintegrated at the edges, and when we listened to our under-water emissions they had a kind of crackling quality which was certainly not identical with that of the recorded fin-strokes. Finally we had to admit that the difficulties confronting us on a primitive ship in the climate of the Red Sea were too great and we had to be satisfied with the technical experience we had gained.

I made further attempts during the *Xarifa* expedition to the West Indies and will refer to them later on—though in a very sad connection.

# Problems Great and Small

THE following remarks and notes may perhaps be of use to those who would themselves undertake such an expedition as ours. When our film *Abenteurer im Roten Meer* (*Under the Red Sea*) won for Austria at the Venice Biennale in 1951 the international first prize for a long documentary film, those present there probably had an idea of the details upon which the success or the failure of such an expedition really depend.

If I may give the best advice I can then it would be this: never believe anything or anybody, least of all one's own preconceived opinions. On an expedition everything must be verified with rigorous care and the only way known to me of effecting this is by drawing up lists. On these lists must be put down, under various headings, everything you must do today, tomorrow or at any other time. The lists must contain everything that occurs to you and they must not be thrown away even if they consist only of black strokes and little red ticks.

To take one example out of many: you may rely for an important shipment on some forwarding agency; you give careful instructions and you may think that is enough. In nine cases out of ten it may be sufficient but then comes the tenth case when a mishap occurs, things do not turn up at the right time and you are plunged into a catastrophe. Therefore it is necessary to get hold of the man who actually sends off the goods and discuss each detail with him personally. On what day will the shipment be made? What is the exact route to be taken? What customs houses will it have to go through and what sort of difficulties may arise in them? Who is to handle the shipment at the intermediate stations and who are the responsible men there? I insist on being given all the addresses and then arrange to receive a telegram from each transhipment point. The date we should receive each telegram is marked on a list and if we do not get the wire on that day, then we start telephoning.

I have learned from bitter experience never to accept as reliable anything that I am assured is sure and certain. What cost far and away the most money on an expedition are mistakes and loss of time. It is only human that the preparedness to accept responsibilities of otherwise reliable people should have its limits —especially in foreign countries and above all in the tropics. There is no use at all in getting worried about some case of unreliability—after it has occurred. The only thing to do is to take all possible precautions beforehand. Of course it is much more pleasant to give orders and then sit back calmly in your chair, but on an expedition that sort of thing will not do. Anyone who does not rack his brains about what may arise from some little fault, some slight misunderstanding, will, sooner or later, come a cropper.

On boat excursions if you have not got a list something is always forgotten. In a hot climate especially your brain is often not in a state for you to be able to check off everything at the moment of departure. It may look rather comical for experienced travellers to sit in a boat and to check off and verify the same thing day after day, but if you are not to have trouble that is the only method. If you fail to consult the lists then often the boat has to put about when she is half an hour out or else you find that at the critical moment something is missing.

There are always some small details cropping up. For instance, we used three Siemens 16 mm. cameras in watertight cases and had chosen Kodak Plus X films. Just before our expedition started we found out that, for some reason or other, Kodak were not prepared to load their film into Siemens

adapters—and Siemens would not do it either, so we had to take
with us a rewinder in order to insert the films ourselves and then
to spool them back onto the Kodak reels. All that meant, in
practice, that in the evenings when I was dead tired I had to
undertake an uncommonly delicate operation in a dark, suffo-
catingly hot room. If one single drop of sweat were to drop on
a film then a whole day's work could be spoiled. A slight scratch
that I might make through unskilful handling would appear
afterwards on the screen as a white line as thick as a man's
finger.

We had furthermore agreed that the films should be sent to
Switzerland by air mail and there processed. We were to get
reports by cable and express mail. Quite by chance I found out
that all mail for Europe went through Cairo where it was sub-
mitted to the Egyptian censorship. We had been assured that
the censors took samples at random and processed them—but
not at all in the way we wanted. Obviously we could not expose
ourselves to such risks. We decided, therefore, to place the films
in hermetically sealed cases, to deposit these in the Port Sudan
refrigerating plant and to take them with us ourselves on our
journey home.

I spent a whole day in the refrigerating plant so as to make
sure there should be no error or misunderstanding. The cases
were to remain in the vegetable room and were on no account
to be moved into the meat room where the temperature was
much too low for films. I talked to each workman on the place,
described the exact location, handed out baksheesh, and asked
every man for his co-operation. In no circumstances must the
cases—even if they hampered the normal operations in the plant
—be removed from where they were or allowed to stay in a
warm place. Neither must they be shifted about since then
sooner or later water would drop on them nor must they be
tilted up because in that way the chemicals which absorbed
the moisture would be spilled inside the cases.

Anyone who had taken the trouble to watch me would certainly have got the impression that I was being altogether
too fussy. I could, nevertheless, cite dozens of instances where,

owing to some circumstance or another for which no one person could be called to account, very considerable and irreparable damage was caused.

It is essential that, before setting out, you should get, well ahead of time, in contact with the officials of the country for which you are bound, since there are always difficulties of some sort or another and you may get referred to people of whom you know nothing. Moreover, there are always some rules and regulations cropping up which you cannot, with all the good will in the world, foresee. Again, spare parts must on no account be omitted from your stores. You must be prepared to under-take repairs in most primitive conditions and to effect these you are in absolute need of blue-prints and special tools. You must check off beforehand whether in the country in question the electric current, the contacts and the plugs suit your equipment. Currency, letters of recommendation, medicaments, snakebite antitoxin, explicit contracts with members of the expedition, insurance, postal communications, customs, immigration and working permits, the local language—all these things constitute big problems which are however not too difficult to solve if you take enough trouble and have some experience. In practice, however, it often happens that it is the small mishaps—to which no one has given much thought because of their apparent in-significance—which find us fully unprepared and helpless.

I should like however to say something reassuring and com-forting. Although in every new place you are bound to run into new snags, you also, almost everywhere, come across men ready and willing to help you. With officials, indeed, things are differ-ent. Laws and ordinances exist and must be obeyed. The minor official moreover is neither able nor is he allowed to exercise his own judgement concerning the aim and object of such unusual phenomena as expeditions always are. You must be patient. With some expenditure of time and some show of tact in one way or another you can generally achieve your aim. Through the mass of complicated ordinances you can, sooner or later, get through to the human being. Then you may find some helpful, unselfish friend, a man whom you had never set eyes on five

minutes earlier, who will, after one glance or a short conversation, put all his influence and energy at your disposal. You do
not have to seek him out—he is always here, there and everywhere. The tighter the jam you get into, the more likely it is
that such a saviour will make his appearance. He may come
upon the scene in strange guise, his face may be of any colour,
he may be of any calling, religion or age, but he is the sort of
man who fills you with pride at being a human being. Amid the
problems and worries of his own life he does not ignore the
quite different reactions of another, a man in whose eyes there
shines an expression like your own, a man, in fact, who under-
stands you though he does not know anything about you.

It got hotter and hotter every day. Gerry went home and he
was followed by Wawrowetz. We had planned a three months'
expedition but we were far from finished and we were to stay
three months longer. July, August, September, the hottest
months in the hottest region on this earth. We were all tired
and almost exhausted but we were determined not to give up.
Leo and Xenophon were suffering from boils. Lotte kept wonderfully well. Her girlish features had lost something of their
softness. There was not—there had not been for some time—any
talk about her not pulling her full weight in all our tasks and all
our adventures. She was much smaller and more delicate in
appearance than any of us, but in strength of will she far surpassed us. Although the hardships and the climate told upon her
she remained cheerful and good-tempered, demanded no special treatment and looked after us in many small ways which I
am afraid we hardly realized.

I could not solve the problem of how our film was to be composed. We were living among astounding, untouched, almost
incredible scenes of nature. We were filming what no man before
us had ever seen. Yet it was clear enough that our experiences
must be presented in the right way, that it was a question of
arrangement, of conception and of the laws of scenic represen-
tation which obey the demands of our human spirit itself and
are always invariable and valid for all artistic creations.

It would be an error to suppose that on an expedition you need simply to photograph all the interesting things you see and that then you will get a good documentary. Obviously, you cannot keep strictly to the events of each day, to each successive adventure through which you live. What is, in actual experience, rich and varied, may well appear repetitious on the screen. Furthermore, what seems interesting, dramatic or comical at the moment may not turn out to be so when the films are projected on a screen. The main problem is this: how can you be in the midst of bewildering reality and, at the same time, transport yourself in imagination far away to Europe, to a cinema and into the skin, so to speak, of a spectator who has taken part in none of the adventures and who may well be, at first anyway, not very interested in what he is going to see? You have to try to get clear in your mind how you can present to an outsider the essence of what you have been through. You have to consider how it is possible to interest him in the scenery, in the animals in the significant aspects of the various problems encountered. I decided that my task was this: to depict reality in a limited number of episodes each one of which should constitute a complete dramatic act in itself.

There is nothing else for it, you have to sit down with a pencil in your hand. We forced ourselves to jot down, as soon as we got out of the water, an account of each scene we had filmed. Otherwise you soon forget exactly what you have got. We recorded in pictures the composition of each sequence so as to be able to judge of its length and technical quality. If you do not do this, then you find that, in a matter of months, you have filmed similar scenes dozens of times, whereas other incidents are quite forgotten, which you find later on are absolutely necessary for the editing.

When any particularly remarkable episode was filmed then I tried to fit it into sections which had already been prepared. I endeavoured to put myself in the place of the editor who has to turn out a whole coherent sequence and I wrote a script for all the scenes we needed in addition to those we already had.

The same sort of proceeding is also useful for photographic

work. After every expedition we found that we had shot thousands of pictures we then never needed, and which no one ever looked at again, while important and often very necessary subjects were just not there. I tried therefore to put myself into the mind of the editor of a magazine who wants to publish an illustrated account of our expedition. In this way I realized what shots we still lacked; I sketched them—and then went out to look for them.

We tried to make up our minds also what we should do when we met with this animal or the other. When you are actually on the spot you are generally far too excited, too absorbed in the preoccupations of the moment, to be able to think things over and to be creative. I made out lists we learned by heart and if many of them proved to be superfluous, still the instances in which our foresight was rewarded fully justified the trouble we had taken.

When you are taking photographs of animals things can be made considerably easier if you can catch up with the creatures and then arrange in some way or other for incidents between them. Many of the most spectacular scenes shown in American and European documentaries are shot in the studio or in an aquarium. In the freedom of nature it is very much more difficult to photograph such happenings—so it is, to say the least, rather disappointing if you have to realize that neither the public nor the critics notice any difference between the two sorts of pictures. I could tell of a whole number of cases in which much more sincere applause has been evoked by trick photography than by work that demanded months in which the operator risked his life. From the scientific point of view, however, scenes photographed or filmed in natural surroundings are by far the more valuable.

We covered endless miles of sea during these months. In the shallow lagoons the water temperature in August rose to $40°$ C., that is $104°$ F. When, at low tide, this water was sucked back into the open sea we would swim at the reef's edge through hot cataracts which mingled in violent eddies with the outer waters several degrees cooler. In the transitional zone there occurred

Filming swirling clouds of anchovy (*Anchoviella*).

the same phenomena of refraction which may be observed also in the deep where different layers of water meet, or again where fresh water flows into salt. On either side of the line of division, which is often sharply marked, the water will be clear and transparent while the transitional zone is, on the contrary, as opaque as a jelly into which the rays of light quiver more or less like warm air over a fire.

Many fish turned away from this water, which they found far too warm. The delicate, variegated butterfly fish moved down to a deeper area at the reef slope as did also the droll trigger fish and the many-coloured host of lancet fish, wrasse and sea parrots. Groupers were rare as were giant specimens of *Cheilinus undulatus,* the largest of all the wrasses, which reach a weight of over four hundred and fifty pounds and may be seen hovering motionless in deep water and remind you of huge, rectangular travelling trunks. We did, however, see on the reef slope numerous small fish snapping at dying plankton drizzling down through the progressively cooler water. There were spread over the surface clouds of small red algae, *Tricodesmium,* which appreciably lessened the visibility despite the vertical position of the sun's rays.

One day, too, all the sharks disappeared. We had got to recognize several which always turned up at the same spot—then, suddenly, not one to be seen. Four or five weeks later, they just as suddenly reappeared. I do not think that they went away because of the heat but because it was the mating season. Captain W. E. Young relates, in one of his books which deals with commercial shark-fishing, that he also had noted the disappearance of sharks from certain areas at certain seasons. At Bill Clark's house the Governor of Kassala told us that once, near the island of Talla Talla, he had seen the sea literally seething with sharks; maybe the creatures had congregated for mating.

The only animals which seemed to have lost nothing of their liveliness in the terrific heat were the dolphins. We always met them in the same place. They must have had quite definite hunting grounds bounded by invisible walls. At one of their frontiers they would welcome us, accompany us to the other border and then when we returned swim with us over the same lap back. There would be fifteen or twenty of them, each about six feet long. They would play about in their usual fashion before the bows and many were venturesome enough to shoot up from the depths and leap as high as six feet above the waves.

We puzzled our heads as to how we should film these creatures. Time and again I would grab my camera and drop from the moving boat into the water, but always when the foam had cleared away the dolphins had vanished. At last we hit on an idea. Leo and I, in diving outfit and with our cameras, were to drop down to about sixty feet in fathomless water and hang there silently waiting. On the surface a floating bottle would mark our position. The boat should cruise until the dolphins caught up with it and lead them right above us. Viewed from below the boat with the gambolling dolphins would make a splendid picture.

We tried this out three times and each time the same thing happened. The dolphins would show no hesitation in making for the boat and in following it. However, as soon as it came to within fifty yards of us, then all the creatures vanished. We hung about the same place under water and watched; time after time the boat came near—but no dolphins. Since those days it has been established by experiments undertaken in the great Oceanarium at Marineland in Florida that dolphins too possess a tactile sense which enables them to perceive objects at a distance—these creatures, indeed, emit squeaky noises that are supersonic for us but the dolphins' ears pick up the echoes.

The last two months of our stay dragged on in almost incredible heat. The natives of Port Sudan lay about in any shady spot they could find, in the streets and in the park, and sprawled as motionless as dead flies. Almost all the Europeans were off on leave. Mahmud could not understand why we did not pack up and get out, but we made off for Shab Amber, a large reef situated some distance from the coast, and here we filmed corals more beautiful than any we had ever seen. As we found no mantas I set out alone in a truck for Mohammed Ghul where I was lucky enough to get some film shots of these animals.

I must say that I no longer had any idea whether what we were doing made any sense or not. In many cases we were foolhardy and just looked for trouble. We harpooned fish in dangerous waters. Once a shark tore a fish and the harpoon out of my grasp. The heat seemed to have purged us of ordinary common sense so that in a curious way and to a marked degree we felt impelled to play with fire. Our diving-gear was coming to bits and our camera cases were patched and soldered up in a dozen places. They looked very odd, covered all over with red lines and blobs since we had discovered that Lotte's fingernail lacquer was the best and handiest stuff for stopping up leaks.

For the last three weeks we were once more in Suakin. Mr. George Sarabis, a prosperous Greek merchant, was kind enough to send us in his car both food and blocks of ice. In fact Bill Clark and George Sarabis were the guardian angels of the expedition. When we got back to Port Sudan we were thoroughly exhausted and had lost a good deal of weight. Here again, George Sarabis helped through with all the formalities and waved us good-bye when we took off in our airplane. When we leaned back in our seats we could hardly realize that our adventures were over. Could there really be such things as soft beds, decent food, green trees, flower-decked meadows?

In Venice, where we were for the world première of *Under the Red Sea* (*Abenteuer im Roten Meer*) in the great Festival Hall, everything we had lived through seemed so remote that our expedition might have been a dream. The film had become an independent entity and did not need us any more. Without any more effort on our part the film went, during the following three years, to all countries of the world (except Russia and China) and contributed to awaken an interest in the world under the sea. For us, however, the best thing was that the royalties went a good way towards the fitting out of a research ship for our institute.

The sailing ship I got this time was twice as large as our *Seeteufel*—she was a three-masted schooner with a steel hull, three hundred and fifty tons, a hundred and forty-three feet by twenty-six feet and a half. She had been built for a member of the millionaire Singer sewing-machine family in 1927 at Samuel White's shipyard in Cowes. She had had several different owners before the war during which she was used for cargo. She had lost her sixty-ton lead keel as well as her mast while her midship had been transformed into a hold. A tall wheel-house, of the merchant vessel type, had been constructed aft so that of the once proud yacht there remained only the steel hull but it was in an excellent state of preservation. Just before we bought her she had been used for carrying coal, but the Danish shipping company that ran her had gone bankrupt. If I have ever shown real courage in my life it was when I took over this sad relic and began the task of bringing back *Xarifa*—her first name—to her original condition.

In 1950 we had accepted an invitation to transfer the head-quarters of our research activities to the principality of Liechtenstein where we found a good deal of support. From our new offices we carried on with our task and worked with great zeal. *Xarifa* was towed through the Kiel Canal to Hamburg where the refitting started.

Our famous lists now became of portentous length. When I had bought the ship I had not had the faintest notion that it would take at least five times the purchase price to put her in a seaworthy condition. The total cost, indeed, not counting supplies, was to amount to more than 600,000 Swiss francs (about £50,000). Most of the firms supplying ships' equipment made us special terms but still we were often at our wits' end to know how and where we should raise the necessary money. Luckily, we had, at that time, not the slightest idea of how much more money would be necessary for the maintenance and running expenses once *Xarifa* was ready to put to sea.

Our enthusiasm and optimism overcame all obstacles. In Hamburg we found invaluable counsellors in Admiral Bernhard Rogge, Count Felix Luckner and Herr Johann Köser. Xenophon, who, as my representative, lived all the time on board, verified every detail himself, and kept me informed of all the new problems as they turned up.

Our finances were looked after by Frau Thea Schneider, a

trusted friend of many years' standing, who has devoted much of her life, her great experience and her astounding energy, to the service of researchers and to the organization of scientific expeditions. She carried on negotiations with all the different firms and took care that not a penny should be spent unnecessarily. We are more grateful to her than words can tell. If a ship can be said to have a mother, then Frau Schneider was *Xarifa's* mother.

So, with what we received from books, lectures and films and with what we could manage to extract in the way of advances, our ship's refitting progressed from month to month.

While all this was going on, I was working out the programme for our first *Xarifa* expedition which was to be composed, in addition to a crew of twelve, of ten scientists, photographers and technicians. As well as a roomy deck saloon and a messroom decorated with pictures of maritime worthies, we were to have a workshop for the technicians, a carpenter's shop, a biological laboratory, a room for microscopical investigations and a photographic dark-room. Our first trip was to be the Caribbean and then to the Galapagos—that most interesting archipelago in the Pacific. We would sail whenever possible but we had a 250 h.p. auxiliary engine for use when the wind was contrary.

As all these projects were whirling round in our heads, a completely unexpected event happened. It was to lead us, before *Xarifa* was ready for the sea, to the antipodes.

...wo red-fire fish
...ve-play. Their
...ly fins are very
...nous.

The even more venomous stone fish can hardly be distinguished amongst the corals.

Lotte among the coral formations.

# To the Great Barrier Reef

I<small>T WAS</small> an evening in October 1952. Lotte and I had been married for two years and we had been invited by an American distributor firm to visit New York and four other large cities for the premières of *Under the Red Sea*. Then I got a letter asking us to bring, at the expense of the distributors, our diving-gear with us; this we were to show on television and at Press conferences.

'That means,' I said to Lotte, 'we and our outfit get free to San Francisco and back. Do you know what we might do?'

Lotte raised her eyebrows at me.

'From San Francisco it is only a hop to Australia. It's a unique opportunity to visit the Barrier Reef.'

Ever since I had taken up diving the Great Barrier Reef had been my Mecca, the place I most desired to see. The Reef stretches—it is the largest coral reef in the whole world—for a length of some one thousand, two hundred and fifty miles along the eastern shores of Australia and, in some places, reaches a breadth of about ninety-five miles. The few accounts available from the reports of pearl and other professional divers who had been down in the Reef's waters led us to expect such marvels and wonders as were to be seen nowhere else in the world. Moreover, in the sea thereabouts lives the legendary, murderous giant clam or *Tridacna gigas*, which has, so it is said, cost many a diver his life. I wanted to be able to check off these stories and discover how the *Tridacna* really does behave. I was, above all, attracted to the outer rampart of the great reef-wall where, as far as I knew, no one had as yet dived. We could make our head-quarters at the small town of Cairns in Queensland, not far from which are places associated with the history of Captain Cook's epic voyages.

The information I was able to get the next morning only made me more anxious to carry out the plan. Since the airlines whose planes flew eastwards or westwards around the globe to Australia were in keen competition, the fares were compara-tively low. The run from San Francisco to Sydney, although as long as from Zurich to San Francisco, cost only half as much. The only problem was that of *Xarifa*—for her refitting was then in its most critical phase. Still, we could take decisions before-hand and leave the carrying out of them to our most conscien-tious and competent Xenophon.

We set off without telling anyone about our plans. After a stay of three weeks in the United States we left San Francisco on 4th December in an airplane of the British Commonwealth Pacific Airways. Our stewardess, a friendly Australian, looked somewhat bewildered at my clothes, which did indeed hang about me in a rather remarkable way. What she fortunately did not find out was that I was carrying in my coat-pockets all the lead-weights of our diving-gear. Indeed, though the price of our fares was quite reasonable, the extra price we had to pay for ex-cess luggage was pretty stiff. The soda-lime we had sent on be-fore by ship, but we had with us not only the diving-gear and the cameras but also over thirty pounds of lead weights. As, how-ever, there were passengers who were a good deal fatter than us and they did not pay any excess fares, I hope that the B.C.P.A., whose officials were so kind to us on our trip, will forgive our behaviour.

We left San Francisco at 6 o'clock in the evening and landed at midnight on the Hawaiian Islands where we put back our watches by two hours. In the warm air perfumed with the scent of tropical flowers, we sat, rather benumbed, on a long leather sofa at the airport and watched the continuous coming and go-ing of Constellations while I told Lotte of my adventures in 1940. Then we had dived off Diamond Head and, shortly afterwards, were, in error, arrested as spies.

Two hours later we were asked to go aboard again. The small sleeping compartments were now made up and we crept into bed. When I woke up it was seven in the morning and we were just over a quite flat coral strip in the middle of the Pacific and losing height. Canton Island—a tiny atoll of the Phoenix Group. The inner lagoon ringed round by the reefs had water of a light green colour, an indication that the sea was shallow and had a sandy bottom. The outer edge of the reefs, bounded by a narrow belt of surf, fell then precipitously down into the abyss. What struck us especially were the numerous channels which, one after the other, showed first in the surf zone and then ran parallel over the brim of the reef into the deep sea. When the plane took off we were able to observe these channels more closely. They oc-curred all round the reef.

'I'm sure no one has ever dived here,' I said to Lotte. 'Maybe we could, on our way back, spend three or four days on the island. We must find out whether the air-line could not put us up in one of the hutments. I want at all costs to examine those channels.'

By noon we had reached the main island of the Fiji group that glittered and shimmered up at us like green jewels, sur-rounded by reefs and small palm-decked isles. We touched down amid meadows and blossoming trees—and put our watches back another two hours. At the air-port rest-house we were served a Fijian meal by smiling islanders. As we looked round at the thousands of blossoms and flowers, as we heard the humming of the bees and the cries of the birds, we said to ourselves, though neither of us spoke a word out loud: 'We'll come back here again one day.'

Then we took off again into the broad heavens while the vast mirror of the Pacific lay far down below us. Since in the mean-time we had crossed the international date-line we also put our date forward by a day. In the airplane the world was not bigger than a globe that you take in at a glance. Geographical concepts became exciting realities. Distances which when we think of them do not seem much less than that from the earth to the moon, shrink and are soon overcome.

As I looked down below me I thought of a small ship—not so long as *Xarifa* but rather broader in the beam—that in 1769 sailed across this ocean and all but smashed on the Barrier Reef. I was remembering the astounding voyage of *Endeavour,* whose track we wanted to follow.

Captain Cook's first goal was the Island of Tahiti which he made, according to programme, and where an astronomer on board took observations of the transit of Venus across the sun's disk. Then, obeying the sealed orders he had received, Cook struck south-westwards into the unknown in order to seek for the legendary *Terra Australis Incognita,* the fifth continent which from purely theoretical considerations was thought to exist in that part of the world. Cook found only endless expanses of sea though he finally reached New Zealand which had already been discovered in 1642 by the Dutchman Tasman. For five months he conducted a careful survey of the New Zealand coasts and then sailed off towards the north so as to be once more in the area of known sea routes. However, on 21st April, 1770, the first officer, Hicks, sighted land ahead. Cook gave the name of Botany Bay to the place where his men first trod Australian soil.

Later on, Cook described this inlet in such glowing colours that the first English settlers were very disillusioned by what is, indeed, a rather disconsolate landscape. The colonists arrived eighteen years after Cook's discovery and they filled eleven ships, but they did not long remain at Botany Bay. They cruised along the coast and found what is today one of the best natural harbours in the world—that of Sydney. Cook had sailed by it without exploring it though he named it Port Jackson. After his two years at sea, Cook, not unnaturally, wanted to get as soon as possible to Batavia and from there to reach England by the route round Africa. So he followed the shores of the newly discovered continent northwards but his progress was more and more hampered by reefs and small islands. Soundings were taken continu-

Botany Bay, where Cook first landed on the Australian continent. Here the under-water hunters of Sydney organized a barbecue.

ously day and night and for much of the way a launch rowed on ahead of *Endeavour*. No one on board had any idea that the ship was sailing into an ever-narrowing funnel, the channel formed by the Barrier Reef from which it was possible only with the utmost difficulty to reach the open sea again.

The story has often been told of how, during the night of 11th June, *Endeavour* struck a reef somewhere to the north of Cairns. Since the ship was a considerable distance from the mainland's coasts and since there was the ever-present danger of an attack by hostile aborigines, it was a matter of life or death to get *Endeavour* afloat again. Everything that was not riveted down, including the ship's six guns, was thrown overboard; despite all this, however, *Endeavour* got clear only twenty-four hours later with the second high tide. Then it was discovered the ship had sprung a leak and that water was pouring in at such a rate that, in the long run, pumping seemed useless. Thereupon one of the mates suggested that oakum, sheeps' dung and any sort of dirt should be mixed together in a sail and that this should be drawn under the ship. Thus the leak was stopped and *Endeavour* saved. Favourable winds took Cook to where now stands Cooktown on the coast. Here *Endeavour* was hauled up on the beach and repaired. Then Cook was able to pursue his adventurous voyage and, through many more hazards, sail right through the length of the Barrier Reef up to its most northerly point.

We glided down and came to a stop on Sydney airfield. The buzzing and humming of the propellers no longer resounded in our ears. At the foot of the stairway there was a group of Press photographers with their cameras at the ready. As we walked down the flash-lights fizzed—behind us a young lady was bowing right and left. She was the Australian Queen of Beauty just back from the United States.

As I could not find my vaccination certificate, the immigration officials took me off into a side office where I was promptly re-vaccinated. In Australia there is no beating about the bush. After our luggage had been examined in the outer hall, we found that ten stalwart-looking men were waiting for us. We shook hands and there and then they made us honorary members of the Underwater Spearfishermen's Association of New South Wales. Dick Charles, the president, told us that the club had over a thousand members in Sydney alone.

'Normally speaking,' he said to Lotte, 'we are strictly a men's club, but we're making an exception in your case.'

The representative of the American distributors had also come out to the airfield and he brought over to us one of the journalists who had congregated round the Beauty Queen. Hardly had the word 'shark' been mentioned than he ran back to his colleagues and called them to join us.

The next morning we saw our names in big print in all the newspapers. Then we realized that we were in a land where sharks are news, where they are a constant menace to the public welfare, where every year many people are badly bitten by sharks—and generally die, where, indeed, the government has set up a special department to deal with the shark danger and try to overcome it. It caused quite a sensation that anyone could speak indulgently about such creatures. Moreover, that we imagined we could, through shouting under water, frighten sharks off seemed almost too much. In the *Daily Telegraph* the well-known Australian naturalist T. C. Roughley wrote that he certainly could not conceive how he could ever come to call a shark a beautiful creature. A Brisbane newspaper asked how long we might be expected to last before we got killed; the paper gave us two weeks. The *Courier-Mail* carried a half-page cartoon in which I was shown in the water calling out to a large shark. On the shark was written 'Income Tax'. The caption was: 'Bet you can't boo that away.'

We got many well-meaning warnings in letters and by telephone, while Dr. Coppleson, one of the leading surgeons in Sydney, insisted on showing me his series of appalling clinical photographs. They were of men whose arms or legs had been bitten off—mostly corpses from which large crescent-shaped portions were lacking. The incisions made by the sharks' teeth were as clean and sharp as though they had been cut with razor-blades.

'It's possible that sharks in some other parts of the world are harmless,' went on Dr. Coppleson, 'but in our waters they are certainly not. Here is a collection of over a hundred reports concerning men who have been provably attacked by sharks. As you can see, 80 per cent of these cases were fatal. We have here in Australia six sorts of sharks that attack men: white sharks, tiger sharks, hammerheads, grey nurse sharks, whaler sharks and makos. Luckily the white shark comes only very rarely near the shores. Most of the accidents can be attributed to whaler sharks and grey nurse sharks.'

I invited Dr. Coppleson to luncheon and was only just able to prevent him from showing his pictures to Lotte during the meal.

'It might interest you,' he told her, 'to know that, according to many people's opinion, a taste for human flesh is harmful to sharks. A few years ago there was caught for the aquarium in Coogee a tiger shark about nine feet long. Soon after he arrived in the aquarium the creature vomited out a human arm and although the limb must have been in the shark's stomach for several days the flesh had hardly at all been affected by the digestive juices. As the police afterwards found out, the arm had belonged to a missing man who had probably been murdered and his body flung into the sea.'

Captain Young, in his book *Shark! Shark!* tells of a similar incident. When he opened up a twelve-foot-long brown shark caught near Key West, he found inside the creature a human arm, other pieces of flesh and a rag of some blue stuff. Young photographed the arm and showed it to everyone he came across who expressed any doubts about sharks really eating human flesh.

Dr. Coppleson warned us not to take matters lightly. From the statistics he had compiled, it would appear that accidents occurred just as often in good weather as in bad, as frequently in shallow waters as in deep, and as many times in calm as in rough seas. Most of the attacks were reported during the months from December to April, that is to say in the Australian summer, and they occurred generally after half past three in the afternoon. Swimmers seemed to attract the sharks most, and once the beast had made one onslaught, then he nearly always returned several times to his victim. The first bite was mostly on the legs or buttocks, then the shark made for the arms, by which the victims tried to ward off the aggressor. There had always been plenty of courageous people to hurry up and try to help. In no case were these injured. The shark always bit again and again into the body he had already wounded. Just as many people with black skins were attacked as with white.[1] Many negroes imagine that because their skins are dark they are safe and some coloured men even go so far as to cover the palms of their hands with black pigment. Captain Young also mentioned that he was able to attract sharks by throwing newsprint into the water, and, furthermore, that the sharks in the waters off Hawaii dealt much more rapidly with a horse's carcass thrown into the sea if the animal was white. It is undoubtedly true that a light-coloured object in water is visible from a greater distance than is a dark one. However, the Australian accident figures prove that too much reliance must not be placed on this fact.

[1]Coppleson 1950, 1953; Whitley 1951.

In three instances several attacks took place at one particular spot—and very probably were the work of one and the same shark. In view of this circumstance, Dr. Coppleson sounded a note of warning in a publication. No one should venture into the water where ,a shark had attacked before the animal in question had been undoubtedly eliminated. He pointed out, also, that attacks on swimming dogs were also an evil omen, for the attackers might be old or sick sharks that could not get enough to eat in a normal way and so had turned into killers, just as do old tigers.

Dr. Coppleson's remarks were still in our minds when, that afternoon, we swam off the great Bondi beach that is visited by thousands of bathers. On a raised scaffolding stood a bathing-attendant keeping a look-out for sharks. He told us that the shore was regularly trawled and that often sharks twelve to fifteen feet long were caught. Airplanes were used for observation and an attempt had been made to frighten off sharks by means of under-water bombs. Exactly one year, day for day, before our visit, the Australian surf-riding champion, Francis Okulitsch, had been killed by a shark two hundred yards out from the shore.

In the Australian Museum we made the acquaintance of Dr. Gilbert Whitley, the shark specialist, and also of Dr. Frank McNeill, the curator of the Invertebrates collection, and of Miss Pope, his assistant. They all warned us, told us to be careful and invited us, on our return journey, to give a lecture before the Royal Zoological Society.

On the Sunday, our last day in Sydney, Dick Charles took us in his car out to Botany Bay where the under-water hunters were holding a barbecue. About a dozen large tents had been set up while in the greenish water many figures of divers were to be seen moving about. We were standing on just about the spot where Captain Cook had taken possession of the new continent for the British Crown. One of the divers hauled out a curiously coloured shark. It was a 'Wobbegong'. The whole body of this animal is, apparently as a disguise, flecked with irregularly shaped blobs or blotches. The head is wide and has a

Dick Charles, president of the U.S.F.A., seen with Lotte and a wobbegong or carpet shark (*Crossorhinus barbatus*).

flattened top, while the mouth—that is fringed with barbels—has exceedingly sharp teeth.

'They hide among the seaweed and the rocks so that often you don't notice them,' Malcolm Fuller explained—he was one of the best divers in the club. 'Not so long ago someone dived under a rock where a Wobbegong was lying, the shark was so frightened that it bit the diver in the face. The poor fellow was a sorry sight . . . we've shot Wobbegongs over six feet long.'

We also went into the water, though it was turbid and rather cold. There were plenty of fish. I was in admiration at the daring of these Australians who hunted in waters where large sharks abounded and where the visibility was obviously poor. Malcolm told us how once, in muddy water, a huge shark had suddenly stopped quite near him. Malcolm felt paralysed and kept so still that the shark swam on without apparently having noticed him.

The next day we flew to Brisbane and there collected our consignment with the soda-lime and the oxygen flasks. We visited the well-known ichthyologist, Dr. Tom Marshall. He gave us more advice and some valuable introductions. Another plane took us farther on and ten hours later we arrived, rather jaded and tired, at Cairns. In a little motor-bus and over a rough road we jolted along to the old-fashioned Strand Hotel. That night we lay long without being able to sleep in the oppressive heat. Dr. Coppleson's statistics had had their effect on us.

There was a fresh wind the next morning but the sun smiled down out of a cloudless sky. All gloomy presentiments were dissipated. We had reached our goal. Before us lay the legendary Sea of Coral and barely twenty miles out there awaited us one of the greatest natural wonders in the whole world.

Cairns attracted us from the first moment we arrived. If Queensland is rightly called 'the Pearl of Australia' then Cairns is certainly the jewel of this province that is so bountifully blessed with natural advantages. The quiet, pleasing little town is bordered on one side by picturesque cane-sugar fields which reach as far as the impenetrable virgin forests of high mountains.

On the other side of the town are mangrove swamps in which the tourist, if he feels like it, can hunt for crocodiles. As we found out, you can, in two hours by car, get to the table-land—famed for its tarns, lakes and splendid waterfalls. Those who want to swim, to fish or to collect souvenirs can take the small pleasure steamer and go to Green Island that lies, decked with jungle, right inside of the Barrier Reef.

We used this vessel for our first excursion. It had been a year and a half since we had last dived and we wanted, before we started operations, to get accustomed to water and sunlight. Furthermore, we had two new under-water cameras and I wished to take a few trial shots with them. The ship slipped out of the harbour to the sound of shrill, friendly whistling, while dance music was relayed through loud speakers. Some of our fellow-passengers looked us over with curiosity, for the *Cairns Post* had heralded our arrival with an article which stated that we were anxious to meet sharks as soon as possible.

After a half an hour the island came into sight. It was flat, had a high growth of trees and was ringed round by a snow-white coral strand. We moored beside a remarkably tall and long jetty. As the helmsman explained to us, the difference between high and low tide is here never less than twelve feet and often enough reaches eighteen feet.

We shouldered the bags containing our gear, and as soon as we were on land, sought out the owner of a boat that was drawn up on the beach. There was a small kiosk where you could eat in the shade of lofty trees and write picture postcards. Here we were directed to a certain Mr. Brett Scott whom we found in the so-called 'aquarium'—a covered concrete pool in which many different sorts of gaily coloured fish and some turtles were swimming about. Mr. Scott greeted us with the broad, amiable laugh that is characteristic of Australians. He was quite ready to let us hire his boat and he took up a pair of flippers and a mask and came with us. Obviously he also had read the *Cairns Post* since he volunteered the information that, the day before, a large hammerhead had made his appearance quite near the jetty.

We rowed out some distance and then dropped anchor in

seven fathoms. Mr. Scott dived in first, down towards the flat bottom strewn with a few dead clumps of coral. He pointed out a serpentine line marked on the sand. He dug about first at one end of the line and then at the other until he pulled out a splendid spotted Auger-shell. I swam towards another similar line and managed to get an even finer specimen. As we soon realized, the Barrier Reef is a paradise for shell collectors. Later on we saw in a small shop at Cairns a collection any museum in the world might be proud to possess.

Mr. Scott had work to do on land so he swam off. We rowed towards some old stakes which obviously had once supported a smaller jetty and made fast. Lotte stayed with a notebook in the boat while I put on my diving-gear and took our new flash-light camera into the water. I could try out the distance to which the flashlight would carry, for the old piles, around which magnificent sponges clustered, were set at regular intervals apart. Some worked well enough, others did not. I surfaced after each shot and dictated the results to Lotte. Fish swam in from all directions and stared at me. As I came up for the seventh or eighth time, we heard excited shouts.

'Hi, hi, Dr. Hass,' came the yells over the water. There was tied up to the big jetty a sailing yacht and on the jetty stood gesticulating figures. 'A shark,' they called out; 'there's a shark swimming about here.'

'Where?'

'Just here, right off the jetty.'

'How big?'

'About fourteen feet; he's a hammerhead.'

I muttered curses on the *Cairns Post*. We had made up our minds to be very careful and I was not at all prepared, when I had not been diving for more than a half an hour, to tackle one of the six sorts of man-eating sharks which infest these waters. Still, all the same, this was a hammerhead and I had been trying for a full twelve years to photograph one of them. I had encountered specimens five or six times already but, on each occasion, either I had no camera with me or I had run out of film.

Lotte looked at me and made no comment while I slipped out of my diving-gear and made loose the boat. Luckily, the day before, I had bought, at a general supply store, some broomsticks and had fitted them with pointed ends and loops. When we got near the landing-stage the hammerhead had already vanished. A woman and four men—including our friend Brett Scott—were standing over us and all gazing intently in the same direction. All at once the woman pointed off towards the right and then the five of them began to call out excitedly:

'There, there he comes; he's swerving round in a circle.'

That decided it. Armed with a camera and a small stick I plunged into the water. The bottom was soft sand and only three fathoms down. Visibility was not very good since there were many particles of sand swirling about and these deflected the sunlight in all directions. It just happened that I had a yellow filter in front of the lens and this proved very useful in the circumstances since it eliminated some of the scattered light.

I could see no sign of the shark. I surfaced and was met with cries from the jetty: 'Right ahead'—'Rather more to the left'—'Still a bit more to the left'—then I saw him.

That had not been such a bad estimate. He was certainly twelve feet long, very fat and massive. The remarkably tall dorsal fin that is such a feature in hammerheads stood up like a sail from the creature's back. He was swimming just within the range of my vision, sideways to me and fairly near the bottom. I dived at once, adjusted the focus and shot. Then I hurried upwards and swam as quickly as I could to the jetty.

What I had seen of that shark was enough for me. He was swimming far too quickly and excitedly for his size. I felt sure that he had eaten not so long before and still had the taste of blood in his mouth.

I had not swum more than a few yards when I heard more cries:

'Look out! There he is again! Be careful!'

I looked round. Sure enough the shark had swerved and was making right for me. Still, there seemed no doubt that he had not yet spotted me. He thrashed along with rapid, powerful strokes, close to the bottom as though he were looking for something.

While my first photograph was practically worthless since the hammerlike excrescences of the head cannot be seen in side-view, I now had an opportunity of getting the picture I had so often dreamed about. The hammerhead stood out splendidly against the light-coloured sandy background. I clenched my teeth, set the focus at two-and-a-half metres, dived under and swam towards the shark. I saw the animal getting bigger and bigger in the viewfinder. I waited until he almost filled the whole of the frame and then I shot. The creature came so close under me that I could have touched his dorsal fin as he glided past.

It was not until he had swum from under me that he spotted me. Nimble as a cat and with an ease one would never have thought possible in such a huge, massive body, he swung right round and turned one side of his misshapen head towards me. To this day I can still see the flat, streamlined section of the hammer on which, like a knob, there was set a round, dull eye. He stared at me with astonishment. Instinctively, my whole body contracted with terror. The effect of this was astounding. The shark became just as afraid of me as I was of him. His body vibrated and shuddered just like mine. He swirled round and shot off like a hunted hare. His fin strokes were so powerful that I could hear them as dull thuds through the water. His mighty bulk vanished in the distance.

On the jetty I was received like a triumphant gladiator. We were introduced to the owner of the yacht—that was called *Mitsu*—as well as to Fred Williams, the owner of the largest slaughterhouse in Cairns, and his wife Peg. It was Fred's yells that had challenged me, and he begged me not to hold anything against him. Only when my shadow melted into that of the shark did he realize the danger into which he had drawn me. Fred and Peg became our very good friends.

They had been fishing early that morning, had cut up a good many fish and thrown the pieces into the water. The hammerhead had obviously been eating these morsels and it was more of them that he was searching for on the bottom. Had I known

The twelve-foot hammerhead shark (*Sphyran lewini*) off Green Island. It came straight at me but did not see me. His small eyes are situated at the ends of the hammer.

all this, I would not, I am free to admit, have ventured into the water.

The incident was reported rather widely in the Australian Press. In one way the adventure was unique for, up until then, scarcely ever had strangers witnessed our encounters with sharks. When, a week later, we got back from our first excursion onto the Barrier Reef, we were shown a newspaper article in which an Australian professional diver advised us to dive near the whale flensing-yard in Moreton Bay. He would not regard us as really daring until we had swum there in the bloody shark-infested water. I replied to him that that sort of thing did not interest us, though, at the time, I could not foresee that, only eight months later, we should be doing just that—swimming about in the water among bleeding whales.

# The Mighty Rampart

THE Great Barrier Reef of Australia is the most stupendous structure which living creatures have built upon our earth. No work of Man's hand can be compared with it. To get things into their right proportions, let us make an estimate of the cubic contents of the reef which is two thousand kilometres long, in many places a hundred and fifty kilometres wide, and, on the outer edge, forms a rampart that drops precipitously to a depth of over two thousand metres.

If we take these figures, then we shall see that the Great Barrier Reef has a volume eight million times greater than that of the Pyramid of Cheops at Gizeh, a hundred thousand times greater than that of the Great Wall of China, and two thousand times greater than the whole mass of the City of New York.

It is generally held today that the eastern portion of the Australian continent once rose considerably higher than it does now, so that the Barrier Reef was formed as land sank gradually under the sea. Originally it was a fringing reef along the coast and since it went on growing while the land dropped, the reef inevitably withdrew more and more from the shore. In the ever-widening channel new reefs were formed so that at the present time the whole expanse of water is filled with innumerable crisscrossing coral chains.

The survey ships, *Fly, Bramble* and *Dart,* were the first to be

employed on the charting of this immense area, but the work is
not yet completed. The earliest comprehensive zoological trea-
tise was that of Saville Kent, *The Great Barrier Reef of Australia,* in which were reproduced photographs taken above water
at low tide, which offered pictures of the emerged portions of
this marvel of the world. We had Kent's book with us as well
as C. M. Yonge's *A Year on the Great Barrier Reef,* in which
the leader of the British Barrier Reef Expedition of 1928–1929
sets out its results in very lucid language. Both of these works
gave us the signposts by which we could, in the short time at our
disposal, find our way about. From these books also we obtained very useful information about the animal life of the Reef.

Fred Williams and harbour-master Captain Barnes helped
us in our search for a suitable motor-launch. As it was already
mid-December, and thus the beginning of the cyclone period—
which heralds and ushers in the rainy season—the fishermen
had just ended their trips out to the Reef. A ship that gets caught
in a cyclone is doomed. However securely anchored a vessel may
be, the whirlwind pulls it down on the anchor chain itself. In
1899 a whole fleet of pearl-fishing cutters suffered this fate.
Altogether sixty-three ships sank and over three hundred men
were drowned. In 1911 an 1800-ton steamer, *Yongala,* rode into
a cyclone and sank without a trace. There were a hundred and
forty men aboard. Later on the wreck was sighted from an airplane. The ship lay broken in two, at a depth of over fifteen
fathoms.

Almost every year Queensland is swept by a number of cy-
clones and many towns and settlements, including Cooktown,
have been devastated. For us, however, this dangerous season of
the year presented one notable advantage. For all the rest of the
year the south-east trade-winds blow uninterruptedly and dash
huge waves against the Reef. It is only during the cyclone season
that there are, in between intervals of white squalls that swoop
down suddenly, fine sunny days without any wind at all. It was on
such days that we were counting, for only then would we be able
to dive on the outer rampart of the Great Wall.

We ended up by finding three boats whose owners declared

The outer fringe of the world's greatest coral reef—the Great Barrier
Reef of Australia.

The seaward rampart of the Great Barrier Reef is pounded smooth by the ocean, though corals grow in a few sheltered spots.

they were ready to risk it. We decided on a nineteen-foot-long motor-launch belonging to a Mr. MacDonald who had been a commercial fisherman for twenty years and made a very good impression on us.

It was a magnificent cloudless morning when we left Cairns and steered northwards along the coast. Steep, uninviting-looking slopes of virgin forest slipped by us. It was twilight when we got to Low Island, a tiny speck with a tall lighthouse.

Here the British Barrier Reef Expedition had made its head-quarters for a whole year. As we drew in towards land we saw shafts of light shimmering through the bushes and heard loud radio-music. A family and a bachelor live here in peaceful soli-tude. The children are taught their lessons over the wireless. Mail and supplies are delivered once a week. We walked round the island in the darkness and then settled down on board, under a swaying lamp, to eat one of those surprising mixed salads the Australians know so well how to prepare.

Early the next morning we had left Low Island far behind us. It was oppressively hot. The mirror-like surface of the sea shim-mered in an immensity of soft haze. About noon we reached the first goal of our trip—the famed Endeavour Reef on which Cap-tain Cook once ran aground.

The six guns he had thrown overboard have attracted divers from as far back as the last century. These guns, indeed, are for the Australians a sort of national treasure, a sacred possession. Every schoolchild learns about their history—only, no one, as yet, has been able to find them. Cook's account of the incident is not very detailed and the reef is, in reality, much larger than it seems upon the map. It extends in a shallow arc for five miles in the sea, moreover many minor reefs lie in front of the main reef. The area, then, in which *Endeavour* may have piled up is of considerable extent.

It was with some discouragement that Lotte and I stared at the blurred outlines of the reefs. The water was, indeed, so tur-bid that there was no sense in making any attempt to dive. MacDonald said that the water hereabouts was almost always dirty, though that particular day was an especially bad one. So

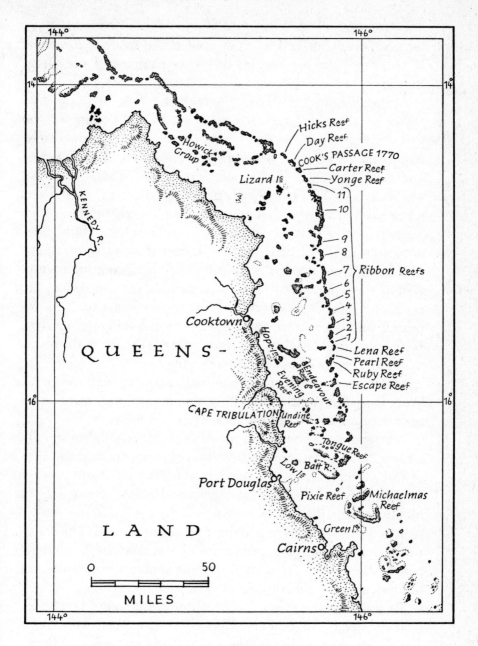

Middle Section of the Great Barrier Reef of Australia

we postponed our investigation and made straight for Ruby Reef, one of the bastions on the outer rampart of the Great Barrier.

Abruptly Lotte cried out, 'There, look!'

Not far off from us, curled up in a ring and floating on the surface, was a huge snake. It was of a brilliant yellow colour with black markings. I wanted to stop at once but MacDonald said he was sure we should meet with plenty of such creatures almost every day. So we pushed on. Never again, during our whole stay, did we catch a glimpse of such a creature.

Shortly after that we witnessed an astonishing natural phenomenon. In the direction of the Barrier there arose quite unexpectedly from above the hardly visible horizon a high white wall of wave that spread as quickly as wind over the sky to the right and left. Several times the strange occurrence was repeated, and later on we were to see the same thing quite often. It is a mirage formed by the projection onto the sky of the much magnified image of breakers beyond the horizon.

The phenomenon seemed to us like a greeting from the Great Wall. Deep down within us we felt both joy and anguish at being near the rampart. What should we find out there?

We stood in the bow and watched the surf becoming gradually clearer. Since the water was so calm we did not notice the leeside of Ruby Reef until we were right onto it. Great pellucid patches showed under the surface, circular coral towers, from sixty to ninety feet in diameter, jutted straight up from the murky depths. We slowed down and drew nearer to the reef. The water was, generally speaking, pretty turbid here also. In the shadow cast by the boat there drifted like snowflakes through the sea millions of minute medusae.

To judge by the colour of the water it seemed to be clearer near the neighbouring Pearl Reef. We went across. Here were just the same sort of coral towers. We tied up to one of them. Lotte and I, in diving-gear, went under water.

The first impression was one of marvellous beauty. The flat roof of the tower—only about six feet under the surface—resembled some magnificent flowering plant in and around which

Forty-five feet below the surface Lotte examines the strange formation of a Montipora coral.

most odd-looking fish were fluttering about like butterflies. However, near the perpendicular side against which we were swaying downwards the water was turbid and there were only a few living corals. Like weirdly grimacing phantoms the dark shadows of grotto and ledge stared eyeless at us. Out of the foggy green, fish came swimming silently. They glanced at us as they glided by and noiselessly vanished.

We came to a halt when we were some six fathoms down and squatted under a projection that was rather like a box in a theatre. Here again there were drifting about innumerable tiny jellyfish. I looked at Lotte. She looked at me. We were rather nervous.

We were nervous lest there should suddenly come sharks up from the murk. We were still more apprehensive about other surprises, about things we could not foresee. Among such menaces there came, first and foremost, the legendary 'sea wasps'.

We knew that as yet no human eye has ever beheld these creatures. Probably they are small medusae. Nevertheless, even those who have fallen victims to these uncanny dwellers in the sea have never seen their tormentors. A typical case was that of a nineteen-year-old lad who in January 1937 when he was bathing in water that hardly came up to his chest—some forty miles south of Cairns—was suddenly stung by something. He dragged himself onto land, collapsed, and within seven minutes was dead. A soldier of the Australian Army to whom a similar thing happened died in three minutes. In Cairns we had talked to Dr. Flecker who had examined these cases. He assured us that death in no single case that had come to his notice supervened later than ten minutes after the attack. All the recorded instances of such accidents had occurred between 13th December and 10th April. Certainly it is not the Portuguese Man o' War (*Physalia*) that is to blame since if it were its striking blue-coloured float would certainly be noticed. Moreover, a Portuguese Man o' War does cause a painful irritation but not death. Dr. Flecker's opinion is that the 'sea wasp' is a comparatively small creature—probably a carybdeid medusa—which lives on the sea-bottom but at a certain stage of maturity rises to the surface. Its poison is more deadly than any known snake poison.

Dr. Flecker also warned us of another animal, not identified, which he called 'Irukandji' after the name of an aboriginal tribe. The Irukandji also stings like a wasp and causes moderate local swelling. The symptoms, however, do not appear until a minimum of five and a maximum of sixty minutes after the stab has been inflicted. Then the victim collapses, without warning, is afflicted with violent vomiting and severe pain in all the muscles. Dr. Southcott, an Australian Army physician, has himself treated more than a hundred cases and all of them occurred between 6th December and 5th February. Although fine-meshed nets have been drawn through great expanses of sea, it has never been possible to catch an Irukandji.[1]

We squatted down as though bewitched and from our seats stared at the murky swirl before us. Then a very remarkable fish with a rounded protuberance on his head came by. I photographed him. Lotte grabbed hold of my arm. Out of a cleft near us there emerged a huge wrasse, also with a knoblike lump on the head; just where Lotte was leaning against the rock I saw a long hairy worm working its way out of a crevice. I pressed her hand and we both swam up to the surface.

'This isn't a very nice sort of place,' I said when we were once more sitting in the boat and enjoying the sunshine.

'No, it's not worth while bothering about; most of the corals are dead anyway.'

Both of us would rather have bitten our tongues off than have talked about the fear that had gripped us down below.

In the evening sky a blood-red crescent moon shone out; we had anchored in the lee of Ruby Reef. MacDonald and the boy were fishing with ground-hooks and pulling up one golden perch after another from the dark water. We could hear the constant thudding of the surf on the outer edge of the reef. Well, we had reached our goal and we felt humble and miserable. The huge, lugubrious reef was getting us down. We had the

[1]Flecker, January and July 1952.

Strange fish shapes loomed indistinctly and threateningly out of the murky water.

impression it was going to be very difficult to probe into its secrets.

The next morning there was a strong wind. Swarms of fish were darting and flashing along the surface pursued by a school of hungry bonitos. The water was a deep blue. The sunlight sparkled in the crest of every wave. We made for Pearl Reef again and tied up where a glistening blue lagoon lay isolated within the great platform of the reef.

We swam against the current, over the reef, and discovered a marvellous, fairy-like landscape of corals. This lagoon was from five to six fathoms deep and in its relatively sheltered waters delicately branched coral trees had grown. Countless shiny blue and yellow fish were swimming in and out of a bouquet of corals that rose in the middle of the pool. Two small grey sharks came quite near, eyed us and then vanished. On every side were astonishing coral formations while the water simply swarmed with fish, large and small. Here also we got our first glimpse of the famed and murderous *Tridacna* clams. They lay ponderous and

A giant wrasse (*Cheilinus undulatus*) emerges from a cave.

immobile on the bottom. The bulky shells were over three feet across and between their half-open wavy edges there bulged out thick fleshy lips like the petals of many-hued blossoms.

We kept at a safe distance and watched. We knew from Young's book that the edges of the mantle were a sort of vege-table garden on which the *Tridacna* grows small algae similar to those which, as plankton, drift about unattached in the sea. The fixed algae, however, settle in the skin and tissues of the gigantic molluscs and provide the creatures with an additional supply of food—a rare example of an animal cultivating its food inside its own body. The *Tridacna* furnishes, as a start in life, a few hundreds of such symbiotic algae, to each one of its larvae. Since the algae need sunlight to flourish, you almost always find the *Tridacnae* in sunny spots where they lie with their mantles widely expanded.

Lotte put her hand a little too near. The giant clam snapped its edges together. At first, however, it stopped half-way so that it could pull in the lips of its mantle. Then the wavy shells clenched together quite tight.

'What do you think?' she said when we had surfaced. 'If I had stuck my foot in I don't imagine that he'd have been able to hold me fast.'

'Better not try. Maybe we can get hold of an artificial leg. You can't be too careful.'

We explored the whole circumference of the lagoon and took plenty of pictures. Then the current changed and the water got dirty again. So we made for the First Ribbon Reef, where we cast anchor on the lee side near some very tortuous coral ravines. I put on my diving-gear and went into the water alone.

The reef was a real labyrinth. The ravines were eighteen feet deep and led into a submarine hall which was lighted from a wide opening in its roof. Other ravines and grottoes led out radi-ally from the hall. One of the passages penetrated far into the heart of the reef, then bifurcated, became narrower and nar-rower and ended in a deep hole. Another gallery led, after many tortuous turns, into a valley overgrown with marvellous corals. I felt pretty safe in the maze of grottoes since visibility was good and I could see all round about me. Little by little I felt my way along and gradually my self-confidence came back. I amused myself by giving each of the grottoes a name. I called the central hall the 'Mausoleum' since in one corner there lay a great pile of empty shells.

Indeed the hall did look just like a mausoleum or the dwelling of some gigantic octopus with shells as witnesses of meals. There were also the empty shells of crawfish but though I explored every nook and cranny I could find no trace of the banqueter.

While Lotte sat in the boat and awaited anxiously for an hour, I posted myself at the opening of the passage leading into the coral valley and delightedly surveyed the scene. Some of the fish I recognized from Red Sea days, but others, with striking markings, were new to me. Arrow-swift wrasses swirled about me. A big Porgy hung motionless before me while he allowed his gills to be cleaned by a small worm-like fish. A globe fish turned around oddly in a circle. High above me glided a school of pencil-shaped garpikes or skipper fish. A couple of trigger fish were engaged in gallant love-making over a huge coral bush. Indefatigable parrot fish nibbled at the blue, reddish and yellow coral buds. I could see a speckled moray eel peeping out of a hole. In another crevice lay sleeping a small grey ray with light blue spots. Wherever you looked there was life in teeming, vari-egated abundance. Nothing was more difficult than to fix one's attention closely on one object out of the multitude.

But I did manage to watch the big Porgy and the little fish that was doing the gill-cleaning. Porgy held his thick-lipped mouth wide open while the little fellow swam busily in and out of the cavity. Sometimes he emerged through the mouth itself and sometimes he made his way through the widely extended gills. I felt a pricking sensation on one of my knuckles where I had a slight graze. There was another wormlike fish calmly nib-bling away at my scratch. Quite deliberately he ripped off a bit of my skin. I chased him away but he soon came back and as often as I kept still to take a photograph there he was renewing the attack.

That evening Lotte and I had dreadful sunburn on our backs.

The ill-reputed giant clam (*Tridacna gigas*) lies like a trap amid the coral. This specimen is nearly five feet long.

MacDonald smeared us with some liquid or other. It worked like magic but burned like fire. He and the lad spent the whole evening at the radio trying to get the weather reports.

MacDonald assured us that a cyclone on its way to Cooktown had swept a piano up a hundred and fifty feet into the air. A cyclone at sea, so he informed us in dismal tones, is something you experience only once. However, that evening nothing could spoil our good spirits. We had had our first glance into the wonderland of the Great Reef and we had, so to speak, taken foothold there. In our dreams we saw gigantic clams surrounded with myriads of very extraordinary fish.

Still, the weather left much to be desired. The next morning the sky was rather overcast. Out in the direction of the mainland there hung a high dark bank of cloud. We went as far as the Fifth Ribbon Reef but it was so windy that we turned and made for our moorings again. Yearningly I looked out over the reef-platform to the great breakers. I wondered if we should ever be able to fulfil our ambition of diving on the outer rampart.

'Saville Kent,' I said to MacDonald, 'tells the story of some divers who reported they had spotted, in the Cooktown area, a giant *Tridacna* over nine feet across. Do you think that's true?'

'Maybe not nine feet but certainly six feet; as a matter of fact I've seen one six feet across myself.'

'Where?'

'Near Lizard Island.'

'Is it there still?'

'I don't suppose anyone's carried it off.'

Splendid news. Lizard Island was more or less on the programme for our second trip after Christmas. In his desperation, Captain Cook had climbed up the thousand feet high granite cliffs of the island in order to spy out some passage for his ship through the reefs. Lizard Island offered us one great advantage. If the weather got worse, we could always dive into sheltered waters either on one side of the island or another.

We dropped anchor near the 'Mausoleum', and I took Lotte through the galleries and passages which I now felt I knew well enough. This time, however, there were considerably fewer fish about. We had often noticed the same sort of thing. If human beings break into an undisturbed area, they upset the equilibrium of nature, and it will be some days before the animals calm down again.

Within the grottoes we felt just as though we belonged to the reef, as though we were two more of the countless inhabitants which live in the protection of the innumerable nooks and corners—guests in a big hotel in fact. We were able to realize, too, how the reef sleeps during the day. It was only in the darkness of the grottoes that we could see the open calices of the polyps. When the light is strong all the coral polyps withdraw into their tiny calcareous holes and venture forth again only when the night draws on. Why?

These polyps, despite their greediness, are peaceful creatures although armed with stinging tentacles. Their principal food consists of animal plankton and this flees from bright light which is too strong and may kill it. Therefore the minute organisms move up and down, in immense clouds, through the water. At twilight they are on the surface; if the light gets stronger then they sink downwards. The clearer are the sky and the sea, the deeper the plankton drift down, for the light penetrates farther and farther. At evening they come up again to the surface and during the night swim about aimlessly hither and thither. That is the moment for the coral calices to open up, and they can eat enough to afford to rest during the daytime.

The minute algae—which live in the tissues of the polyps just as they do in those of the *Tridacna*—behave in a diametrically opposite manner. For the algae the daytime is working time. They feed on the water matter in the cells, they relieve the polyps from their 'fatigue', as one might say, and supply them with oxygen which the algae, like all plants, give off. Much discussion has taken place as to why the reef-building corals are only found down to a maximum depth of twenty-five fathoms. The little algae may well be the determining factor. There are so many coral polyps present on one coral tree that possibly they can only obtain sufficient oxygen if the algae are there to provide it. All plants need sunlight and cannot flourish in water that is more than twenty-five fathoms deep. So here may be the explanation of why, too, no reef-building corals are to be found at greater depths.

The sun disappeared behind a cloud and it became quite dark in our grotto. We waited a little while and then swam up again to the surface. The sky was covered. The heavy wall of cloud over the mainland had visibly increased in size. Then it began to rain and MacDonald made it quite clear that he no longer felt safe at our anchorage.

However, we spent the night there though the waves got higher and higher. A strong wind whistled over the sea and fine spray whipped past us. In the early morning the sky was grey and quite overcast. Still, we dived in a small, sheltered lagoon, but there was a strong current running and the water was rather opaque. MacDonald urged us to leave. He had not been able to tune in to any weather forecasts for a whole day and he was getting upset. With a rather heavy heart I agreed and we set our course for the Hope Islands, two thickly forested spots of land well within the channel. Between them, so MacDonald explained, there was excellent anchorage.

From afar we could make out thousands of white specks in the trees—doves. MacDonald had a gun with him which I borrowed. Half an hour later we were stalking through the matted tangle of astoundingly tall trees. After that we sat in a row on the beach while we busily plucked the birds.

Pitch-dark clouds hemmed us in on all sides. The sea was like glass and the air tingling with electricity. MacDonald let down another anchor and showed me on the map how the boat now lay in the protection of a narrow passage between the reefs. Only weather coming from directly north could touch us. He wanted to give us, after the doves, a special pudding he called 'pantaloons'. He was just getting down to this interesting occupation when the storm broke over us.

The floodgates of the heavens were opened and a waterfall engulfed us. The lightning flashed unceasingly. The thunder rumbled and rolled continuously from all directions. MacDonald had stowed away everything. Then, there he was, standing pale-faced in front of me. The storm had veered round and was now attacking us from the north. There was nothing for it but to pull in our anchors, set off in complete darkness against the wind and out of the shelter of our channel, to make our way round the island so as to seek protection on the opposite side.

Then it became clear we had made a good choice both of master and boat. Except for the compass we had nothing to guide us but the snow-white outline of the island as it was visible, for a fraction of a second and through a wall of rain, at each flash of lightning. In these circumstances, it was a masterly achievement to find the course through the reefs and to reach a sheltered spot on the far side of the island. Lotte and I had done what we could to help, were wet to the skin and thoroughly exhausted. The thunder crashed on all through the night. However, in spite of all this, we insisted that poor MacDonald should produce his 'pantaloons'.

The next morning was so still, so sunny, so reassuring, that we almost felt that the storm had been a figment of our imagination. There was a very strong ebb-tide running and the broad reef-platform, to the south side of the island, was quite exposed and dry. We walked about on it through puddles and pools, we threw stones about and found some wonderful shells. We also discovered Cone shells, which you can take hold of only at the ends since these creatures have a poisonous sting they dart out, quite without warning, from their apertures. Then, as all the clouds had rolled away, we hastened on board and made for Ruby Reef once more.

Now, for the first time, we could see the outer rampart of the Barrier in comparatively calm weather. We approached it from the outer side. There was still a very heavy swell, so that we could advance only to within thirty or forty yards of the broad band of foam that indicated the reef-edge; still, from the purely technical point of view, it would have been possible to dive. I should have had, however, to plunge into the deep sea and to swim towards the rampart under clouds of foam. The boat could only have kept on turning round in circles and could not have kept near enough to me to be of ready help. MacDonald

A unicorn fish can defend itself with the sharp spikes extending from the tail-fin, as well as with its horn.

Cone shells from the Great Barrier Reef. They can be picked up only from the ends as they have a poisonous sting.

and the boy let down drag-hooks and we coasted along Ruby Reef. I kept a sharp look-out to see if some more suitable place could be found, but finally had to give up. As things were, the undertaking would be too hazardous and we would surely have a better opportunity later on. Very reluctantly I told MacDonald to put about. We took the same course back.

MacDonald told us that often very large sharks came up when he was fishing off the outer rampart.

'I saw one,' he said as he reeled in his line, 'that was so big you wouldn't believe me even if I told you. But it's true. I had been fishing for about two hours at the same place. There were a few sharks about. Then this monster came out of the depths. I've never seen anything like it. I can't even guess how long he was. He was just enormous and incredibly fat.'

'What colour?'

'Dark. The things that struck me most about him were enormous gills. The water was pretty calm and I could make him out quite clearly. He rose slowly, a real monster, a bit clumsy and cumbrous too. Then he turned round and vanished. He was surely over thirty feet long.'

It might have been a basking shark which, after the whale shark, is the largest of all the shark tribe, but these animals live in northern seas, feed also on plankton, and are easily recognizable by their long and striking gill apertures. That such sharks should be found in tropical water seemed very curious.

Up to then MacDonald had been most good-tempered and amiable, but now he and the lad were obviously upset. We knew the reason. The next day would be Christmas Eve and the day after that the greatest holiday at Cairns in all the year. But we had firmly agreed that if the weather was good we would remain out even over the holidays.

By now we were anchored on the inner side of Ruby Reef. There Lotte and I swam to a glittering blue lagoon I had espied from the roof of the cabin. The first thing we saw was a large shark. The water of the lagoon was fully fifteen fathoms deep and out from the depths he came obliquely towards us. When he got quite close he remained still, just about at the limit of visibility. He was a whaler shark. While Lotte kept an eye on him, I took as many photographs as I could since here were coral formations such as we had never seen. Then we left the lagoon to the shark. It was obviously his domain anyway. We swam to the boat, changed our diving-apparatus and then went under at a break in the reef somewhat farther to the west.

What surprised us most of all was the size of the animals we saw. Not only were the corals and clams on the Barrier Reef strikingly large, but all the other sorts of animals seemed to vie with each other in size. There would be pale yellow seacucumbers resembling pumpkins or gourds, and deep blue coloured starfish, some of which were sixteen or twenty inches across. On a coral wall was an ugly black lump. Lotte touched it with the tip of her finger when the black skin contracted on both sides and a most delicate white porcelain was revealed. It was a white cowrie shell as large as your fist. We turned over some of the coral clumps and found under them a number of tiger-cowries. Then, abruptly, Lotte caught hold of my arm and pointed to a not very pretty but rather deformed seriatopora coral. She guided me nearer to it and then touched a lumplike formation. Only the day before we had been reading and talking about it. The lump was none other than the strange dwelling of the small gall-forming crab *Hapalocarcinus marsupialis,* the female of which allows itself in some unexplained way to be overgrown with branches of coral. The coral growth, however, leaves a number of interstices free which are large enough for the considerably smaller male crab to make his way in. The young crabs too slip in and out through these openings. I took my knife and carefully opened the gall. The little creature squatted, quite astounded, on the bottom and made no attempt to hurry off. Its whole way of life had been destroyed. An odd case, that of a female building its own cage and never leaving it.

When we surfaced an hour later we heard the rumble of thunder and saw to our astonishment that the sky was quite overcast. It had been marvellous weather but now it started to rain. With some show of regret MacDonald informed us that this sudden change had made it quite necessary for us to put back to Cairns.

The lad was so overjoyed at the idea of getting home in good time that he steered us to within a hair's breadth of Undine Reef. We heard a grating sound, then we were all clear and on our way. If we had been only three feet more to port we should have bashed right onto the reef. MacDonald, who had been repairing a fishing-line, leapt aft and seized the rudder.

That night we slept once more on Low Island and reached Cairns the following day at noon. There were no less than thirty empty beer-bottles near the bed in our room at the hotel. The place which had before seemed so quiet and respectable was unrecognizable. Nearly every guest had drunk more than was good for him and no one knew which room belonged to whom. Everyone was hugging and embracing everyone else, and sounds of gay song echoed through the hall.

On MacDonald's invitation we ate our Christmas pudding at his home; then Fred and Peg fetched us and we moved from one house to another. Everywhere we met new faces, and everywhere we heard some tale or other about sharks. There was hearty laughter when we told about the Brisbane's diver's challenge. No one wanted to believe that we had already dived among the outer reefs.

The next morning Fred and Peg took us in their car to the tableland where we spent two wonderful days in splendid weather. Everything, however, indicated that the rainy season that year was setting in earlier than usual, and if it did begin to rain in earnest then it would never leave off. In Cairns the water would rise to a height of sixteen inches in the streets and the tradesmen would have to lay down sandbags to prevent their shops being flooded.

As soon as we got back to Cairns I contacted the 'bush pilot' who, with a small plane, maintained communications with outlying places. If we wanted to do what we had set out to do, then we had to survey the endless chain of reefs from the air, get a bird's-eye view, take photographs from a plane and find out where were really the best spots to set to work. The bush pilot agreed to fly us over the whole range of the reefs from Cairns up to Lizard Island. As the small sports plane was open on either side we could easily peer down below and take photographs. We took off early in the morning and flew first of all to Evening Reef over which we cruised for half an hour. MacDonald, who had never been up in the air before, came with us.

By closely studying Cook's journal, I had come to the conclusion that perhaps the general opinion was wrong and that his ship had not piled up on Endeavour Reef at all. Two hours before the catastrophe, indeed, *Endeavour* had already struck shallow water which, however, soon fell again to sixteen fathoms. According to the traditional account this shallow water was over the outermost platform at the end of Pickersgill Reef. Still, there was the possibility that it might be a small elevation marked on the maps as Bonner Rock. If this latter supposition was right, then the course would have led not to Endeavour Reef but to Evening Reef.

We flew about over both reefs and I took several hundred shots. There was the tedious labour of fitting them together, like a jigsaw puzzle, but we got an accurate outline map of the lines of reef as they exist today.

Next we hovered over Ruby Reef, which we knew well enough from the water, and then flew farther and out over the long chain of the Ribbon Reefs which looked, from the bird's-eye view, for all the world like a string of sausages. Each of the reefs made an arc against the sea. On the inner side everything was flat and sandy, while on the outer side against the deep water there were tower-like formations resembling those near which we had already dived. Within the narrow channels rather receding smaller reefs were visible; these were obviously young and in full development.

What interested us most of all was the outer rampart where the wide stretching white chains of breakers rolled over the reef platfrom close to which the sea was black and of abysmal depth. In some places, notably at the Third, Fourth and Fifth Ribbon Reefs, there ran along, before the edge of the rampart, a clearly visible dam which did not, however, reach to the surface of the water. Through this dam a longitudinal channel had been formed. I could not understand what could be the explanation of this and made up my mind that, come what might, I would get a good look at the formation.

We flew over Cormorant Passage and the twelfth ribbon reef which has been called Yonge Reef, over Carter Reef and Day Reef. It was between these two that Cook managed to get out into open sea once more. The whole endless line of reefs here swerves in an arc so that the two latter reefs, Carter and Day, run in a north-westerly direction. The terminal reef, Hicks Reef, seemed especially interesting. From its western end there opened out onto the outer rampart many small promising-looking inlets.

We flew in an arc to Lizard Island, circled over it, and then set off back towards Cairns. Our pilot took us over many of the inner channel reefs among which were the blob of the exposed Pixie Reef—to whose singular beauty Saville Kent makes allusion—and the vast flat expanse of Tongue Reef and Batt Reef whose platforms lie like slabs of concrete under the surface and have a diameter of between four and a half and five and a half miles.

On the way in from the airfield, Lotte pointed to a haberdasher's shop. In its window were a number of artificial legs on which ladies' stockings were displayed. We stopped the car, went in and, amid general astonishment, bought one of the legs. It was made of plastic material and in the hotel I filled it up with plaster. Here was our instrument for trying out the strength of the murderous clams' bite. Maybe it was not quite fair to experiment with a peg-leg for it had hardly any joint and besides that was much too hard. All the same it was a leg and we could not find a better one.

# The Goal

SINCE the early days of the great maritime discoverers, those
strange formations we know as atolls have aroused the curiosity
of man. They rise out of the ocean, rings of reef dotted with tall
palms, and enclose a shimmering blue lake—the lagoon. What
is the origin of atolls? Formerly it was thought that they were
sunken volcanoes around whose craters' edges coral reefs grew.
Then Darwin put forth a hypothesis which, because of its sim-
plicity, soon found general acceptance.

It was well known that fringing reefs occur along tropical
coastlines. If land sinks for any reason (and we know from
geological evidence that land often does sink) then, through
the upward thrust of the fringing reef which goes on growing as
the land sinks, a barrier reef is formed. If, however, the central
island disappears completely below the surface of the sea, then
there remains only the ring-shaped reef above the waves.

Today Darwin's theory is by no means generally accepted.
Part of it, however, the division of coral reefs into fringing,
barrier and atoll reefs is universally adopted. This classification is to be found in every school-book and in every work which
provides a summary of scientific knowledge. The classification,
nevertheless, is very liable to induce erroneous conceptions, for
there are, indeed, many coral reefs which fall into none of the
three categories.

I had already thoroughly explored many of such 'nonclassi-
fied' reefs in the Red Sea. Here they lay within the real barrier,
and it was easy to see how they had formed. I was able to observe a coherent evolutionary chain which started from a small
mushroom-like formation and then spread out upwards into an
ever-wider reef-complex until it presented the appearance of a
huge concrete pavement under the surface. It is on such pave-
ments that islands are formed.

From some elevation down in depths where reef-coral can
still thrive there develops upwards an ever-spreading reef. According to the elevation the reef may be a cupola, a long-drawn-
out strip, a sickle-shaped arc, or of irregular branching outline.
Since in the depths living conditions are more or less uniform,
the reef pushes upwards with the shape it has fortuitously assumed.

As soon, however, as the reef nears the surface of the water,
the influence of wind and wave begin to make itself felt. On the
Queensland coasts, for instance, there blows for eight months
out of the twelve the regular south-east trade-wind. Thus, the
reefs show a corresponding orientation. Wind and wave bring
nourishment and oxygen so the corals display luxuriant growth
towards the south-east. They spread out farther and farther
into the sea and thus is formed a slope which becomes ever
steeper until it is a perpendicular wall which in some places is
topped by a projecting ledge.

Pieces of coral broken off by dashing waves during a storm are
rolled and swept by the sea over the reef and so there is formed
on the opposite side—that away from the wind—a rubble slope
that increases in size and on whose surface, in sheltered spots,
much sand accumulatae. The shells of the tiny plankton animal-
culae—the *Foraminifera*—purl around and are reduced to sand.
Dead coral blocks are crushed and pounded by the waves and
also become sand. Sea parrots and other animals eat coral-buds,
crush them and leave sand.

With the flow of the tides this sand is whirled about over the
reef, whose crevices and interstices become filled in, while, at
the same time, calcareous algae combine to cement the rubble

together. There is thus formed between the perpendicular wall on the one side and the rubble slope on the other a rather smooth, very hard platform with only a few corals on it. During heavy storms the sea sometimes hurls blocks of coral against this bastion. They lie on the platform and appear above the water's surface. Since there is a strong back and forth wash over the platform, only very robust animals can thrive there, animals which are able to hold on fast. The older the reef gets, the wider becomes the platform.

However the reef does not—as is generally thought—grow farther in the direction of the breakers, for once the perpendicular wall has been constructed no more extension on that side is possible. The reef grows much more on the other side where is the spreading declivity of rubble. From among the sands arise coral bushes in clumps and trunks. Since these live in protected water which affords them what they need for life, the growth of the new corals is regular in all directions. Trunks and clumps near together unite so as to constitute labyrinths, mazes and enclosed pools, an Eldorado for all animals that like best still waters. Since, finally, it is the corals on the surface which thrive most luxuriantly, the clefts and crevices grow together above and become more or less roofed in to form grottoes which often lead deep down into the interior of the reef platform.

Moreover, the coral animalculae are engaged in a constant struggle with the sand. If the sand gets the upper hand, the corals all die off. Since on the lee-side, that is to say away from the wind, there are much less oxygen and nourishment in the water than on a reef's edge which is constantly swept by the waves, the coral colonies are not so resistant. Small parasitic algae worm their way into the lime and kill the corals of which some sorts altogether disappear while only a few can hold their ground. Thus wide expanses become barren and get clogged up with mud so that the water is dirty and turbid. The rocks take on a desolate, calcareous appearance. In the last stage the reef is almost entirely desolate.

Above, however, on the reef platform, where the currents pile up sand, there is formed a sandbank. Winds and birds bring

The sunlit coral garden at Pixie Reef.

seeds and soon plants are growing. The soil gets firmer and
humus is formed. A few coconuts will be washed up. The first
palms push their way aloft. A new coral island has been born.

On the morning of 2nd January MacDonald and I left Cairns.
We had been advised that a new camera would arrive any
minute, so Lotte stayed behind to get it. She would then fly to
Cooktown and meet us there. We made first for Green Island
where a gentleman from Cairns said he would show us a shell
six feet across, but he sought for it in vain for three hours. We
then took leave of him and went to Pixie Reef where we arrived
while it was still broad daylight.

Pixie is a typical young reef, an isolated dome rising from a
bottom about eighteen fathoms down. The surface of the reef
was a splendid garden bedecked exclusively with crown coral
among which, since there was a strong current, the fish whisked
about as though they were being blown in a high wind. I grabbed
firmly hold of a coral branch, for I wanted to take some photographs, but I was soon torn loose by the current and swept right
across the reef. The water swirled like a river's stream through
clefts and channels. Everywhere there hovered fish with their
tails wagging as they tried to make headway against the current.
Two tiny sharks were amusing themselves by shooting hither
and thither crisscross through the bushes. Everything was moving, flowing, except the corals standing stiff, motionless, calmly
majestic, spreading out their table-like branches and offering
their delicate petrified buds to the confusion around them.

We passed the night in the lee of Cape Tribulation. The air
was damp and the atmosphere heavy with approaching storm.
By sunrise we were at Evening Reef over which we had circled
round several times in the plane. Using the maps we had assembled, I explored the projecting portions of the outer rampart,
but they dropped away so precipitously that they could hardly
be identified with any area mentioned by Captain Cook. If
*Endeavour* had indeed run aground hereabouts then she had
hung over the edge of a wall of rock that dropped down sheer to
the depths.

It must then be in the turbid water of Endeavour Reef that the famed guns lay. Two hours later we were there. I had plotted out seven areas over which the boat was to drag me in my diving-gear, back and forth. Nowadays there are quite comfortable devices you can use in doing this sort of job, but in those days I had only a small board attached to a rope. I grabbed each end of the board with my hands and so steered my way up and down. I do not think I have ever been frightened for so long as I was on this and the following day.

The water was so dirty that you could not see more than six yards before you. And six yards in the sea, especially when sharks are about, is very little indeed. I kept well down close to the bottom and glided above astonishing coral formations. In many places the corals lay in confusion like heaps of ruins. Not so long before a cyclone must have ripped through these waters. Tall trunks like those of the giant trees of a virgin forest had been overturned, while clambering over them were young coral bushes of the most singular shapes.

My prospecting had little chance of success if one judged by results of explorations in the Maldives and Samoa. It has been estimated that in a thousand years corals can build up a layer seventy-five feet thick; therefore, if we follow this reckoning, since the shipwreck of *Endeavour,* the reef had increased in depth by fully four and a half metres or about fourteen feet. On the other hand, however, I had observed sunken ships on which the growth of coral was not nearly so rapid and did not reach a tenth of the rate mentioned above. Furthermore, on a sunken ship the corals constitute a highly peculiar living complex composed of many more different species than in a reef. Even then, if the guns were completely hidden by over-growth, I might, I thought, be able to recognize their position by such differences in the nature of the corals.

I clenched my teeth and glided along at one or two knots through endless expanses of turbid water. Very large *Tridacna* shells lay with their massive mouths wide open scattered about among the ruined corals. The murderous clams looked like uncanny blossoms of the underworld as they lurked and displayed their enticing snares among the surrounding destruction.

As I went gliding along a large mako shark swam right before me. He swerved politely aside and I saw him no more. During my second towing trip two whaler sharks followed me which took a similar attitude to that of a pike with spoonbait.

I got so nervous that I stopped and considered sailing on to Cooktown before evening; still, there still danced before my eyes the coral-encrusted guns of the famous sailor. So I overcame my feelings and by the next noon had completed our programme. Alas, I found nothing, but I must say that I did my best. May the guns long lie in peace, enclosed in their elaborate tomb down amid the chaos of intertwined corals.

The sun was just sinking when we entered the deserted harbour of Cooktown. Once it had been a flourishing place but it shows no signs of its former prosperity when it was a gold-rush town. The workings have long been exhausted and the port is unsuitable for large vessels. Moreover, the decay of Cooktown was hastened by a cyclone that ripped up most of the houses. Once there were twenty thousand inhabitants. Now there are three hundred and fifty.

Down a long, deserted street, bordered here and there with tumbledown dwellings, Lotte came to meet us. She seemed to be very relieved when she caught sight of us.

'I've taken a room in this hotel,' she informed us. 'Nearly everyone here is drunk.'

MacDonald gave us a lamp in case we might want to come back on board that night. He warned us of the wild pigs that attack people who wander about after dark.

This hotel, the only one in the town, was exactly like the plank or log cabins you see in the Wild West films. Some not very reassuring-looking men were lounging about in the bar. A great giant of a man with several days' growth of stubble on his face lurched up as we went in. He shook hands with us, insisted that we drink a beer with him and then told us about a certain Mike Buzzarton who was a tourist guide on Daydream Island.

In order to impress the girls this fellow would stand on his head on the top of his ship's mast. If he was sitting in the bar and was called away, he would take out his glass eye and put it beside his glass so that no one should drink up his beer in his absence. His greatest stunt was to put on a knife-battle with a shark. Of course he invariably picked out harmless varieties with thin skins. With them he performed spectacular struggles.

'All until one day he made a mistake and got held by a grey nurse shark,' added the giant, grinning. 'Then he gave up that sort of thing forever.'

All the other beer-drinkers seemed to be well informed about us and our plans. They had been reading the newspapers. One of them told us about Otis Barton who had dived off Lizard Island and was there attacked by a shark. Quite recently a young married couple had been gobbled up by sharks in Cooktown harbour. All those present grinned and drank to our health.

The landlord showed us an inscription commemorating the tragic events that took place on Lizard Island in 1881. In those days there lived there a certain Watson and his wife with a baby and several hired hands. They gathered *bêche-de-mer* which they cooked in a big trough. They also collected mother o' pearl which in those days was to be found everywhere on the reefs, so that at ebb-tide you had only just to bend down and pick up the shells.

One day, however, while Watson was absent, some aborigines came rowing out from land. They attacked the camp and killed one of the Chinese servants. The other, who was badly wounded, managed, nevertheless, to flee with the woman and the baby. At nightfall they clambered into the trough and let themselves drift. The wind drove the trough against Howick Island, thirty miles distant, but all three perished. When the trough was found later there was in it the diary of the woman. It ended with the words: 'Almost dead of thirst.'

After I had stood beer all round we went to bed. Outside, the clinking of glasses and the hoarse brawling and shouting lasted far into the night.

Fish-hunting armed with a Rolleimarin in a Caribbean coral reef. Lotte drives a black-and-yellow angel fish (*Pomacanthus paru*) toward the flash.

The following morning we got to Lizard Island and anchored in a sandy creek on the west side where the ruins of Watson's house can still be seen. During the night there was a terrific storm with torrential rain. MacDonald, whose thoughts were still in Cooktown, told us some yarns about gold-digging and how some men are patient while others are not.

A man employed in a mine struck a rich vein off the main gallery. Without saying a word to anyone, he quickly filled in the hole he had made. He then waited for forty-five years until the mine was thought to be worked out; all the claims had expired, so he bought the mine for a song and became rich. Another man dug for three whole years on a claim and then gave up and sold out; the man who bought it pushed his shovel down into the sand on the very first day and struck a rich vein of gold.

As the morning was very cloudy and windy, I asked MacDonald to show us the six-foot-long *Tridacna* he had told us about; we anchored near the spot he had mentioned, then he and the boy paddled about for over two hours in our tiny dinghy while they peered down to the bottom that was only some twelve feet below the surface. But the clam had disappeared. It just was not there, so to console us MacDonald took us to the coastal mangroves on to whose woody roots very tasty oysters clung. Since the hold was full of ice for the fish that were caught on the trip, we enjoyed for dinner that night some excellent *hors d'œuvres*.

On the second day the weather got fine again though there was a stiff south-easterly breeze blowing. This, however, was of no importance for our plans which were to get to Hicks Reef. We had seen from the airplane some small indentations on the outer edge of the reef but as these pointed northwards we should be protected from the wind there.

We cast anchor off the north-west point. I put on my diving-gear and plunged into a seascape of breath-taking beauty. Through a tortuous ravine about forty feet deep I reached a veritable temple of the seas. It was some sixty feet in diameter and the perpendicular walls were covered with a fantastic ornamentation of blossoming corals. The roof was a silvery, luminous ceiling of water, the floor was a flower garden shimmering with every kind of colour. This spot had, indeed, attracted us from the air, out of a thousand others, and the fish seemed to share our tastes for they looked as though they had gathered from far and wide into the temple. In the crystal-clear dayshine of the sea there hung, almost motionless, swarms of the strangest denizens of the ocean.

I swam back for Lotte who armed herself with the newly arrived *Rolleimarin* flashlight camera, which had been developed after my design. I took an under-water Leica equipped with a tele-lens. This was for taking portraits of fish. At the temple's portal we both stopped and gazed as you do before a great masterpiece of art. It was, we thought, almost a profanation for men to intrude into such a scene of peace.

We swam about under the fish and got to work. I used my small spear as a ruler, for in order to get sharp definition with the tele-lens I had to judge the distance to within five centimetres—that is a shade under two inches. I set the lens in accordance with the length of my stick, held it sideways and then took a shot when I saw the fish in about the same distance.

Twice a shark made his sudden appearance. He was some four and a half feet long and uncommonly shapely as he rushed at breath-taking speed diagonally through the temple. Like a shower of many-coloured fireworks the fish burst away from the shark's path. The shark made a weary movement and disappeared through one of the crevices leading to the outer slope of the reef.

Lotte was using her flashlight close at hand. Her first subject was a grouper which took fright at the flash and made off almost as fast as the shark and through the same gallery. She then snapped two pictures of wrasse which strangely enough did not react at all. A *Tridacna,* just beside us, did however jolt together with a clearly audible snap. Just as the smaller *Tridacna* the giant murderous clams are also very susceptible to light and perceive a swimmer's approach even from some distance. Very often our first intimation that there were giant *Tridacnae* about was the sound of their shells cracking together. In fact, surrounded as they were with coral branches the *Tridacnae* were often hardly visible.

One of the coral-bushes towering up in the middle had an ugly grey mass stuck to it. I gave the thing a shove with my stick. To our astonishment it jumped off. It was the most poisonous of all fish, the ill-famed 'stone fish'. The points of its sharp dorsal fins convey a nerve-poison that is reputed to be fatal. The creature is so aware of its formidable nature that it scarcely moves if you touch it or step on it. And that is what is so dangerous, for only a very practised eye can distinguish a stone fish from its surroundings.

Another clump sticking out between two bouquets of coral I was able to recognize on close examination. Two slitlike, very wily eyes were staring out at me from the middle of the mass. A little prod with the stick worked wonders. The lump shot out like a rocket, squirted out an inky cloud and made off on its way jerking through the water. It was an octopus about eighteen inches long. Swerving through a swarm of fish, it disappeared under an overhanging ledge of coral.

That even these animals are not quite harmless is shown by an unusual incident reported, some two years later on, in the periodical publication of the Australian under-water hunters. A young man from Port Darwin who had captured an octopus in shallow water took it to the shore and let the animal climb over his arm up to his neck. Quite suddenly it dropped off. Shortly afterwards the young man complained of pains, vomited, and two hours later was dead. It was found that the octopus had nipped a bite in the lad's neck. The tragic effects were attributed to the position of the bite on the backbone and also to some allergy for what is otherwise the rather harmless venom of these animals.[1]

We swam right up to the farther wall of the temple, crossed a narrow barrier and found ourselves in a neighbouring ravine whose walls dropped down steeply to a depth of some nine fathoms. The bottom was sandy and the ravine widened out towards its end where we discovered a grey shark over nine feet

[1] *The Skin Diver,* February 1955, p. 22.

long around which circled a small one. They looked like mother and child.

We dived some fifteen feet down, when the little shark noticed us and through some movement or other drew the big one's attention to us. It turned round and, at an oblique angle, made for us at top speed. You could easily see from the form of the tail, the short snout and the rounded pectoral fins that this was a grey nurse shark. Behind us the passage narrowed. I pushed in front of Lotte and held out my stick towards the shark. He pushed his head so near that I gave him a shove with my weapon, whereupon the creature whisked around, described an arc, and then tried the other side. It did not seem to be interested in me but clearly wanted to get at Lotte. Apparently it was the reflector of her flashlight that attracted him. When I gave him another blow he opened his mouth like some huge, vicious dog. The whole thing occurred so rapidly and so unexpectedly that it was not until afterwards that we realized the danger of the situation. Suddenly, there was a blaze from behind me and at headlong speed the shark swerved away from us.

Lotte had let off a flash. We had not often seen a shark make off so quickly and in such a straight line.

Down below us, and about thirty yards away, he turned round and came back for us once more. In the meantime however we had reached the upper ledge of the wall and slipped over the slight barrier back into the big temple. There we climbed up on the rim, got our heads above water, took the breathing-tubes out of our mouths and panted for breath.

'Did you get him?' I said to Lotte.

'I've no idea. I was holding out the camera in front of me and suddenly the flashlight went off . . . did you see his teeth?' The sun was on the fringe of a huge, black cloud. After we had calmed down a little, we went under water again and swam through the passage that led to the outer slope of the wall. With our backs pressed prudently against the wall we rounded the corner.

We had reached our goal. This reef was, it must be admitted, one of the few whose outer declivity was not touched by the trade-wind, yet, despite that fact, we were undoubtedly on the wall of the outer rampart. Before us lay the vast expanse of the yawning abyss. Under water it got suddenly dark. The cloud had drifted over the sun. Now stretched before us the murky, ghostly reality we had tried so often and so long to picture to ourselves.

The reef rampart fell steeply like the bulwark of some ancient fortress, a bulwark river through with fissures and cluttered with climbing and blossoming plants, it is true only small, coarse sorts of coral which clung to the rocks as might lumps of moss. The view was far from being as magnificent as that in the sheltered waters of our temple. Now that the scattered sunlight had disappeared we could see considerably farther down; far below us there projected a slab formation and close to it paddled along a large turtle.

We swam down deeper, watched the fish and examined all the corals we could see. A swarm of King mackerel was just streaming by. We saw it through a veil of smaller fish which hung like frozen star flakes in space. For the rest, the fish life off the outer rampart was not especially interesting.

We did not see a single shark. Since Lotte's manometer showed now only ten atmospheres of oxygen, we took a last glance at this millenial marvel we had been the first to see, and swam through the ascending passage back into the sea-temple, now all murky, and thence through the winding passage up to the boat once more. Now, for the first time, we felt as though we had been able to measure up with the Great Barrier Reef.

The weather turned uncommonly sultry and oppressive. The air seemed to press like lead upon us. Our every nerve was tingling. Rains and storms were certainly closing in on us. It was with a good deal of unwillingness that MacDonald was persuaded to carry on with our trip according to the programme we had agreed upon between us. Some hundreds of miles away in the interior of the continent a cyclone was raging. If it were to change its direction it might well strike us.

In a perfectly calm sea we got to the Tenth Ribbon Reef. However, there was heavy surf on the outer edge. I had the boat taken to one of the subsidiary reefs in the passage between the

Ninth and Tenth Ribbon Reefs and there invented a new method of diving.

Since there were some unpleasant-looking sharks near the steep precipitous side of the reef, I let myself down into the shallow water over the reef platform and there looked for an opening which might lead into the maze of grottoes that honeycombed the reef. I found a veritable rabbit-warren of passages and galleries, one of which branched off and, after a great distance, led at a depth of some six fathoms to the outer and steeply dropping wall. When I had thoroughly explored the caves, I ventured along as far as the exit and sat down on the edge of the opening. I felt absolutely sure of the hole into which I could, at any time, drag myself like a snail into its shell.

That day and the following day I got to learn a great deal about the behaviour of whaler sharks and grey nurse sharks. These, quite unlike their congeners in other seas, did not show the slightest fear of man. They came up calmly and pushed their heads so close to me that it looked as though they wished to shove their noses right against my skin. I do not think that they really wanted to bite me, but certainly sharks that come so very near to a human being might easily be led to try out how such a strange creature tastes.

Very curious indeed was the behaviour of one grey nurse shark that I warded off three times with my stick before he moved away diagonally into the distance. I looked carefully around me and under me and thought I was quite safe—then, all at once, I saw the white belly of the shark pass by hardly more than eighteen inches from my face. When I had lost sight of him he must have swum up into the shallow sea covering the reef platform, then reached the water just over me and plunged down vertically to where I was.

When the tide ebbed or flowed the sea rushed powerfully along past the various places I had chosen to sit down. As the Tenth Ribbon Reef—which measures from tip to tip not less than eighteen sea-miles—is the longest of the chain, a very great amount of water is massed at its extremity. Fish and sharks, as though carried along by a river in spate, washed past me. There is a very ingenious theory that these openings formed at places where, when the continental land mass was higher than it is now, and when the Barrier Reef was only a fringing reef, the river-courses debouched. This theory is based on the following considerations: where fresh water falls into the sea no corals can grow and therefore in such places there must be a gap in the fringing reef. If, then, the land sinks so that the reef becomes farther removed from the shore-line, then the water of the spreading lagoons pours, with increasing force, in and out through these openings. Thus it is the tides that prevent the gaps from becoming filled in, long after the rivers which formed them have disappeared or have now their outlets in quite different spots along the coast.

The weather got worse and worse. MacDonald and the boy spent hours listening to the radio so as to get the weather forecasts. Almost every hour the wind veered about to a new quarter while from time to time we would be drenched by unexpected showers of rain. On the morning of 10th January the sea lay absolutely still and calm, just as it will before a storm. High black walls of cloud piled up in the direction of the continent.

Now or never, we decided, and set off round the reef on whose outer side the sea was also perfectly calm. Quite near the edge of the reef I went down into the water. What I saw then was perhaps the most disconsolate vision ever to meet my eyes. I was staring down at an immense declivity that slid away into the depths and on which not one of the larger sorts of coral bushes could be made out. The whole thing reminded me of a rocky Mediterranean coast. The stupendous impact of the waves and the force of the surf had here shaved off smooth the entire sloping shelf. The water was gloomy and far from clear. With the exception of some groupers, at a pretty good depth, I saw almost no fish at all. I plunged as deep as I could while I turned round and round on myself. If a shark had come along there would have been no hiding-place for me on the barren slope. But no shark appeared.

I explored as much of the incline as I could in my nervous condition and then was uncommonly glad to get up to the boat again. Now our job was to make for the Fifth Ribbon Reef and to inspect its remarkable outer channels.

During the following two days it rained almost incessantly while a cold wind whipped over the sea. We anchored in the shelter of the Fourth Ribbon Reef but MacDonald became ever more insistent that we should set our course for home. Indeed, there was no doubt about it, the rainy season had set in, heavy breakers were dashing against the outer rampart of the reefs. In these circumstances I made up my mind to have one desperate try with our tiny dinghy and to push right across the reef-platform.

It was raining hard. Half-way across the outboard motor gave out, so I left the boy with the boat in water that did not come up higher than to my chest. I struggled into my diving-gear and with a spear in my hand made my way as best I could through the powerful current towards the breakers. After several falls, I managed to get through under them. At last I was actually in the channel. Here everything looked as cheerless and desolate as off the Ninth Ribbon Reef except that there was a broad dam that rose before the actual slope itself. I have no sort of idea as to how this dam was formed, but undoubtedly it must have been in existence for a very long time.

At last my nerves could stand it no longer. Although there was no actual reason I smashed my way, in a sort of panic, back through the breakers. I knocked against spikes of coral, slipped my mouthpiece and had to swallow water. In some way or another I did manage to make my way through the heavy white squall. I was quite giddy when I got to the dinghy. The boy helped me in and with the current running with us we soon reached the boat. I told MacDonald then that there was no more any reason why we should not make for home.

As it was difficult, in the rain, to spot the reefs, we made very slow progress. We anchored for the night in the lee of the Second Ribbon Reef while a terrific storm raged. The next day the sky was quite black though there were only intermittent showers. We reached Low Island and the next morning set our course straight for home.

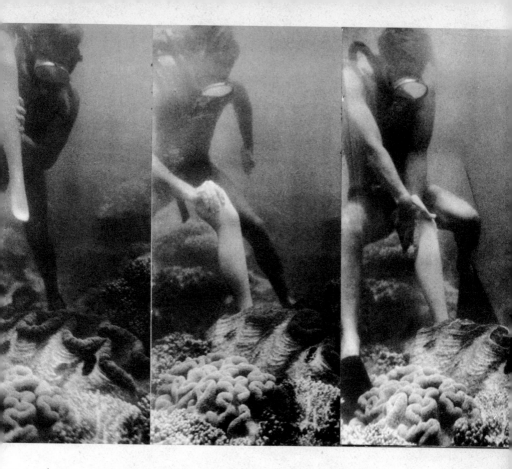

As an experiment I push a dummy plaster leg into the opening. The shells snap shut in a flash before I can pull the leg out.

All at once Lotte said, 'You know what we forgot?'
'Well, what?'
'Our leg.'
The fact was that in our endeavour to find an especially large *Tridacna* we had let our experiment quite slip our minds. As the sky had by this time cleared a bit, we made for Michaelmas Cay, a large sandbank on which thousands of wideawake terns breed. After a good deal of search we did end up by discovering, in the rather turbid waters on the lee-side of the reef, several middling-sized giant clams. We chose one of them for our experiment.

While Lotte photograped I shoved the leg in between the open shells and then pulled it—as quickly as a man might do who inadvertently steps into a trap—out again; or, rather, I

Even with a harpoon I cannot lever the shells apart.

The giant clam and the captive leg have been dragged ashore. I release the leg by cutting the clam's muscles with a long knife. The cracks on the plaster show how firmly the thing was held by the clam.

tried to pull it out, but the clam had snapped together and held on fast. The more I tugged, and wrenched and hauled, the tighter the edges of the shells stuck together. The creature had certainly no evil intentions but was just upset by the alien object and wanted to close itself up!

I had to wait until I noticed some signs of relaxation and then I gave a sudden jerk, but the clam was quicker than I was. After thirty-five minutes we decided to give up so we attached the *Tridacna* to a rope and hauled it up into shallow water. I fixed a knife to the end of a stick and then pushed it between the edges of the shells and through the powerful constrictor muscles. Finally we got the leg free and could see what had happened to it. The edges of the shells had cut right into the plaster on both sides.

So it seems that the stories about the murderous clams really are true. If a *bêche-de-mer* gatherer, at low tide and in breast-deep water, were to get caught by a *Tridacna* it is very possible that it could hold him fast until the incoming tide would drown him. In the same way a diver unlucky enough to get his hand into one of these creatures might very well suffer a painful death.

A week had gone by. We were on Heron Island, in the southern area of the Great Barrier Reef and well over six hundred miles away from Cairns. We had been told that the rainy season set in later on down there and we had hoped that we might be lucky, but it was raining when we got to Heron. At night Lotte and I, armed with pocket-torches, went along the steep sandy beach around the island. Out from the giant trees of the interior came piteous cries like the wailing of little children. Maybe a million birds breed here, for Heron Island is a nature sanctuary; the cries came from the young mutton birds in holes in the ground. The little creatures were calling out for their parents which had gone off to seek for food.

This was the time of year when the big sea-turtles creep onto land and lay their eggs. Formerly there was on the island a factory for the manufacture of turtle-soup tins, but the buildings have now been transformed into a boarding house for tourists.

Leaving behind her tracks like a tank, a huge turtle (*Chelone mydas*) drags herself up from the beach at night so as to find a spot to lay her many eggs.

After scraping out a pit some eighteen inches deep with her hind flippers, the turtle deposits from eighty to one hundred and forty eggs, which are about the size of a ping-pong ball and have a parchment-like shell.

After ten weeks' incubation the baby turtles crawl out and make their way to the sea. In some mysterious manner they know the road to take. If they are picked up they make instinctive swimming movements.

We were about the last visitors of the season and we hoped
to be able to watch the turtles laying their eggs. When we had
wandered round nearly the whole island we spotted a line of
wide tracks leading up from the water. They looked like the
marks a tank makes and between the two lines there ran a
lighter track made up of strokes and dots; from them we concluded that the animal had crawled up from the sea, since, in
order to get up the slope the turtle has to make a great effort and
uses all the means at its disposal, including its little tail. Thus are
the small dots formed. When, however, the turtle blunders back
down the slope towards the sea, then the tail describes an un-
broken line.

We followed the tracks and saw that they ran in a number
of curves up into the bush and then downwards towards the
sea again. Either, then, the animal had laid its eggs or had
found no suitable place for them. A little farther on, however,
we spotted a second track and it led us to a turtle that was just
engaged in digging. It was a huge creature, certainly over a
hundred kilogrammes, or, say, two hundred and twenty pounds.
She had scooped a hollow in the ground and now was plying her
hind flippers to make a regular circular hole quite sixteen inches
deep. The flippers were bent at right-angles so as to act as
shovels and they worked alternately.

The turtle scooped out one little dollop of earth after another,
laid them on the edge of the hole and then smoothed them away
on one side. There was a root in the way so that a little sand
kept on falling back into the hole, but the turtle meticulously
tried again and again. Our presence did not seem to disturb her
in the least. Finally to help her we tugged the root out. As soon
as the hole was nice and clean, she began to lay. One egg after
another dropped into the nest. Altogether there were eighty-
nine eggs. Then the turtle covered in the hole, pounded about
on the surface for some ten minutes so that the nest should be
quite unnoticeable, and then ambled off contentedly towards
the sea.

In about ten weeks the heat of the sun hatches out the eggs.
When the little turtles come out, they stay under the sand until

it is night for their instinct tells them that dangers lie ahead. Nevertheless, at most one out of every ten baby turtles reaches the sea. Big land-crabs lie in wait to snap them up, birds swoop down and bear the tiny creatures aloft in their beaks. The tragic thing is that both crabs and birds have designs only upon the eyes of the baby turtles.

Much discussion has been aroused by the mysterious instinct which guides these animals towards the sea, for even if there are sand-dunes between the nest and the shore, the small turtles always succeed in finding the right road. We were lucky enough to discover some living babies—for dead ones with their eyes bitten out lay all round—and, the next morning, experimented with them in the waters of the lagoon which were from six to nine feet deep.

Although the ground all around for a hundred yards was quite flat the little animals at once recognized, even in the lagoon, the direction of the open sea. We turned them round time and again but they never made a mistake. They swam round, without hesitation, in an arc, and then took the shortest and most direct route to the edge of the reef that was four to five hundred yards away.

Despite the bad weather we dived among the neighbouring reefs. We found that below a depth of fifteen feet most of the corals had died off and were choked with sand. On the other hand, by the edge of the reef itself there was plenty of life. Here again was proof of the rule that in colder climates the number of species diminishes but that the number of individuals greatly increases. In striking contrast to the most varied formations in the Cairns area, the reefs here were made up of a much smaller number of species which, however, extended over wide expanses.

Sadly we took leave of the Great Barrier Reef. We journeyed back to Sydney where, at the invitation of the Royal Zoological Society, I gave a lecture on our adventures. Two days later we were two thousand miles away on Canton Island where the reef channels had so struck us when we were on our way from America to Australia.

On the outer rampart of Canton Island atoll, where we met with a variety of shark (*Carcharias*) having a black and dorsal fin.

We were greeted by a cloudless sky. A few friendly Polynesians looked on while we loaded up our much increased lot of luggage into a car the aviation company had placed at our disposal.

Through the low bush and scrub that cover the atoll we drove and then explored. We waded through the shallow water of the outer reef platform as far as the beginning of the slope. The channels we had sighted from the airplane began in the zone of the breakers and were from about three to four and a half feet deep. They had been obviously scooped out by the backwash of the waves and they afforded an easy way of reaching the depths under the breakers. You just have to find the extremity of such a channel, then to lie down and you are automatically, and very quickly, drawn along by the thundering suction of the waves.

The edge of the outer reef dropped at first rather gently and then broke off into a steep declivity that reminded us rather of conditions on the outer rim of Hicks Reef. A special sort of shark with dorsal fins marked black and white seemed to be common in the waters off Canton Island. We spotted as many as ten individuals at once. They were visibly sensitive to noise and were easily frightened off by our cries.

On our third plunge out we were accompanied by Jim Beudecker, a Dutch employee of the air-line, who up to that time had only ventured to swim in the shallow waters of the inner lagoon. He wrote to us, afterwards, that he had quite overcome his fear of sharks and sent us under-water photographs he had taken when he had dived alone on the outer slope of the reef.

We stayed at Canton Island three days, spent another three days in Hawaii and then flew back to Europe once more.

# After the Sperm Whale

Six months later came the moment for which we had waited so long. Our proud *Xarifa,* in full sail, swept out from Hamburg towards the open sea. She was to take us on an eight months' voyage to the Caribbean Sea and the Galapagos Islands. Thousands of people watched our departure, for nowadays there are only a very few sailing ships as large as *Xarifa.* Those who waved to us all along the banks of the Elbe as far as Cuxhaven must have felt that they were paying homage to a symbol of bygone days.

Our main mast was thirty-three metres high and we carried an expanse of sail of five hundred and fifty square metres. With the aid of our auxiliary engine we could make from eight to nine knots. We could carry with us twenty tons of oil fuel and water and that meant that our radius of action, when we were using the engine, amounted to four thousand sea miles—about the distance from Hamburg to the West Indies. Moreover, the water supply would last for as much as five months, if you count six litres daily for each person. However, as we were to call at a number of ports on our way, we did not have to be sparing with water.

As soon as the last guests had left the ship and the coast had faded away behind us, there began the daily routine that was to bind together twenty men and one woman into a closely knit society. Each one of us had his own definite job. Dr. Heino Sommer was our physician and radio specialist. In his former capacity all he had to do at first was to prescribe for his own seasickness; as a wireless operator, however, he was, for a time, the busiest of us all since we had an amateur station and kept in touch with a number of amateurs all over the world. The biologists took up their quarters in the small laboratory on deck. Dr. Georg Scheer was zoologist and also electrical engineer. These double qualifications promised well for our researches into the physiology of fish. He was an assistant in the Hesse Provincial Museum at Darmstadt and had brought with him some thirty cases of scientific equipment, gear and instruments, all of which had to be sorted out, after they had been unpacked, and then stowed away. Dr. Irenäus Eibl von Eibesfeldt was an animal psychologist from the Max Planck Institute for animal behaviour. He had on board a good supply of cages for we wanted to bring back alive specimens of tropical animals, especially lizards and iguanas. Professor Dr. W. E. Ankel, director of the Zoological Institute of the Justus Liebig University in Giessen, came with us, as our guest, as far as the Azores. Not only did he want to study surface plankton but he was keenly interested in sperm whales.

Konstantin Tschet, the camera-man, stowed away the cameras and stands in the equipment-room. Kurt Hirschel, the engineer, took over the dark-room and made himself familiar with our workshop, for, so that we could undertake repairs and make some spare parts on board, we had a special machine which could perform almost every sort of fine mechanical work. Lotte had her typewriter in our cabin so that she could deal with all the correspondence by the time we got to the last port of call. Xenophon and I crept about in the hold and supervised the stowing away of all the equipment which had come on board at the last minute.

Captain Johannes Diebitsch, the master, had had much experience commanding windjammers and he had sailed on the navy training-ship *Grossdeutschland*. Under him there served as first officer Count Marsil Geldern and as second Herr Hein-

rich Becker. The engines were in charge of Herr Biastock. In
addition to a cook and a steward we had also five sailors including a carpenter and a cabin-boy. Most of them were sons of sea-
captains and the time they spent on board *Xarifa* counted as
part of their course at the School for Pilots.

The weather was alternately good and bad as far as London,
where we took on board our second camera-man, Lieutenant-
Commander Jimmy Hodges, R.N. Then we tacked down the
English Channel in stormy weather and, after that, sailed
through the Bay of Biscay. We were all reading books on sea-
mammals and on whale-hunting, for at the Azores, our first
stopping-place, we wanted to watch sperm whales and to film
them under water. The more we read about these, the greatest
of all extant predators, the more excited we got at the thought
of meeting them.

The way of life of the sperm whale is one of the most extraordinary in all nature. He dives straight down into the black
depths of the open sea and there hunts the ten-armed squids
which he grabs with his serrated lower jaw. Then he dashes
right up to the surface, takes about seventy breaths, and again
plunges down in the abyss. Once while a cable was being hauled
up from a depth of five hundred fathoms, the carcass of a sperm
whale was found entangled with the line. There is proof then
that the animals get down to stupendous depths. Every diver
must wonder how the sperm whale manages to do what he does
and still not contract the bends.

A man who spends half an hour thirty fathoms down must,
as he comes up again, make a number of stops amounting in all
to some ninety minutes. If he does not do this, then nitrogen
that was dissolved into the blood under the pressure of the depth
forms bubbles and so produces an embolism which leads to
paralysis and even death. But the sperm whale, a warm-blooded,
air-breathing mammal like ourselves, dives ten times farther
down and then shoots back up to the surface without any pause
at all. One theory has it that the nitrogen is absorbed by the
sperm-oil contained in the head of the animal, another hypothesis is that bacteria do this job. But, since the sperm whale does

not breathe while he is in the depths and as he exhales his breath before he dives, then it may well be that the nitrogen content in his blood is not sufficient to cause bends.

If we consider the difficulties marine animals once had to overcome in order to fit themselves for life on dry land, then we cannot but wonder that those which subsequently turned back again to an existence in the water encountered difficulties no less great. Dolphins and whales are descended from terrestrial predators which adopted a life in the sea about 50,000,000 years ago. Since they were warm-blooded animals they had to protect themselves with a thick layer of blubber against the cold of the water. Furthermore, as these creatures could not recover their lost gills they had to content themselves with a strictly limited length of time under the water. Dolphins can dive for twenty minutes, sperm whales can remain for over an hour under the sea. These creatures owe this ability to a special network of blood-vessels which extends all over their bodies and in which can be stored great amounts of blood and consequently a very large supply of oxygen which in a highly peculiar manner serves the needs of the central nervous system.

The layer of blubber which originally was a necessary pre-requisite for a marine life proved, later on, to present one very great advantage. In arctic waters where, owing to the extreme cold, fish and sharks are doomed to a much diminished activity, whales, with their 'central heating' system, have an advantage. Therefore, whales could establish themselves preferably in the cold seas and, indeed, apparently, it is from there that these marine mammals later spread out over the whole globe.

The mating of the sperm whales takes place on the surface. The females give birth to living offspring—generally a single calf. As with dolphins, young whales can swim as soon as they are born and also take air. They are protected and trained by their mothers and suckled under the water.

Whales keep together in schools and their wanderings are subjected to a regular annual cycle. A young English zoologist, Robert Clarke, who was in the Azores a year before us, had told me that August was the best month for making observations on sperm whales. Unfortunately we could not get to the Azores as early as that, but we hoped we might still find good weather in September.

It was darkest night when we got to St. Michael's. We cast anchor in rather deep water off Capelas and we were at once surrounded by a circle of lights which closed in towards us and looked like a garland of glow-worms. These were the boats of the fishermen who were using carbide lamps. We tried out our Portuguese in conversation; both the islanders and we laughed a good deal and we let down from the deck bottles of beer. The boats stayed quite near us and we were able to see the nets hauled in full of squirming fish.

The next morning we got quite a different impression. Instead of murky silhouettes there in the bright sunshine lay the friendly, glittering white houses of the little fishing village standing out against steep, green slopes covered with vegetation. Between the rugged, black cliffs and the rocks of the coast there was a tiny harbour where many boats were drawn up on the beach. Captain Diebitsch and I went ashore and visited the police station where, however, we were informed that we must make our clearance at Ponta Delgada, the principal town of the island; so we took *Xarifa* round the coast.

St. Michael's is the largest and most prosperous of the Azores and like all the other islands it is of volcanic origin. According to an old chronicle, there was in ancient times, in the western part of St. Michael's, a high mountain which, as late as 1432, served the Portuguese as a landmark. During a terrible eruption the mountain is said to have disappeared and seven towns to have been engulfed in a crater that was no less than three miles wide. A little later on we visited the Sete Cidades or 'Seven Cities' which, nowadays, seems a very peaceful place. The spacious sweep of the circumference is covered with the lovely blooms of ginger-lilies while at the bottom of the crater are two charming lakes, one green and the other blue.

As soon as we had finished off the formalities in Ponta Delgada, we made enquiries as to the whereabouts of the brothers Cymbron Borges da Sousa who direct the whaling of the islands. Clarke had found them very helpful and they welcomed us also in the most friendly fashion. The first whalers in the Azores came from Brittany in the sixteenth century and settled in the north-east of St. Michael's, but today Capelas and Ponta Delgada are the centres of the whaling industry.

The whales keep to a distance of from ten to fifteen miles out and are sighted by look-out men posted on high points of the island. Senhor Pedro Cymbron assured us that he had two old men who could, at this distance, judge to within a yard the size of a whale just from the shape and the height of the spout of water emitted.

'When a whale surfaces, we get a telephone call,' he went on, 'and at once send out the boats.'

On both sides of the island, in fact, there is a fleet consisting of two launches and from six to eight rowing boats ready for action.

'The crews keep in radio-telephonic communication both with us and with the look-out men and are thus guided towards the whales. When the men get near the animals, then the motorboats cut off their engines and the rowing boats try to catch up with the whales. If you like, we will put one of these boats at your disposal so that you will be right in the middle of the chase. However, whether you will like running the risk of getting a ducking I can't say.'

'Do you use harpoon-guns?' I asked.

'No, we don't. Since guns have been used whales have altogether disappeared from off the Portuguese coasts and we don't want to frighten them away from here. The whaling you are going to see takes place just as it did three hundred years ago, even the specially built whaling boats are made in the same way as of old. But it's a pity you didn't turn up earlier. We have had a good season, but if you are patient I think that you are still going to see some whales.'

We set up a special watch on board so that we might know at once if whales were sighted. Jimmy Hodges and I got everything ready for taking under-water pictures. The first attempt

This fifty-foot sperm whale (*Physeter*) drags the harpooners' boat behind it.

we would carry out alone and then, if everything went well and things did not look too dangerous, Lotte could dive with us. Tschet was to photograph the operations above water. The other members of the expedition were to explore the coasts and get acquainted with the use of diving-gear.

It was not until the fifth alarm that the chase was on. We took a hired car and dashed as quickly as possible to Capelas where, clutching our gear and tackle, we ran down the steep path to the sea. One of the motor-boats was waiting for us but the other had gone off with the whalers and was already out of sight. A big male had been spotted out to the north-west. While the female sperm whales and their calves congregate in schools, large males are almost always found alone.

The wind and spray whipped around us as we cut right out into the open sea. The sky was cloudless and all signs were favourable; then, I could not have wished to have with me a better diver than Jimmy. During the war he had trained British frog-men and later on had specialized in under-water photography. He was the first to go down in a search for the British submarine *Truculent* sunk in the mouth of the Thames. For a film company he had dived alone off Zanzibar and, during the war, he had done a good deal of skin-diving in the China Sea. He was calmness and self-confidence personified. When we set out on this really dangerous task of filming a sperm whale we could not suspect that, during our expedition and on a quite easy under-water operation, he would meet his death.

'The question is,' said Jimmy, 'whether the fellow is going to take us for a squid or not. I must say that I'd rather he didn't. We mustn't stick out our arms and legs too far or he'll surely think they're tentacles and he'll swallow us up.'

After we had gone twelve miles we sighted the boats. They were far apart from one another and floated almost motionless on the sea. Also the launch lay still. We learned that the whale had already been hit by a harpoon and had dived. We hurriedly got our tackle on to the whaler reserved for us and were rowed to the spot where it was thought that the whale would surface.

The question now was: what should we do? We were all prepared to swim in the wake of an unwounded animal, but since the whale was already harpooned, the situation seemed rather different. He had, it was true, as yet only one harpoon sticking in his blubber but he might well be rather excited by this nuisance.

We waited. The oarsmen glanced curiously at our flippers and little spears. They laughed and lighted cigarettes. Then, all at once, came yells over the water. Half a mile away from us could be seen the oblique spouts rising above the waves. He had come up again. The boat which held the harpoon-line began to move forward drawn by the long rope. Some of the other boats quickly set their sails and flew with the wind towards where the whale was and tried to head him off. Like a ship's figurehead in the bows of every boat there stood a harpooner.

Our men too pulled on their oars and no university crew could have shown more keenness than did those Azores fishermen that day. The chase was, for these tough fellows, more than just a job; their eyes glistened and they seemed to be quite oblivious of our presence.

Suddenly they stopped. One stood up and they all began to jabber away at once. The whale had doubled back and was making straight for us. What we saw was a huge black back

I photographed the huge animal under water.

bulging up from the water. The thing might have been an immense locomotive rushing along just under the surface and bumping up from time to time to the surface. That is what this whale looked like to us. When he rose then he projected a tall spurt of water into the air, just as a railway engine lets off clouds of steam. I looked at Jimmy. He looked at me. Then with no more hesitation I jumped with my camera into the water.

I swam off as rapidly as I could, diagonally, so as to hit the line of the whale's advance. It was all a matter of seconds. The whale was now hardly fifty yards off and was again hunching up his back. I plunged down to about twenty-five feet and waited. I was now right in his course. I had just time to adjust my camera and he was onto me. He looked quite different from what I had expected.

A thick, clumsy mass, yards broad, swooped towards me but it moved with the agility of a tadpole. It was huge and awkward-seeming and though it did not appear to possess any defined form or definite shape, the whole dreadful thing was instinct

A close-up of the sperm whale's head. The small eye lies back twelve feet from the snout.

with life and movement. The wide-spreading, obliquely held tail churned on with resilient power that rippled throughout the whole colossus of flesh. The monster rushed towards me. It was as though some phenomenon of the heavens were upon me. Life embodied in a mass of incredible unreality.

I took a shot, wound on the film, took a second one—and the whale heard the minute clicking noise of the camera. The entire gigantic body reacted. If it were not ridiculous to say that a house could twitch together, then I would describe this whale's movements just like that. He made off obliquely into the depths. He had done no harm to me, but the clicking noise of my camera had frightened him. The rope to which he was attached whizzed by. The last I saw of the colossus was the seesaw movement of his immense tail-flippers.

When I surfaced I was greeted with a confusion of shouts for the boat towed by the whale was coming through the spray and waves right towards me. I dived under at once and saw the boat, like a dark bird, shoot by over my head. Then, at last, I could get some fresh air. I clambered up into our boat again and told Jimmy what I had experienced.

Jimmy Hodges close to the whale. The harpoon looks like a pin stuck in the blubber, but the whale is doomed.

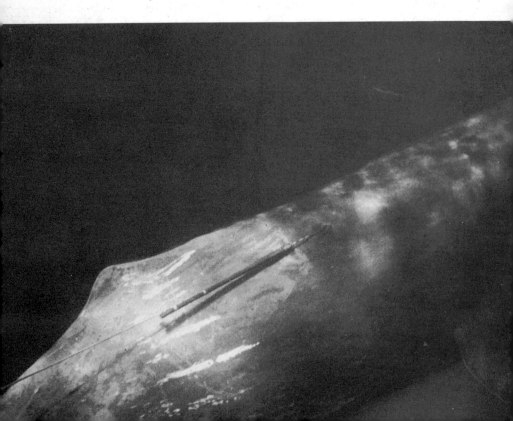

A second harpoon harnesses another boat to the whale, which has now to surface more often to breathe.

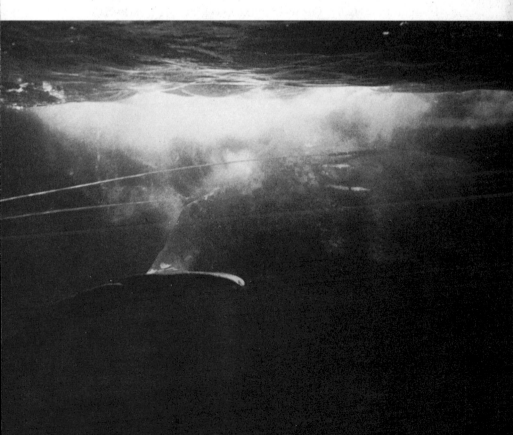

The whale fighting for its life. (BELOW) I photograph the struggle from under its belly. The teeth in the lower jaw are clearly visible.

It was only later that I came to realize why the animal had seemed so dreadful. I had seen neither eyes nor mouth. An animal without eyes is no animal at all. We look on a sea-urchin or a starfish more as a kind of living ornament. Only when a creature turns its eyes towards us is its individuality, its soul, if you will, revealed. Even when an animal attacks us we do not look at its mouth or paws but at its eyes.

But what I had not seen came out clearly enough on my photographs. The eyes of the sperm whale are very tiny and are set right back from nine to twelve feet from the front of its head. He can see with them a little on either side of him but nothing at all that lies in front. Melville in his wonderful novel *Moby Dick* refers to all this and remarks that the position of the eyes may well be responsible for the way in which the whale observes the world around him. Although men are the most evolved spiritually of all creatures, we can fix our attention on only one spot at a time. How then can a sperm whale find his way about when he receives two quite different pictures of his surroundings? Melville says that he must, so to speak, switch his eyes off and on. He pays attention either to what is to the right of him or to what is on the left. So would be explained the panic-stricken behaviour of sperm whales which are attacked simultaneously from several sides.

The motor-launch took us in tow and brought us back once again to the battlefield. The whale, in the meantime, had been struck by a second harpoon. He was now dragging two boats along behind him and he was surfacing much more often. The other motor-boat had cut off his retreat so that he was circling round as in a circus. When he neared us again we could see that instead of a clear stream of foam he was now spurting up to the heavens a blood-red fountain. He had been hit in the lungs and was now, as the whalers say, hoisting the red flag.

The spectacle was so frightful that we could not make up our minds to plunge into the sea; nevertheless, when the whale circled near to us again we were both in the water. The same being that only a short time before had seemed to me so alien, so terrifying, now aroused our sympathy and pity.

The colossus indeed was distressed and helpless. More and more frequently the need of air forced him up to the surface where his torturers awaited ready to drive more cruel javelins into his body. Nevertheless he was able to notice us and to avoid us. He surely could not imagine that we also belonged to the army of his hunters. He lunged forward, a wide, dark wave of blood streaming from his body, then he swerved away as though he would not hurt us with his massive might.

A sperm whale can never know what the enemy looks like who menaces him from above. Probably, for him, it is just the boats that are the foe. He may sense them as narrow, pointed malevolent things that shoot out projectiles over the water, missiles that fasten into his flesh and slow him down.

Although our sympathies lay rather with the beast we could not withhold our admiration for the men. Their boats darted swift as arrows over the mounting waves. Skilfully they avoided his tail if the whale in his desperation thrashed about him too near to the boats. The whalers were incredibly nimble in preventing anyone from being caught in a running rope and thus being dragged into the sea. The men drove their boats with crazy daring right against the whale's broad back, the better to hurl the flat, twelve-foot-long lances through the blubber. At the same time the harpooneers exercised the care of surgeons in seeking out the most vital spots in the beast's body. They laughed coarsely as they beat their bent spears straight again on the boats' sides. They were all sweating—as much with excitement as with exertion. Each boat's crew was a unit, an organized death-dealing unit, and there was to be no cessation until the enemy was vanquished.

Then the whale broke out of his circle and the hunt went on for many miles in a straight line out to sea. He seemed to draw on some mysterious reserves of strength for now he remained under water for longer periods. One of the motor-launches took over two of the ropes and was also pulled by the whale. We yelled and waved but the men in the second launch had apparently forgotten our existence. So, for a time, we were left to ourselves while the wild chase careered off over the horizon.

After about a half an hour the boats reappeared. The whale was still alive. He was still full of power. He dragged along the heavy launch and appeared hardly to notice it when the motor—like a brake—was put in reverse.

The struggle altogether lasted over four hours. The sun was sinking and the wind had freshened a good deal. Slowly, very slowly the whale tired out. More and more often we saw him raise his gigantic tail fins in the air and dive, but he could not stay for more than two minutes under water. His body quaked as he rolled about one spot around which a brilliant blood-red circle spread. The boats closed in from every side and sought to deal the death-blow. Once more the whale reared up and the great tail swept laboriously over the surface.

The whale was dead. He had come to his final rest and had tilted over helplessly on his side.

'Look there!' shouted Jimmy.

Just under our boat several sharks had appeared and were swimming right into the bloody circle. The tips of their fins were white and each shark was accompanied by a dozen pilot fish. As the whale was dragged off and the water became clearer we could watch the sharks biting bits of blubber off the body. We did not feel at all inclined to take a closer look at those sharks under the water.

A week later we joined in another hunt. This time it was a school of female sperm whales that was attacked. These were only about half the size of the male and they met their end much sooner. The longest struggle lasted only half an hour and the shortest but seven minutes. Altogether four females and young whales were killed.

This time we did remain in the water when the sharks turned up. They rushed from the ocean's depths, savaged the bleeding bodies and ripped at the wounds. I had, up to then, always found sharks rather beautiful creatures, but here we learned to look on them as repulsive and horrible monsters. They behaved as if they wanted to drink the blood and they paid attention to nothing else but the gaping gashes on the whales' carcasses.

These sharks were uncommonly insolent. They were hardly

White-tipped sharks (*Carcharinus*), surrounded by pilot fish, close in on the dying sperm whales and rip pieces of flesh from them.

more than six or seven feet long but they nosed up to us like inquisitive dogs and neither our shouts nor our stabs with poles could drive them off. Since they make their appearance only when there is a good deal of blood in the water, I got the impression that this sort of shark, anyway, is attracted not by the noise of the struggle but by the smell of blood. This fact might also explain their complete indifference to our shouts and yells.

Most striking was the number of pilot fish that hovered like a cloud around each shark. Lotte was with us in the water when some of these fish broke away from one of the larger sharks and made straight for us from a distance of about twenty yards. They peered and snuffled around us and then hurried off, in close formation, back to the shark. Maybe it was such behaviour that gave rise to the legend of pilot fish informing sharks that booty is about and leading them to it. But, in fact, these particular sharks were so over-populated with pilot fish that it is possible they came up to us in order to find out whether we were not sharks to which they would switch over.

We got close to one harpooned female when to our astonishment we saw two other whales. One of them was a young animal that belonged apparently to the wounded mother, while the other was a fully grown whale which, for some mysterious reason or other, seemed to have owed some debt of fidelity to her. This was the only opportunity we got to film unwounded sperm whales. They let us come quite close to them, then got frightened and dived off again into the depths.

Shortly after that we were the witnesses to an astonishing incident. A dying beast snapped open its lower jaw almost at right angles, and a most curious noise echoed through the waters. It sounded like the creaking of a huge barn-door turning on rusty hinges. It was a quite deep, harsh, vibrating tone carried clear and powerful through the sea. Naturally, we thought at first that the sound was emitted through the opening of the mouth, but later on we saw and heard another whale making a like sound with the mouth closed.

This cry of the sperm whale—which, as far as I know, we were the first to hear—may, perhaps, explain how these animals

The size of the whale's tail-fin compared with Lotte.

find each other, for normally they swim so far apart that it is quite impossible for them to see each other under the water. Often the males are miles away from the females. How, then, do the sexes discover the way to each other? How do the herds of females manage to keep together and how, during their diving operations, do they succeed in remaining in contact? Dolphins also emit sounds but these are much less strange and rather resemble the squeaking of pigs. The voice of the sperm whale, on the other hand, is just as unreal as everything else about this astounding monster. The very penetrating sound must be audible for a great distance.

It may be possible, also, that the whales make use of this sound for the locating of squids. The sperm whale must have some sort of means of effecting this else it would be hardly possible to catch the swift swimming molluscs. Obviously it is not sufficient explanation to say that the whale just swims with open jaws through the darkness of the ocean depths.

At São Vicente in the whaling station we watched the last acts of the tragedy. The same beasts that we had seen alive in the water were now hauled up by cranes, dumped on land and cut up by huge knives into slices. First of all a powerful circular incision parted the head from the body. Then one gang of men with a crane began to strip off the blubber while another gang used axes to crack open the head.

A sperm whale's head makes up a good third of the length of the whole body—that, in the case of a large male, is not less than from eighteen to twenty-one feet long. The striking bulge that humps out over the forehead is from four to six feet high, is hollow and divided into several compartments which contain the precious sperm oil, a viscous substance whose biological significance is unknown. The men filled bucket after bucket full of oil from the heads.

When we saw the whales' carcasses cut up it was easy to note the difference between them and the bodies of a fish. In these latter the main muscles are on either side and this arrangement accounts for the meandering motion described by a fish when it

*From left to right:* Tschet, Scheer, Hodges, Xenophon, Hass, Sommer, Lotte, and Eibl

swims. However, when the first fish crept out of the sea and gradually developed limbs from fins, the back and belly muscles became all-important for progression on land. The muscles on the sides were greatly reduced. It was with such a heritage that the marine mammals had to be satisfied, so these creatures do not move their tails sideways but up and down. The evolution of the tail-fin was also complicated. In whales and dolphins it arose from an obliquely placed skin-fold which is not supported by any bony structure and which, in large whales, reaches an over-all width of up to fifteen feet. The fore-fins or flappers are transformed fore-legs and in them may still be found hidden the wrist and metacarpal bones. The hind legs, on the other hand, have been entirely lost and only a small remnant of the pelvis remains.

All the hair disappeared with the exception of a few bristles on the snout. The nose was transformed into a breathing-hole and for this reason it has been assumed that the sperm whale has no sense of smell. The ear has no external opening and is therefore invisible; the skin is so delicate that the slightest blow grazes it. The real protection for the body is the thick layer of blubber. If a shark bites into a whale it is like chewing into a piece of cheese.

Inside one of the females we found an embryo. It was only about three feet long and therefore was in a very early stage of development since young whales when they are born measure about twelve feet. Professor Ankel and Dr. Scheer preserved this foetus and it was later on the subject of close examination. Furthermore we found in the whale's belly numerous more or less digested squids. The late Prince Albert of Monaco, a passionate marine biologist, extracted from whales' bellies a number of species of deep-sea denizens which, up to that time had been unknown. We had a great surprise when the belly of a male whale—some fifty feet long—was opened. In it were two half-digested sharks. One was two and a half metres long and the other three metres and ten centimetres. The legend of Jonah assumed a new significance for us. A big sperm whale would be quite capable of swallowing a man whole.

After the flesh had been flensed and removed to the cauldrons, men came with mops and buckets and sluiced the bloody slaughter-place clean. They dragged the serrated lower jaws to behind the factory where there were forty or fifty others piled up decaying. They are left to rot until all the forty-two teeth—they have the shape of a blunt cow's horn—fall out. From these ornaments are carved.

Two years later, in London, John Huston invited Lotte and me to the Elstree studios where *Moby Dick* was being filmed and showed us the big model of the legendary white sperm whale. As I watched the mechanically operated huge mouth—which in the picture smashes in two a whaler boat—I thought of the cemetery behind the factory in São Vicente where lay the last remains of so many of these proud, uncanny creatures. As long as they survive they will be, for all mankind, symbols of the daemonic powers that reign in the dark depths of the ocean.

# Old Scenes Revisited

Xarifa glided like a bird over the deep blue waters of the Caribbean, her slim white body cutting through the waves and her unbleached sails all set. After we had left the Azores a heavy storm obliged us to make for the Canaries. Then she had to sail southwards as far as the 23rd latitude so as to get the trade-winds, but she made slow progress on account of lack of wind and a bearing that turned hot. The first island of the Antilles at which we touched was fairy-like, thickly forested St. Lucia, but it was on the out-of-the-way reef of Los Roques, off the Venezuelan coast, that we made our first trial-dives. Soon, however, owing to the turbid water and the unpleasant working conditions, we moved off farther away. We headed for the Dutch island of Bonaire, where everything was to remind me of earlier days.

I had come back after an absence of fourteen years. My feelings, I must confess, were rather mixed, since during my first stay the Second World War had broken out and we had been treated in not very friendly fashion. We were, indeed, taken for spies and accused of having maintained contact with U-boats under the water! I had given some account of these happenings in two books which had been translated into Dutch. Was the *Mijnheer Gezaghebber* still holding down his job? Had he taken amiss my descriptions of him?

The familiar flat coast drew near. Every inch of the ground held memories for me. Towards the left lay the island of Little Bonaire where, under an isolated tree, Jörg Böhler had put up the tents of our first camp. Off to the right was Punt Vierkant, where we had landed Alfred von Wurzian when he was struck down with an embolism. Little dream-like Kralendijk, with the *Mijnheer Gezaghebber's* mansion, which we had so often visited, seemed to have spread a good deal. The strip of houses had lengthened and on a newly constructed airport a plane was just landing.

When we three adventurous students had come to Bonaire years before, we carried all our belongings—in haversacks— and our equipment consisting of a few spears, flippers and goggles. Now I was appearing on my own ship. Here, I could not help thinking, was tangible proof of the work which had started on this little island.

Words of command roared over the deck. *Xarifa* glided alongside a brand-new, spacious landing-stage. Among the crowd of inquisitive sightseers there were some who recognized me. Old Engelhart, who had gone quite white, came tottering up and stretched out his horny hand over the rail. A friendly Dutchman came up:

'*Mijnheer Gezaghebber*—our Governor—is expecting you. I am to take you to him.'

I followed my guide and said not a word. At the top of the step leading to the terrace we had so often trodden there stood a new Governor who was, however, in some way familiar to me. He made a pleasant sign of greeting:

'Hullo, Hans! How are you?'

It was still a little time before I caught on to who he was. Quite near to one of our camps on the neighbouring island of Curaçao there had been the tents of a group of boy scouts who often brought us our letters and gifts of fruit. The scoutmaster in those days, a slender young man, was now the Governor of Bonaire. We shook hands and Heer de Hazeth introduced me to his wife and then called for his five children. The others back on board had begun to get anxious because my visit was lasting

An ill-matched pair of sea perches glided in front of my camera.

Tiny silver fish playing about between the delicate feathery branches
of a colony of *Hydroids*.

so long. Still, when eventually I did get back, I was able to announce the good news that we should find all the help and assistance we might need.

*Xarifa* dropped anchor in Slag Bay, a charming, picturesque inlet on the north-west coast of the island. Here the sea is almost always calm and protected from the wind. Cacti as tall as trees dotted a plateau bounded by rugged, rocky cliffs. The inner lagoon is completely land-locked—a lake between the cactus slopes. Here fiery-red flamingoes strutted about on stilt-like legs while swarms of chattering, shrieking parrots whirled about in the air. Before a tiny hut on the strand, fishermen's nets were spread out to dry. There were a few picturesque boats hauled up on shore.

Our first task—and it was a most disagreeable one—was that of examining our ship's bottom. At the request of a German firm we had painted beneath the water-line with ten different 'toxic' colours and now we had to investigate the plants and animals which might have become affixed to the hull. Since such growths can very markedly lessen the speed of a ship, it was a matter of some consequence to determine, once and for all, how colonies of living creatures developed on the various coloured surfaces. During the voyage we had noticed certain forms develop and then disappear. Some sorts of living creatures which, at first anyway, defied the toxic paint were, so to speak, the pacemakers. On these or round them other organisms fixed themselves.

The work was unpleasant, most of all because the vibration from our electric-light plant throbbed so powerfully through the steel hull that, in many places, it was a hard job to keep one's mouthpiece between one's teeth. The paint was applied in regular strips or panels on both sides of the ship. We would swim down along one of the strips and prize off with a small knife specimens of the various growths. These were then placed into bottles numbered so as to correspond with the notation on the relevant strip.

Since at Los Roques all members of the expedition had

familiarized themselves with diving-gear—and with sharks—
we were able, in Slag Bay, to begin our zoological investigations
without any delay. We were anxious to find out just exactly how
a Caribbean fringing reef is formed and we chose as the most
suitable spot the west side of the little bay. Here the sea bottom,
decked with magnificent corals, sloped down at first gently and
then dropped precipitously to a depth of some two hundred and
twenty feet. We fixed a halyard to the shore and laid it down so
that it stretched right over the slope. Then we set to work to collect specimens of all the corals that we found within a yard's
distance to the right or the left of the line. We made sketches
on aluminum plaques so as to indicate the emplacement of the
various coral bushes. We also photographed, in detail, the
whole of this six foot wide segment. We tried to secure specimens of the animals which lurked in the corals and also to note
the kinds of fish which swam past us in open water.

For work in greater depths we used compressed air, otherwise
we employed oxygen. We hammered and chiselled away up
and down the declivity. A large grouper which, at first, had regarded all this noisy toil with some astonishment soon got used
to it and would swim towards us each morning as though in
greeting. In open water he would not let us get to within a yard
of him, but if he was resting under a rock then we could touch
him with our hands.

Once when Eibl and Scheer were diving with compressed-air
equipment there was almost a serious accident. The anchor-
cable broke and Xenophon drifted away in the boat without his being aware of anything amiss. Then both men came to
the surface. They held pails full of coral but saw no boat. They
were thoroughly exhausted, but did not want to let go of the
buckets. They flopped and struggled about on the surface while
they yelled for help. As his motor would not start up Xenophon
had to row back against the wind. Eibl and Scheer had not only
to let go of the pails but even the diving-gear pulled the two of
them under the surface. They were swallowing water when they
were just able to throw away the flasks. Such an incident goes

to show how easy it is for the slightest oversight to have serious consequences.

But the greatest of all dangers is panic. The beginner who is generally slow in his movements and very careful what he does is less subject to panic than the man with enough experience to make him think that he is a really good diver. Jimmy and I were forever urging our people never to feel too sure of themselves. We made a habit—it is also a custom in the Navy—of taking off and putting on our face-masks under water, of swopping gear and of removing our mouthpieces. Jimmy even let the others stand on their heads and do somersaults on the sea's bottom.

Eibl made himself independent and would sit for hours on one spot among the corals. In this way the fish got accustomed to his presence and he was able to study the normal course of their daily lives. His remarkable powers of observation were especially directed towards those small, wormlike fish which clean out the mouth and the gills of larger ones.

He noticed that the little fish lived in a certain coral bush and that the larger fellows regularly resorted thither when they felt the need of a wash and brush-up. If the large fish saw that another customer was being dealt with then they would swim about nearby and patiently await their turn. Things went on indeed much as in a barber's shop. One client was attended to after another.

What was particularly interesting was that the big fish—they were mostly groupers—assumed a definite stance whereby they invited the smaller fish to get to work on the cleaning job. The perch hung motionless above the coral bush; they opened their mouths and they stretched their gills. At this signal out came the cleaners from among the corals and set to work with a will. The little fellows chased after the small crustaceans that Eibl could see scurrying about over the bodies of the groupers. In addition to this (and as I had myself seen in Australia) the small fish swam through the mouth and gills and cleaned up the back part of the gullet. If the grouper had had enough and wanted to close his mouth, he made another signalling movement. He jolted his jaws until there was only a small slit of mouth remaining open, and then parted his jaws again. Thereupon all the mouth-cleaners hurried out of the cavity. Even when, inadvertently, Eibl frightened the perch, it never forgot to give the signal. Both groups of fish understood one another by means of a strict code whose rules were carefully observed.[1]

The animal psychologist refers to such things as examples of 'innate behaviour pattern'. Such patterns are, indeed, as has been shown, just as characteristic of different species as their bodily peculiarities. All the five different kinds of 'mouth-cleaners' distinguished by Eibl displayed striking yellow designs on their skins. Eibl concluded from this that this colour was, so to speak, the sign of their 'gild'.

During our under-water filming we made use of mirrors to direct light onto areas which lay in shadow. As soon as the first fish saw himself in a looking-glass he rushed up to it and began to attack his image—another incident of great interest to the animal psychologist for one could conclude from this behaviour that the fish had their well-defined territories in the reef which the animals regarded as their own property to be defended from intruders. When they beheld their reflection in a mirror, they took it for a fish of their own species which wanted to contest their rights—therefore they made furious bites at their own images.

A large grouper rushed with such energy against one of the mirrors that he splintered it. We left the broken pieces on the sea bottom and thought no more about them. When we returned to the same place two days later, the fish were still fighting. Some of them were quite exhausted and had their heads hurt, so we had to pick up the bits in order to restore peace in the coral reef.

While all this was going on, Scheer and Hirschel had pre-pared our floodlight equipment. In order to film the corals for the first time in all their natural and magnificent colours, we had installed on board two thirty-kilowatt generators which could supply a number of floodlights under the water. Our range of action was limited by two cables, one three hundred and the

[1]Eibl-Eibesfeldt 1955 (Über Symbiosen ect.).

Shooting our colour film *Under the Caribbean*. Lotte lists the scenes on an aluminum sheet. Our five-thousand-watt floods reveal for the first time the glory of colour in the twilit corals.

other five hundred yards long which could be used separately or one joined up with the other. They weighed over a thousand kilogrammes—that is a ton—and to every six yards of length we attached a buoy so that the cables hung just below the surface. Switchboard cases were placed on board the boats and from these thinner cables a hundred and twenty yards long led to the projectors. On board we generated two hundred and twenty volts but at the lamps themselves—mostly because of the great resistance of the cables—we arrived with one hundred and ten volts.

I signalled by signs under the water to the divers how they should hold and move the floodlights during the filming. Everyone, including Lotte, had to set to work as an 'illuminator'. The floodlights had a power of five kilowatts; nevertheless the light they gave was sufficient for taking colour-photographs only up to a maximum distance of about ten feet.

As soon as we flashed the rays on to the coral bushes the most incredible hues were revealed. Dull, muted greens and browns blazed suddenly into glaring reds, yellows and orange. Why nature has created such splendid colours down in the depths is a mystery. Since from a depth of only thirty feet or so, all the red and yellow rays of light get absorbed, these colours can never show themselves and no denizen of the sea can see them. It is only in artificial light that the sparkling hues spring into life. Many flared with such an intensity that one felt they had been awaiting since their creation for this one moment when they might display their beauty.

We had promised the distributor firm which had contributed to the financing of our expedition to bring home a film of our doings and adventures. There was to be no commentary but a scenario with dialogue was to furnish explanation for the various incidents. This was no easy task without script-writer, actors or director, but we did our best. When we lived through any exceptional experience then we endeavoured to translate it into a scenario. I spent nights in making up dialogues and everyone on board had to play his role, either a major or a minor one.

In order to satisfy our backers we even recorded underwater

dialogue. In our film the divers chatted about what they saw and so we had to study roles, rehearse under water and shoot scenes over and over again—in fact to train ourselves as actors. The fish watched all this drama with increasing astonishment.

One day Tschet told us that he had had enough of being the odd man out of the water. He was an ardent fisherman and pointed out how useful it would be, once in a while, to put out his hooks not from above but from under the surface of the water.

Jimmy gave him diving-gear and led him down to a depth of about fifty feet. There Tschet sat himself down on the edge of a steeply falling coral rock, opened up his little box in which was every imaginable sort of bait, and put a fine little fish on the hook. While we were busy filming, he cast out his hook—in slow motion.

As under the water he could see everything clearly enough he directed his bait right before the mouth of a grouper that was discoloured (which meant that he was resting) but as the bait waved continuously to and fro before his mouth he at last could not resist and gobbled greedily. In true professional manner Tschet wound in his line. We sat round in a ring among the corals and applauded—in slow motion.

Lotte dived in with another hook to which, in place of bait, she had fixed a glittering Christmas tree tinsel ball she had carefully filled with wax and shot. She wanted to hypnotize fish with this gadget, for many animals—like men—allow themselves to be put to sleep if their attention is directed towards a glistening object.

I did the filming and the joke nearly came off. Lotte held her ball right before the eyes of a trumpet fish. At first he was just irritated at being disturbed. He swam about in curves to free himself from the fascination of the shining object. While he was doing this he turned his eyes upwards. Gradually he got accustomed to the globe and his movements became slower. Finally the globe swayed backwards and forwards over him and the fish, as though bewitched, followed every movement. Lotte could not be persuaded that she had not really hypnotized the animal.

One day while Eibl was working under water we got news he had become the father of a strapping baby boy. Without a moment's hesitation Dr. Sommer jumped overboard with a bottle of champagne and congratulated Eibl on the sea bottom. That was another scene for our film. Bit by bit we were getting it together.

My main task was to co-ordinate the film with our scientific activity. We worked in shifts and often the ship's deck looked like a witch's cauldron. Dr. Scheer remained marvellously calm and did not allow anything to upset him. He sat down amid the corals and animals that we brought up daily. He sorted them out, he wrote descriptions of them, he took colour-photographs and put away each piece, carefully packed in strips of tissue, into various containers.

All the same, from time to time, we would hear him yell out, run excitedly across the deck and climb up into the rigging. We knew what had happened. Our ship's cat, a fine Persian called Mouche, took also a great, if quite unscientific, interest in fish.

During the evenings we sat in the deck saloon, discussed our work and made plans for the next day. Then work proceeded in the dark-room and in the laboratories. Cameras and floodlights had to be cleaned, script written and plans prepared for the shooting. Xenophon was indefatigable in ordering, arranging and watching over all supplies and equipment. Then of course there was the menu of the day to be settled. Often Lotte and Dr. Sommer, who were promoted to be entertainment officers, organized concerts on L.P. records, devised parlour games or arranged for a gay evening. At other times we read or played chess. When he was in a particularly good humour Sommer would strum his guitar for us.

During the third week the wind began to blow from another quarter so we moved *Xarifa* over to Little Bonaire and anchored just off the self-same solitary tree under which my first tent had been pitched years before. Here it happened that while filming was going on down upon the reef's slope, the projectors suddenly sailed off into deep water, but the divers held fast and rode them like Münchhausen did his cannon-ball.

What had happened was quite easy to explain. *Xarifa's* anchor had slipped and the strong wind had blown it off the coral slope right out to sea. From the ship hung the main cable to the boat with the switchboard cases and to these were attached the subsidiary cables, the floodlights and the divers. The whole of this was swept off at great speed out to sea.

Furthermore *Xarifa* swung round on herself and since the anchor chain then hung perpendicularly down into the water without touching the bottom, the main cable got twisted up in the chain and was brought dangerously near to the propeller. We had to disentangle ourselves in very deep water. It was two hours before we were once again securely anchored on the reef.

A whim of Jimmy's also caused us an unusual experience. We had worked until quite late in the afternoon and the projectors were just about to be hauled in. Then Jimmy proposed that at sundown we should dive again and let ourselves be overtaken by the rapid onset of darkness in the tropics. We should then be able, in night conditions, to flood-light the sea's bottom.

Four of us went in, Jimmy, Hirschel, Lotte and I. It was an eerie and uncanny world into which we had ventured. In the murk, shadows flitted ghost-like, as the light of the floodlights blazed out stronger and stronger. Hardly ten minutes had passed before it was black night above, but the cones of light cut sharply into the darkness while fantastic forms and shapes loomed around us.

Since we were very familiar with the ground, we moved with a good deal of self-confidence through the reef. I broke away from the others and tried to film a picture of the rotating floodlights and the black silhouettes around them. Then, all at once, I realized how very imprudent we were being. Often towards evening, we had seen large sharks cruising about off the coast. It was true that not one appeared but the light of the floodlights did not reach far and I was convinced that some sharks were watching from fairly near.

Whenever we illuminated the reef we got exactly the same scene as during the daytime. The fish were not still or resting, but many of them were swimming and darting about busily here

A blue parrot fish (*Scarus vetula*), a hogfish (*Bodianus rufus*), and a trumpet fish (*Aulostomus maculatus*) attacking their reflections.

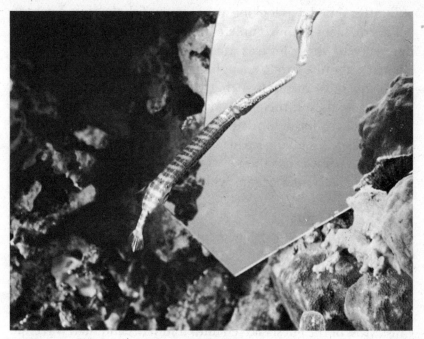

All these fish have their special territory in the reef and will attack any intruder of the same species.

and there. This again made it obvious that fish can find their way about with the aid of other sense-organs than those of sight.

Close to a *Gorgonia* coral bush that rose to a height of over six feet and whose long thin branches quivered and dipped in the current, there hung, just like a stick and parallel to one of the branches, a trumpet fish. The astonishing thing was that he was settled in exactly the same way in relation to the branches as he held himself during the day.

Fourteen years before I had already been struck by the behaviour of these animals. They keep a look-out for the small reef fish which they outwit in the following manner. Either the trumpet fish stays stiffly close to the corals so that he looks like a sprig or branch, or, again, he may ride on the back of a harmless parrot fish—just as a sucker fish does to a shark's body—and thus gets near unperceived by the smaller fry.[1]

[1]Hass 1942, p. 32, 122 ff.; 1947, p. 234 ff. Eibl-Eibesfeldt 1955 (Über Symbiosen ect.).

But this time I was looking at a trumpet fish that was carrying out his manœuvres in complete darkness. He must intentionally have stayed where he was among the coral branches, for the current was quite strong enough to have swept him away.

All this must mean, first that the trumpet fish could clearly 'see' the corals and their position in the darkness, and secondly that his concealing of himself at night also has some signification. Indeed, since his taking up his stance is in order to deceive small fish, obviously it is not their eyes alone which play a part in the contest but also their organs which allow them to perceive at a distance.

The weather was getting steadily worse and worse. We decided, therefore, to set sail, earlier than we had planned, for the Galapagos Islands and to call again at Bonaire on our voyage home. For our farewell party we decked *Xarifa* overall and invited the notabilities of the place to come on board for cocktails. Most of the guests stayed until midnight and then waved to us from the landing-stage as we slid clear and disappeared into the night.

The next morning we were off Curaçao. The old swing-bridge at Willemstad opened for us and *Xarifa* sailed into the Schottengatt. My thoughts went back again to Jörg and Alfred. We had spent over six months together here.

Lotte and I walked through the old streets and visited old friends. Pepe Schemel was dead. Fischer, the photographer, had now his own studio and a fine house. From Dr. Diemont I learned that he had become the official adviser on fishing.

It was a bitter disappointment for me when I saw once again Jonghoudt who had been so kind to us. In those days he had been an important police official. When Holland entered the war, however, he was interned on Bonaire. He had been too friendly with us it seemed. He spent five very difficult years on the small island and just managed to keep his head above water by the sale of coral. In fact he did just what we had done in the past. Now he stood before me again. He was broad-shouldered and cheerful and he shook my hand with all his old cordiality. In the new governmental set-up of autonomous Curaçao he was the leader of the Christian Party and one of the five ministers in office.

In a car we toured the island and visited our old camp sites. On the second day we went out to the northern coast as far as Ronde Klip. Poor, crazy 'Nigger Arnold' was not any longer alive, but the crashing roar of the waves against the high cliffs was as wild as it had ever been.

Captain Lenderink, a friend of Jimmy's and a trainer of Dutch frog-men, accompanied us. Just as in the old days, but this time with diving-gear, I swam through the breakers to the edge of the submarine shelf. Then we shot a grouper. Not more than ten seconds later the sharks were there. Perhaps one of the old-timers was among them. Since sharks have their definite hunting-grounds this was not impossible.

On the third day amid farewells and much hand-shaking we said good-bye to Curaçao. Favourable winds took us to Panama in four days. We spent the Christmas holidays in Cristóbal. Then we passed through the Canal and, in full sail, moved out onto the vast, gently swelling expanse of the Pacific. On 4th January we crossed the Line and on the following morning sighted land ahead. We could make out vaguely, against blood-red evening clouds, the forms of tall craters.

# The Galapagos Islands

THE Galapagos Islands, or 'The Isles Bewitched', as the
Spanish discoverers named them, are, both for the student
of nature and for all who are interested in man's knowledge of
himself, a historical area. It was here, indeed, that in 1835
Charles Darwin, during his voyage round the world on the surveying expedition of the *Beagle,* received the impressions which
led him, later on, to formulate his doctrine of the Descent of
Man—and of other animals. Here, then, took definite form the
fundamental concepts of 'Darwinism' that was to be combated,
and misunderstood, more than almost any other scientific tenet.
How, we may ask, did the Galapagos Islands come to interest
Darwin so deeply?

These isolated, volcanic rocks rise like slag-heaps from the
ocean, but what most astonished Darwin about them was the
great number of different sorts of animals which live, almost
within sight of each other, on the various islands, each one of
which, in fact, has its own peculiar tortoises and mocking birds,
its own special finches and its characteristic plants. Darwin
could not help wondering just why on these small and barren
fragments of land there should have developed such a remarkable creative activity.

The same species of animals are found spread over whole continents while here, on a few mounds of ash, the caprice of the

Creator had, apparently, formed a surprisingly large number of different sorts. It had been held, partly from interpretation of Holy Writ, and partly from the teaching of Linnaeus, that an animal species was something fixed and unalterable. If this point of view were adopted—some scientists even before Darwin's time had already questioned the doctrine—then the conditions obtaining in the Galapagos Islands were very puzzling indeed.

It was strange too that all the living beings showed a clear relationship with those of the American continent. Darwin asked himself why life in the Galapagos did not rather resemble that in the Cape Verde Islands. They also are of volcanic formation and present comparable conditions with those in the Galapagos, but the animals and plants of the Cape Verde group are nevertheless obviously related to those of the African continent.

However, all these apparent contradictions could be easily explained if 'species' were not something fixed and unalterable —if, indeed, during long epochs of time, one species had evolved from another. Certain animals and plants brought by the winds, on driftwood or through other fortuitous circumstances, to these volcanic pinnacles in the sea, might, in the course of time, have become adapted to the special conditions prevailing in the islands and there have developed into new species. If such were indeed the case, then it would be quite understandable that each individual island might have forms peculiar to it, forms which had evolved there. So, depending upon the circumstances, the various sorts of living creatures would have become modified in this direction or in that.

In fact, such an evolution was clearly to be seen in the case of the Galapagos finches. There were finches on all the islands but there were no less than thirteen different species of finches and each one had a beak of a peculiar form and used this beak in a special manner. One kind of finch pecked on trees—as woodpeckers do with us. Another sort of finch displayed the large, powerful beak of the grosbeak. A third had a beak like that of a parrot. The beak of a fourth kind of finch resembled that of a starling. Still a fifth species of finch possessed a beak as delicate and thin as that of a warbler. What had occurred was easy enough to understand. At some time or another finches from the mainland had been driven—maybe by a storm—out to the islands and since there the birds found no rivals in the air, the finches had become specialized for different methods of getting food, methods which elsewhere are employed by other groups of birds. Indeed, what had happened might be compared to the behaviour of a merchant who, in his own country, keeps closely to his own speciality, but who, in some hitherto inaccessible land, suddenly sees a dozen new ways of getting a living which he can exploit because there is no competition to hamper him.

Darwin then tackled the next problem. How did such a transformation of species really occur in practice? The answer he thought out to that question was this. New species develop from already existing species wholly by natural selection in a continuous struggle for life. Nature did not make each finch exactly like another one. There was variation. Some had a rather larger or smaller beak than others, or again some had a specially formed beak—and the fittest variation persisted. A finch with the beak of a grosbeak was obviously fitted to obtain nourishment not accessible to others. So he prospered and he transmitted his physical improvements to his descendants. Thus arose a new species. What, however, did not prove so useful was not transmitted to succeeding generations. Thus nature favoured those forms most suited to conditions of life in a certain environment.

What had occurred on the Galapagos Islands could surely have taken place also on a larger scale. Maybe, during the course of exceedingly long periods of time, all kinds of living creatures had developed from other kinds. Perhaps all animals—and all plants—were just branches of one and the same trunk of life.

After Darwin returned to England he spent twenty-two years in applying and in trying out his theory—in the whole realm of nature. He assembled an incredible amount of evidence so that when he did finally announce his theory to the world, his doctrine was so well founded and buttressed that it soon attracted supporters.

Research in natural science took a new direction. If all species really had arisen from others, obviously the task now was to trace relationships step by step. Fossils—which hitherto had been regarded as 'freaks of nature' or as the remains of 'antediluvian' animals—assumed outstanding importance since they would be witnesses of the past as well as links in a chain connecting extant animal groups with one another. In many cases it did become possible to determine not only how one sort of living creature had arisen from another sort, but also it was possible to ascertain how organs had been transformed and adapted to new functions.

Let us take one example, that of the appearance and the development of the fin-rays of fish. The story begins with the worm-like ancestors of fish in which (for the better maintenance of equilibrium) from a fold in the skin there evolved a fin-edge —whose final development was the human hand!

While primitive fish were aided in their swimming by the fin-edge still this needed some sort of prop or support. Nature produced as a 'mutation' fish whose fin-edges were stiffened with horn-like or cartilaginous spokes and since these presented an obvious advantage they were retained and further developed.

With some fish the rays hardened into spikes which, since they were furnished with a poison-gland, could be used as weapons. In other fish the supporting rays became extremely long and held up wing-like fins which enabled the fish to glide along the surface of the water. With the sucker fish the rays of the anterior part of the dorsal fins developed partly to the right and partly to the left and thus became the transverse of its sucking-disc. In the deep sea some fishes developed rays like long threads which they use as organs of touch while at the ends of these threads in some cases, indeed in many, there formed a small, feather-like organ by means of which small fish can be attracted into the mouths of large fish. In such cases, indeed, we can say that the rays are used as 'fish-hooks'.

One of these transformations was to be of immense consequence. From the fin-rays of those fishes which crept onto the land (and whose fins were eventually transformed into legs)

there were evolved small, articulated bones—the forerunners
of the fingers and toes of the vertebrates.

The five-finger and five-toe arrangement appears already
in the amphibians. In the reptiles the former fins became
clawed feet. In birds wings and in mammals paws, hoofs and
hands.

Each of these groups produced, furthermore, species which
returned to the sea and re-transformed their 'land' extremities
into fins. Among the reptiles it was the now long extinct *Ichthyo-
saurus* which lived in the sea much as a dolphin does. Among
the birds it is the odd and amusing penguins who have, so to
speak, pocketed their wings and used them as fins. Among the
marine mammals it is the seals, the sea-cows and the whales.

However, the transformed fins reached, of course, their peak
of significance as the hands of Man. Hands were not a whit less
important for our evolution into what we have become today
than was our highly developed brain. If dogs or cats possessed
the same mental powers as ourselves they could never attain to
anything like our degree of culture for they would still lack the
indispensable implement of hands with which can be created
what is imagined and invented by the spirit. If we had no hands
we could not use a hammer—or play the violin. We could not
clothe ourselves and, above all, we could not write and second
only to speech itself writing has proved to be the most significant
instrument of human progress. Writing alone has made it possible to preserve for later generations the experience accumu-
lated by earlier ones. We have thus been able to build ever anew
on old foundations.

Several generations of researchers have by now expanded and
strengthened the doctrine of evolution as originally propounded
by Darwin. It is today taught in every university as the very
foundation of biology and the doctrine has even been accepted,
in principle at least, by the Church. Such differences of opinion
as still exist relate to origin and nature of the transformation of
species. That such transformation does take place is now everywhere accepted as a fact.

Nevertheless the doctrine of evolution cannot be said to have penetrated into the consciousness of the average man and woman. If one mentions the *Descent of Man* or if one pronounces the name of Darwin then most people conclude that one is referring to the question as to whether or not Man is descended from apes. Yet this point is perhaps the least important of those connected with the doctrine of Evolution. Indeed, in the light of the latest conceptions, it may well be the reverse and apes descend from man-like ancestors. Undoubtedly we are fairly near relations of the apes and as we hold these animals to be 'ugly and comical' the thought of such cousinship revolts us. Nevertheless, what in the doctrine of evolution is much more important is this: we, together with all other mammals, are derived from reptiles and we, together with the reptiles, arose from amphibians; furthermore we and all amphibians come from fish, from worms and finally from unicellular protozoa.

According to the doctrine of Evolution, life on this earth is one great and marvellous process. In the first most primitive living being 'creation' (in whatever way we conceive it) must have laid the groundwork for all the possibilities of life.

That is the truly stupendous concept which formed in Darwin's mind on the Galapagos Islands.

We were soon to learn why the Spaniards called this archipelago the 'Isles Bewitched'. We had sighted them at sundown, we had approached them during the night. Yet in the morning they had disappeared. One of the strong currents that flow hereabouts had swept us many miles off our course.

Soon after we had left Panama we had organized, from among members of the expedition, an additional watch to keep a close lookout for the confluence of currents sighted by Beebe in 1925. Not long after we had left the dirty, turbid waters of the Gulf of Panama we had noticed several currents unite, but nowhere did we see any marked line. The temperature of the sea had regularly diminished and now that we were in the vicinity of the Galapagos there was no doubt that we were already in the cold waters of the so-called Humboldt current.

The Galapagos archipelago is composed of ten large and

many small islands and islets and lies just at the confluence of this cold current that sweeps in an arc from Peru towards the South Seas and the equatorial current which is from 8 to 10 degrees centigrade warmer. Thus it may happen that from one island you dive into cold water whereas off another island the sea is tropically warm.

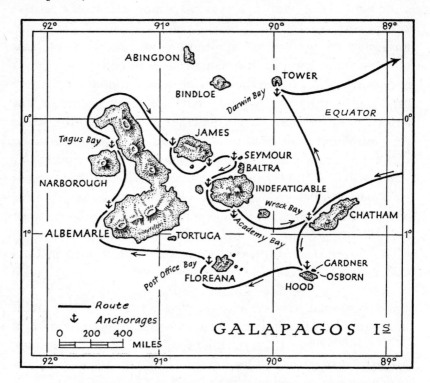

The remarkable geographical position of the islands is reflected in their animal life. Though the equator runs right through them they are the home of penguins and sea-lions. On the other hand there are tropical animals such as large iguanas and tortoises. And, as we were to see for ourselves, there are also corals and coral fish.

It was about ten o'clock in the morning when the islands came clearly into view. The even ascending slopes of the Chatham and Indefatigable volcanoes rose higher and higher up from the sea. Through our field-glasses we looked out on the patches of withered underwood and scrub that dotted the lava slopes which, as we knew from written descriptions, are uncommonly difficult to climb.

When Darwin visited the islands there were clearly visible paths cutting through the thorny bush up the slopes. The Spanish pirates who came this way knew these paths well and knew also that they led to the rare water-points situated in the higher parts of the islands. These tracks were traced out by the elephant tortoises after which the archipelago is named since *galápago* in Spanish means 'tortoise'. Darwin watched these creatures in great numbers crawling up or down the paths. Since his time, however, the crews of passing ships have taken so many of the tortoises on board as fresh provender, that the animals are almost extinct.

Formerly there were specimens so large that it needed from six to eight men to lift one up. The beasts were deaf and when Darwin came upon them from behind they did not notice him until he was right on them, whereupon they emitted a hissing sound and let themselves collapse as though they were dead. When, however, he got on their back and rapped on their shells, they stood up again and carried him forward with them.

Large specimens furnished up to two hundred and twenty pounds of flesh and their fat produced a clear and limpid oil. The tortoise hunters were accustomed to make a cut in the skin near the tail and then peer in to see if there was enough fat collected under the dorsal shell—if there was not they let the animal go free. It is stated that the tortoises always recovered from this strange operation.

Skirting Kicker, a picturesque rock that rises perpendicularly to over four hundred and sixty feet, we sailed close to Chatham. The water was a milky green and quite opaque. Then we made for Wrack Bay and let down our anchor.

The Ecuadorian commandant came on board himself and invited us to go towards sundown and have a drink in the military club. We all, therefore, got into the launch and made for shore. About fifty dismal-looking huts bordered the colourless and dusty strand. They were just shacks of planks and sheet-metal roughly nailed together. The 'capital'—Progreso—with five hundred inhabitants, lies in a less arid region high up in the mountains.

We bought some of the locally grown pineapples. We made a pilgrimage to Darwin's monument which is surrounded by a neat fence. Then we went to the pleasantly furnished and equipped club where the commandant showed us his gramophone. Our sailors wandered about sullenly in the open. They had seen everything that was to be seen in this god-forsaken place and they had bought everything that was on sale. As far as one's eyes could reach there was nothing but dirty sand and black lava scoriae patched with a thorny, leafless scrub in which a few birds were chirping.

By the next morning Chatham lay behind us and we were nearing Hood Island which Beebe has called the most beautiful of the Galapagos. Many boobies and sea swallows kept us company; dolphins and large mackerel leapt around us and some way off we could see a solitary shark-fin streaming along the surface. After the damp heat of Panama and the desolation of Wrack Bay we breathed freely in magnificent, inviolable solitude. We made for the little island (which Beebe baptized Osborn) lying between Gardner and Hood. It shoots up like some petrified garden over a hundred and fifty feet from the sea. In the interstices of the riven lava-blocks sprouted cacti and bushes while the dark rocks were patched with variegated mosses. White and pitch-black birds circled round and round.

'Do you see them?' Eibl called out excitedly while through his field-glasses he examined a flat spit of land on the south side of the island. There were brown blotches there down among the black crags and rocks. From time to time the wind carried a bleating noise towards us. Sea-lions.

As soon as *Xarifa* was anchored we put off the boat and rowed towards the animals. There was a heavy swell and it was not too easy to land. A male sea-lion, a good six feet long, was swimming about restlessly in the shallow water. He roared at us in a very uninviting manner.

We gathered up our many cameras, both still and cine, and

Family life among the seals on the black volcanic rocks of the Galapagos Islands. A mother seal barks at strange babies but tenderly nuzzles her own.

sprang on shore. A few females that had been sleeping in the sun looked up astonished but did not stir from their places. The bewhiskered calves were playing and scuffling about in the shallow pools. Hardly ten paces away there sat, on a high mass of lava, a Galapagos buzzard. He looked at us with a good deal of interest but no animal displayed the least anxiety or sign of fright. This tameness of the animals on the Galapagos has been noted ever since the discovery of the islands. As there are no carnivorous land animals there, the creatures have developed but a very slight flight-reaction. One can approach as near as six feet to almost all the birds as well as to the sea-lions and other animals. The only exceptions to this rule are the goats, swine and cattle—which have on many of the islands greatly increased in numbers—released by pirates and whalers. After the thin varnish of domestication has been shed by these beasts they display once more the normal flight-reactions of their wild ancestors. The islands are indeed bewitched for here the wild animals are tame while the tame animals, introduced by man, remain wild.

When we walked upright then the sea-lions did not let us get very close to them, but if we went down on all-fours we could get near enough to touch them. While Master Tschet set up the cine-camera Eibl got to work with his note-book. He first established that all the animals on the western side of the spit belonged to one herd under the command of the old male who was vigorously roaring away while he wallowed in shallow water. There were twenty-one females each with a young calf and three females who appeared to be without offspring. Some way off there sat a young male on a rock and squinted in melancholy fashion at the harem of the old tyrant. He was alone. He looked as though he was biding his time.

With the old male we soon came into contact. We noticed some females playing about in the water and we swam, armed with our spears and under-water cameras, in their direction. We wanted to observe their antics while they were diving. The sea was opaque and the bottom consisted of black lava with a moderate amount of vegetation. We judged that we were quite close to the females when the fat old pasha suddenly appeared

This six-foot-long male sea-lion is drifting asleep in the water.

under the water swimming right for us. It was quite clear from
his behaviour that he was not at all playful, but that he meant
business. As he rushed towards us he was showing his teeth, so I
gave him a jab with my harpoon. He roared out and bubbles
came rising from his mouth to the surface. Then he swerved
round and made for Lotte, so I hit him again and gave him
another scratch. This offended him very much and he retreated
to some distance. He looked indeed as though he had been
grievously insulted in the performance of his duty. He saw
clearly enough that he could not carry on a struggle with my
spear, but he showed plainly that in the sea-lion code a spear was
a forbidden weapon.

Eibl wrung his hands and besought us not to upset the whole
colony, so we took pictures of what we needed for our film and
then left the field free for him. During the next few days he was
hardly ever on the ship. He had been a pupil of Professor Kon-
rad Lorenz, the eminent animal psychologist, and so he did not
carry out his observations in any half-hearted manner. We had
to send his meals in the launch and also provide him with
blankets for he wanted to sleep with his sea-lions—in this way,

Lord and master of twenty-four females and twenty-one youngsters, he wakes up and roars in all directions.

in fact, he was able to study the whole daily routine of the animals' life.

In the early morning, at sunrise, it was the old male who woke up first. He slipped into the water, swam about a bit up and down while emitting his husky roar. His roaring was especially energetic and imperative on the border of his domain and near where the young male had his solitary resting-place. In this way the old fellow informed all and sundry who cared to listen that this plot with all the ladies on it belonged to him and to him alone.

After that the females stretched themselves and then took their ease in the water where they hunted a little, threw stones up in the air to amuse themselves and just enjoyed life. When they met the old male they swayed their heads in greeting and allowed themselves to be sniffed. Some of them went a little farther and took a playful nip at the nape of the old tyrant. But he was not as yet disposed for any dalliance and sporting. If a female swam out too far she soon found that he pushed her back again towards the shore.

In the meantime the calves had also woken up and were playing in the pools. When the mothers got back they snuffled at the young sea-lions and each female sought out her own and suckled it. While all this was going on Eibl noticed that the mothers saw to their offsprings' manners. Each calf had to greet his mother with mooing and movements of the head. If one of the young creatures made a mistake and nestled up to the wrong mother, he was promptly chased away.

As the heat of the day increased the females and calves lay out in the sun and slept or scratched themselves with evident enjoyment in the oddest parts of their body. The old male also let up on his patrol duty and fell asleep while swimming. From time to time he would shove his head above water and take a breather with his eyes closed. If a wave pushed him towards a rock he would avoid it without waking though when he did come out of his slumbers he emitted a powerful roar.

The ladies of the harem would quarrel a little and spit at each other. During their less serious differences of opinion they confined themselves to giving out calls of 'Ek—Ek,' but if things got more lively then they roared 'Öü—Öü—Öü.' This would bring the old male hurrying onto land to make them see sense.

All the time the young male, sad and melancholy, watched from afar and let out a long-drawn note 'Oa—Oa—Oa.'

It was not until evening that the females got really active again.

Before sundown they go hunting once more and are quite tired when they come ashore—the sturdy old male bringing up the rear. The calves would wander from one female to another, snuffle at them while searching each one for its mother. If they could not find their own dams, then the calves would set up a cry of complaint—'Bööö.' That would bring an answer from the mothers, a reply couched in the same tones as the calves' wail, only deeper and more grave—'Bööö.' Then gradually all became still, but the old male would look up every fifteen or twenty minutes and gaze round him over towards the young male in his solitude. After that the old fellow went to sleep—and Eibl also.

When we got to the east coast of Gardner Island we saw there several other colonies of sea-lions. The water just offshore was dirty but became crystal-clear a short way out to sea. Here we swam about, with our diving tackle, on the surface and tried to attract the attention of the ladies of the colony where we saw the male sleeping on a rock. We bleated out an inviting and melancholy cry—'Oaa—Oaa—Oaa.' At once the females obeyed our call. They cast but one look at their sleeping lord and master before they flopped into the water. We dived down about forty feet to the bottom and waited. The sea-lion damsels came gliding towards us. It is difficult to imagine anything more elegant and gracious than these supple beasts. They seemed to defy all the laws of gravity and their delight in the water's impact on their bodies was obvious. The creatures twined and twisted in charming harmonious movements. The fore-flippers served them as oars as well as rudders.

Lotte and I stood near to one another on the sea bottom. Jimmy with the cine-camera was about fifteen yards away from us. When we heard the animals squeak, Lotte and I squeaked

Young female sea-lions circle gracefully around us under water, while they watch curiously with their brown eyes.

too. The seals came up quite close and circled around us barely a yard away. Their big brown eyes, which on land seem so dull and short-sighted, flashed with curiosity and intelligence under water. One of the females paused near me and emitted a bubbly squeak. I could do that also and I put out smaller bubbles and gave my voice a real seductive tone. The creature came and pushed her muzzle against my outstretched hand while I heard the happy sound of whirring made by Jimmy's cine-camera.

Then the sea-lion lady swirled off in a joyous movement to the surface, took a deep breath and came, describing a great arc of a circle, back again. Another animal almost touched our diving-masks with her charming moustached snout while she stared inquisitively through the glass. A rapid turn and both flew over towards Jimmy, who went on filming. They slipped by close above his camera, and circled around him before they darted off to the shore. We saw Jimmy performing a sort of St. Vitus's dance on the sea bottom. To judge from his gestures he had just made the film of his life.

We took full advantage of the wonderfully clear water and filmed the huge swarms of coral fish and surgeon fish swirling about quite close to us. It was a most astonishing thing, but these fish showed just as little fear of us as did the birds and sea-lions on land. Such lack of any anxiety could be explained for terrestrial animals, by the absence of carnivores, but, on the contrary, under water there were sharks and carnivorous fish in any quantity. Yet the fish at this spot were much tamer than we had found anywhere else. A kind of *Anisotremus,* of which a school hovered slanting near us, allowed itself even to be touched with the finger. There seemed to be only one explanation for this state of things. There was such an incredible wealth of fish that the carnivorous sea animals must be satiated and weary, so that individual fish remain comparatively secure and therefore fearless.

We dived in a strong current off the eastern point of Gardner Island whose coast is bounded by a great lava cliff. What we were here able to see under water can hardly be believed. The

A swarm of cat fish or barber fish (*Plotosus anguillaris*), in search of food, seethes over the sand like a breaker. Surgeon fish (*Xesurus laticlavius*) and coral fish (*Holacanthus passer*) pass by in the cold currents of the Galapagos.

flat sandy bottom, some sixty-five feet down and dotted with blocks of rock, was literally blanketed with fish. Ten to twenty-pound groupers rushed towards us from all directions as though they wanted to offer themselves for luncheon.

Behind a wall of rectangular stones Lotte discovered a huge sleeping stinging ray. She frightened him with her harpoon and he was so bewildered that he smashed into a stone and broke it. At this very moment Jimmy gave me a shove in the ribs. No fewer than sixteen large Eagle rays were swimming towards us and in close formation. With true British calm Jimmy set to work with his camera. The heavy animals glided like archaic, flying saurians, right over our heads—then, without any warning, sea-lions appeared and circled about us. When, a little later, I happened to peep down into a crevice in the lava I discovered as many as twelve large crawfish. They might have been sitting in the stalls of a theatre. Each was closely jammed against the other and their long antennae trailed out before them.

We called to the boat and Xenophon handed me down one spear after another. In the space of five minutes I had got out all the crawfish—they weighed altogether thirty-eight pounds. The creatures were of magnificent red and blue hues while two of them had just cast their shells and were still soft and armourless.

We also touched at the tiny island to the west of Osborn and baptized it 'Xarifa'. Here too the sea was seething with fish. Since, in the neighbourhood of the Galapagos, cold and warm currents meet, incalculable quantities of small floating animal-culae die off and their bodies attract billions of fish in whose wake come great carnivorous denizens of the depths.

We sighted also a number of sharks—some of them of noble proportions—but they did not appear to be much interested in us. No doubt they had so much to eat close at hand that it was not worth their while having any dealings with intruders.

A week slipped by all too quickly. We dived and we watched. We collected specimens and we photographed. Then the current changed and the water became turbid and dirty. We had a farewell picnic on the beach. We had shot a couple of wild goats and barbecued them. The sea-lions watched us from afar. Some-

I had to wait a long time before this shy *Priacanthus* made up its mind to emerge from among the polyps of an *Alcyonaria*. Photograph taken with flash-lamp and close-up lenses.

This picture of a "hair-star" looks like an abstract painting. The photograph was taken at night and shows ruby horn-coral and orange sponges.

thing of far-reaching importance had taken place in the colony. The old male had been dethroned.

One morning, indeed, Eibl saw that the young male had taken over command of the herd. Now it was the turn of the old fellow to sit in solitary state where once the young rival had languished. Maybe that, indirectly, I was responsible for the change-over. It is possible that my spear thrusts had broken the old pasha's spirit. I could not forget the look he had given me. Something novel, something overpowering had come into his life and so, perhaps, the young supplanter had got the opportunity he needed to assume the lordship.

A fortnight later, on Seymour Island, we sighted a huge colony of over a hundred animals. Quite apart, and in a clearly de-limited small area, sat a few decrepit, half-blind males who, like the inhabitants of an old people's home, were awaiting their end. These aged sea-lions had been conquered, repudiated, cast forth. They were ancient, exhausted and close to them were the desiccated carcasses of others who had already died. Probably these poor old fellows were dreaming of the days when they were strong and lusty and swam proudly to and fro before their coastal domain and when the lovely females had nestled close to them and nipped them in the nape of the neck. The old sea-lions' day was, however, over. No one cared anything more about them. Nature that favours the strong and the young and ruth-lessly rejects the old and the weak had, as a special measure of grace, left the ancients a small plot on which they could die off in peace.

On Floreana Island we visited the tomb of the celebrated Dr. Ritter whose fate once so keenly excited an interest that was echoed in the world's Press. What was once a cultivated plot has reverted to bush and of Ritter's house nothing more is to be seen. Hidden away beneath the scrub I found the small stone seat on which he used to sit and meditate. He settled in the Galapagos Islands in 1929, there to lead a healthy life and to philosophize in solitude over the world and its affairs. Maybe he took as his model Nietzsche who found the inspiration for his 'Zarathustra' on lonely rocky cliffs near Rapallo. But for Ritter things turned out quite differently. For him and his lifelong companion Frau Dora Körvin the first two years were very hard indeed. They had read Beebe's books on the islands, but they had not realized that Beebe, as a zoologist, had seen the archipelago through rose-tinted spectacles. The arid, dusty reality was appalling. Ritter discovered water high up on the island but it was a long time before he managed to wrest any subsistence from the barren soil.

In the meantime, however, rich Americans came in their yachts and exercised their curiosity on a man who wandered naked about the island and wanted to live to the age of a hundred and fifty. They left him some preserved foods and various utensils. Then, attracted by all the newspaper publicity, there appeared an Austrian Baroness and three young men who settled down near Ritter. She dubbed herself 'the Queen of Floreana', but when more yachts brought more gifts the two groups of settlers began to quarrel.

After two years everything came to an end. The Baroness and one of the young men disappeared without leaving a trace. The second young man went home and the third was found half-rotted on a sandbank, while Dr. Ritter, the vegetarian, died from food-poisoning—after eating meat.

Down by the shore of the bay there still lives the Wittmer family who have indulged in no extravagant ambitions but run a plantation and engage in fishing. Frau Wittmer very kindly invited us into her charming home. The last sailing-ship flying the German flag which had touched here before *Xarifa* was Count Luckner's *Seeteufel,* the very same vessel which I had acquired and then had lost possession of at the end of the late war. Frau Wittmer had a grown-up son and a young daughter. Another boy had been drowned while fishing. Despite the bitter loneliness, they all seemed more or less happy.

Our next call was at Albemarle Island, the largest of the whole archipelago, and where in quite recent times a volcanic eruption took place. One could distinguish the newly formed crater near the older ones. Owing to the swirling lava dust the water hereabouts is never clear and from the murky depths a good many large mantas shot up quite close to *Xarifa*. The powerful currents prevailing here—as everywhere between the islands—made navigation very difficult. We coasted along the rugged shore of lava, put into Tagus Bay and there anchored. It is a real little crater on whose sides many a ship has left traces of its passage.

Fish that were no fish at all but lively penguins plashed about in the turbid water. They plunged boisterously up and down. On the dark cliffs and rocks along the coast were lying everywhere large, dull-green iguanas, the famed swimming iguanas of the Galapagos.

They reach a length of nearly five feet and look like antediluvian dragons. Their head is knobbly and the males are markedly larger than the females and have a much taller crest. Just like the sea-lions, each male iguana had his harem of females and a quite clearly delimited domain that he defended with energy against all intruders. As we drew near the reptiles showed no signs of fear at all. The males looked up in menace and nodded their heads. This is the sign that they are ready to fight. If another male dares to attempt an excursion into the domain, the animals stand on either side of the border-line nodding at each other. Then one of them makes a sudden dash at the other and the armoured heads clash and bump. Each one endeavours to force the other out of the way. With a few pauses for rest such a struggle may go on for as much as two hours. When one of them has had enough he lies down flat on his belly in an attitude of inferiority. He is then no more attacked but crawls defeated on his way. In these tussles the creatures make no use of their sharp teeth.

From our anchorage in Tagus Bay we rowed over to the completely barren, steeply rising island of Narborough where the cliffs were swarming with hundreds of such iguanas. They lay quite motionless on the rock until we got fairly close, then all the males began to nod their heads, but we could go right up to them and even lift them up by their long tails. In the surf we could see them browsing on sea-weed and some of them were swimming as far as a hundred yards out to sea.

Like most creatures on the Galapagos, penguins have little fear of man.

The marine iguana (*Amblyrhynchus cristatus*) actually let themselves be touched.

While Tschet was busy filming and while Scheer was observing the bird life, Eibl made an experiment to resettle male iguanas in other domains than their own. At once there was a very serious battle. Since intruders had not, according to the rules, approached the border-line and there nodded their heads the invaders were pitilessly bitten. Moreover, it was obvious that they felt themselves in the wrong for they made efforts to get back into their own territory. If they succeeded—and they would find their own domain even if it was thirty yards away—then they would regain all their self-confidence and were ready to stand their ground. Here they were on their own rightful soil. Here they were at home.[1]

In addition to many pelicans which nested in the mangroves

[1]Eibl-Eibesfeldt 1955 (Der Kommentkampf ect.).

Male marine iguanas in combat. With nodding heads they charge each other, each trying to drive his opponent away with blows from his armoured prow.

and the penguins which stood like porcelain figures on the rocks, we noticed a number of flightless cormorants with wings reduced to mere stumps. Only here, where there are no carnivorous animals, could such a condition of degeneracy be maintained. Elsewhere cormorants like these would long since have disappeared.

It was unfortunately impossible for us to watch, as Beebe did, a penguin from under the water since it was far too murky. When, however, later on, we ran into Academy Bay, there to buy potatoes and fresh meat from the settlers, we noticed a captive penguin which was kept in the kitchen and seemed very miserable there. So we bought him and gave him the name of Benny. He soon became the most important member of the expedition. Our ship's cat, Mouche, would arch his back at the sight of Benny and run off up a mast. Benny was always in high spirits as he waddled proudly about on deck. We all loved him except the officers, who liked clean decks, and the cabin-boy, who had to clear up after him.

From Albemarle we sailed to Seymour Island on which, during the war, a large American military camp was set up. Next we touched at Indefatigable and visited the picturesque Guy Fawkes rocks. We dived a good deal, added to our collections and took photographs of the world of the sea, but nowhere did we find such clear water as off Hood.

Our last call was at Tower Island where, despite the difficult passage, we managed to get *Xarifa* into the spacious Darwin Bay. In the bushes and trees that dot the walls of this former crater there live thousands of boobies and frigate-birds while between the rocks we found some of the rare sea-bears which were for long thought to be extinct. Eibl made an excursion to the Arcturus crater lake—discovered by Beebe—and there found a hitherto unknown form of plankton.[1] Scheer carried out here, as he did everywhere on our voyage, and in addition to his investigations into bird life, some geophysical surveys which resulted in interesting additional information regarding the degree of twilight illumination on tropical islands.[2]

[1]Triebel 1956.

[2]Scheer 1955.

It was with heavy hearts that one day we watched Tower Island disappear behind us. We had no more time at our disposal.

In addition to a live pig, two giant tortoises and the penguin we had also on board a good many large sea-iguanas. Captain Diebitsch looked on, with patience and resignation on his face, when the cages were opened and the animals were fed on the deck.

The Isles Bewitched faded from our gaze in the delicate rose-red light of a magnificent sunset.

# Treasure Island

IT IS NO easy matter for a ship to find the far-famed Cocos Island upon which, it is said, there have been hidden no less than three different hoards worth altogether between $40,000,000 and $60,000,000. The islet—for it is quite tiny—lies about three hundred miles north-east of the Galapagos and is, for most of the time, wreathed about with heavy rain-clouds. It often happens, indeed, that when a ship is quite close to the steep coasts clad in impenetrable virgin jungle, the island looms up phantom-like from among the grey mists as though it were the Flying Dutchman itself.

We were unusually lucky, for when we approached the island it was basking in the beauty of a summer's day. Girdled with a snow-white ring of breakers, Cocos rose iridescent, arsenic-green, from a deep blue sea. We made, first of all, for Chatham Bay but there was a very heavy swell there and we finally anchored in a small inlet between high walls of rock and sheltered by an off-shore island. I had a distinct feeling that here there was going to be something unusual to be seen. So, as soon as we were fast, *Bill I* was lowered into the water and not ten minutes later Lotte, Hodges, Hirschel and I, together with the big cine-camera, went under water on the left-hand side of the inlet. The first objects to meet our eyes were three hammerhead sharks at least twelve feet long.

One following the other they were swimming just under the surface. We squatted down on the bottom in twelve feet of water and amid coral bushes while I filmed the stately procession. I got the first hammerhead into the picture, then I let him swim out of it and turned my attention to the second. The third was some way behind. The monsters glided like heavy bombers over us as they went on their way. They did not pay the slightest attention to us and when they had disappeared we held an excited meeting at the sea bottom at which we gesticulated like deaf-mutes and expressed ourselves in sign-language.

Then only did we have the leisure to examine more closely the ground on which we were standing. It was covered with coral that grew up into high curved tops of from six to nine feet. I looked at them with feelings of some awe and reverence since they represented the farthest-flung easterly outpost of the great Indo-Pacific coral area whose western extremity lies in the Gulf of Suez. While in the Caribbean a quite special coral fauna has developed in which soft, flexible horn-corals are predominant, the coral formations from the Red Sea right out over the expanse of the South Seas make up one great complex. Just as off Heron Island—where we had dived in the southern extremity of this vast area—there were here only a few kinds of coral, but these had spread out abundantly. Among the coral boulders we saw only a few fish but, on the other hand, plenty of sharks.

No fewer than seven small, slim sharks with white-tipped fins, swam into our view. They were from four and a half to six feet long and circled about us at a prudent distance.

Then Lotte pointed excitedly to behind me. The hammerheads were coming back again. They must have been swimming in a circle since they approached us from exactly the same direction as before. One of them, with a bite-scar over his gills, I recognized at once. This time I swam with my cine-camera diagonally up to meet him. When he noticed me he made a frightened movement and then went on straight ahead.

The three came back yet a third time, still from the same direction. I shot a whole roll of film and then we surfaced quite well satisfied with ourselves. My presentiment had not deceived me. It is only too often that on a first visit to a new place one sees things for which one is not prepared, things which may well never appear again. But I learned the lessons of experience and this time everything was in readiness. Lotte had photographed and I had filmed a scene that we had been waiting for through fifteen years.

Since *Xarifa* in the side-swell was heaving about a good deal, we moved her into Wafer Bay whose natural beauty is outstanding. We all stood on deck and gazed up at the rocky wall nearly a thousand feet high that rose, covered with velvety green vegetation, on the right-hand side of the inlet. Over the precipitous cliffs long silver streaks of waterfalls plashed down into the sea while on the summit of the walls a primeval forest towered up towards the heavens. The level sandy beach before us was fringed with tall coco-palms behind which virgin forest slopes stepped up to the high summit of the island.

Through our telescopes we could make out the remains of the huts left by Captain Giessler who for twenty years, solitary and crabbed and self-willed, lived on the island. The Costa Rica government had accorded him an exclusive concession to search for treasure but, despite this privilege, he was to witness countless other treasure-hunters come and go.

As soon as we had made fast with two anchors, we all landed. Indeed we were seized with an attack of the fever that does not fail to make victims of everyone who gets near to Cocos. Since the island measures hardly more than five miles across you would think it would be impossible to miss the treasures. It is only when you land that you realize how elusive the hoards really are.

In nearly each one of the many books which have been written about the island we get a different story about the various hoards. The first treasure is said to date from as far back as the seventeenth century and to have been hidden by a certain Captain Edward Davis who commanded a whole fleet of pirate ships and is reported to have had, at times, over a thousand men under his orders. Among his exploits was the storming, in 1685, of the

City of León in Nicaragua, and he captured many richly laden galleons. His ship *Bachelor's Delight* became a subject of legend and struck terror into the Spaniards. Davis brought his treasures to Chatham Bay. They are said to have been so immense that during the share-outs gold piastres were scooped up in jugs. It is probable that not only Davis himself but also many of his men cached their illgotten gains on the island, so it may well be that smaller hoards also are hidden away on Cocos. Perhaps it was one of these that was struck by a sailor named Bob Flower in

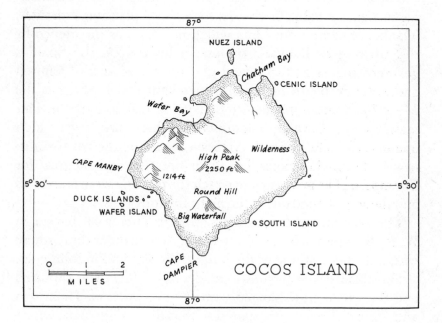

1875. He skidded down in a thicket and fell right into a trove. He carried off as much as he could carry, but apparently never had any opportunity of coming back for the rest. With regard to the site of the main treasure only the vaguest clues exist, but, anyway, Captain Davis spent his later years in Jamaica where he lived as a much respected and very wealthy man.

Rather more details are available about the treasure of Benito Bonito, one of the most cruel and bloodthirsty pirates of his time. He had been an officer in the Portuguese Army but had been dismissed from the service. The first theatre of his activity was in the West Indies; then he shifted his operations to the West Coast from Peru right up to Mexico. His treasure, also worth several million dollars, he hid in 1820 on the north side of Wafer Bay, the inlet where *Xarifa* lay. The steep cliffs rise precipitously from the water and do not become wooded until quite a height. Through the promontory there is a picturesque natural gateway so that one can see between the cliffs into the neighbouring bay. Here some of our crew went on shore.

The greatest treasure of all, however, was the third. Concerning its size and value there exist some fairly plausible estimates. The hoard came from Lima which in 1821 was threatened by the advance of Bolivar's troops. In his distress the Spanish governor conceived the idea of placing the treasure of Church and State on board an English merchant-vessel. She was the *Mary Read* and happened to be lying in Callao harbour. Her master was a Captain Thompson. In those days a very high opinion was held in South America regarding the trustworthiness of the Anglo-Saxons, but the temptation was too great for Thompson. The guards set to watch the treasure were murdered and the ship slipped out in the night fog for Cocos.

The accounts of the precious objects Thompson buried in Wafer Bay seem to be hardly credible. Among other things there was, it is said, a statue of the Virgin, life-size and in solid gold.

Shortly after the cache was made, *Mary Read* was captured and the whole crew hanged with the exception of Thompson and one sailor who were spared so that they might show where the treasure was hidden. Both, however, managed to escape. The sailor died but Thompson lived on for a considerable time in Newfoundland at the house of a man called Keating. Thompson never got back to Cocos Island but spent his days, a gloomy and self-centred man, who never dared to leave the house in the daytime. On his death-bed he told Keating—with whom he was on very friendly terms—the secret of the treasure and handed over a map showing the position of the cache. Keating found a rich merchant who financed a trip to Cocos but the expedition ended in mutiny and murder and Keating got away with only a small part of the buried riches, though this was enough to afford him a good income. The details of the story were overheard by a man in a San Francisco bar and served him as the groundwork of a story. Thus it came about that Robert Louis Stevenson wrote *Treasure Island*.

Of caches two and three there exist several maps which in devious ways came into the hands of men thirsting for adventure. Cocos indeed has known many illustrious treasure-seekers, among them a British admiral and the well-known sportsman Sir Malcolm Campbell. It is the physical conditions which oppose the almost insuperable difficulties met with by hunters after hidden riches. The volcanic soil is cut up into hundreds of ravines and clefts and pierced with many caves. The whole surface is covered with an almost impassable, matted, tangled and slippery wet virgin forest. Moreover, it rains almost unceasingly. It is quite possible also that in some places earth and stones from the steep slopes may have slithered down and filled in caves. Some of the recent expeditions, furnished with all sorts of modern equipment, have dug broad trenches and driven galleries into the mountain sides. Then it may be that one of the treasures has been found long since and no news has been noised abroad about it. A finder might well be careful to tell no word of what he had found. Still, all the same, it would seem that nothing like this really has happened, for to get to Cocos one must have a ship and ships have crews. And when the glitter of gold is actually seen then it does not often come about that the discoverers part and go peaceably on their several ways.

Dr. Sommer was the only one of us whom the thought of treasure left cold. In his role as our radio-operator he experienced on Cocos the culminating triumph of his career. With the collaboration of amateur radio enthusiasts in Panama and Costa Rica who had furnished some equipment he set up in Wafer Bay the first amateur radio-station in the history of the island. Many radio fans in all parts of the world had followed on their sets the fortunes of our expedition and had indeed given us valuable help. These amateurs did all they could, on three successive nights, to contact our Cocos Island station TI9AA, but owing

*El Xarifa* at anchor in Wafer Bay in the Treasure Island of Cocos.

Dr. Sommer sets up the first radio transmitter in the history of the island.

to the shut-in position and the high mountains, only three stations were successful in getting us.

Despite his achievement however Dr. Sommer on the second morning of our stay seemed very pale when he got on board. During the night suddenly the side of his tent had been raised and a huge trunk had appeared close to his body. Two large wild swine and eight young ones had rooted about all round the tent, and they had come back several times.

Our first officer, a keen shot, at once shouldered his gun and set off to spend the next night on shore. He was indeed the only one of us who clambered up high onto the slopes. He did not, however, come back, as he had hoped, with a wild boar but with a young deer. Which of the ships had put off deer onto the island we have never been able to find out.

No one appears ever to have climbed right up to the top of the thickly wooded mountains. We had the best of intentions and were indeed all prepared for the excursion when the rain set in. Sir Malcolm Campbell has ventured to suggest that up on the heights there may still be living Incas who ages ago sought refuge on the island! He seems to have heard in the night some very remarkable noises outside his tent and noticed that his dog

Small Cocos sharks in sight.

showed signs of unusual and marked distress. Perhaps, though, such noises may have been caused by deer.

We worked hard with our cameras from early to late so as to take advantage of every sunny day and indeed of every hour of sunshine. Three times we went back to the little inlet and once we saw hammerhead sharks but never in such a slow and majestic procession as the first time. In another bay, a little farther on, we met many grey sharks with white fin tips, which were appreciably larger and thicker than the smaller sort which was common almost everywhere. In Wafer Bay itself we discovered right under our ship a most interesting coral formation and a short way off the remains of a sunken ship. We added to our collections all the time and removed large lumps of coral from the sea bottom. While this work was going on Hirschel came one day up to the surface. His face was deathly pale. He told us that he had seen an enormous shark motionless just behind him and gazing at him. The creature had obviously been attracted by the hammering noises we had been making.

The number of sharks to be seen on all sides was astounding. In their spare time the crew amused themselves by pulling one after the other out of the water. If we fished with a spoonbait and got a bite almost always immediately afterwards would come another bite and then we pulled in just a fish-head hanging on the hook. Cocos may be the prototype of all treasure islands but it is surely also to be reckoned as the foremost of all shark islands.

Jimmy and I set off each morning round the promontory of Wafer Bay in order to see if the heavy surf around the small island of Nuez had abated. Beebe likened this gloomy crest of rock jutting up from the waves and magnificently clothed with vegetation to Böcklin's *Toteninsel* or Isle of Death. Nuez remains in my memory above all as the main meeting-place for the sharks of Cocos.

It was clear to both of us that there, if at all, we should be able to find the huge tiger sharks mentioned by visitors to the island. If you dive all the year round off remote coasts, then you get, as far as sharks are concerned, a sort of sixth sense. After a glance at a map or an air photograph I can generally point out at once the spot where sharks may be found.

With two cine-cameras ready for action in the boat we got quite close to the steep walls of Nuez and gazed down into the deep blue waters streaked through with foam. Since Cocos Island is so tiny it does not afford, on any side, protection from the far-reaching swells that roll across the Pacific. Out at sea one does not notice them much but when the swell comes against a shore then the water dashes with incredible force while the gargling waves lash high up against the rocks.

It would, nevertheless, have been possible to dive, but neither of us could make up his mind to take the plunge just as I had hesitated to do when, some time before, I had made my first approach to the outer rampart of the Great Barrier Reef. Here the heavy breakers and the surf would not have allowed our boat to remain near us and our heavy cine-cameras would have been a great encumbrance. In what may be called normal waves you can, through appropriate swimming tactics, so counteract the influence of the tide that you keep your balance. With a swell that rolls along forty or sixty yards in breadth, however, the waves keep on pushing so long that finally they get you and roll you imperturbably over the rocks.

We drove up and down along the cliff and then our unspoken decision was to be prudent and careful that day. At heart we were angry with ourselves as we made our way back to *Xarifa*. I suppose that mountaineers experience very much the same sort of feeling when they find a climb too much for them and cannot make up their minds to risk their lives in an attempt.

But there did come one day when the swell was noticeably less. There was rather a strong wind, but it was blowing from a different quarter and the island offered some shelter from the weather. Dark, strangely shaped clouds were scudding past against the sky and were so low that they seemed to touch the tip of the island's summit. From time to time the clouds parted and then brilliant sunshine streamed down on us. At such moments the whole island glistened and shimmered. Owing to the great humidity and to the dew that sparkled on all the leaves, every hue was so intense and so luscious that the scene looked more like a painting than reality. But it was the sea that gleamed with the most magnificent colours of all. Right round the steep shore and up to the seething white zone of foam the water was so luminously ultramarine that no precious stone could have been more intense in brilliance, more lovely to behold.

The many dead birds and leaves that drifted on the surface bore witness to the fury of the thundering waves. We sailed right past the little inlet where the hammerheads were probably swimming round in their eternal, circular procession. This day we realized that we could not find any specious excuses. We had to conquer Nuez. The waves, it was true, were still whipping and hissing and dashing against the crags but they were shorter, less dangerous. It was, indeed, compared with what we had got accustomed to at Cocos, a remarkably fine and auspicious day.

About ten yards off from the reef of the rocks we throttled down and drifted about to and fro. We still had a short respite for a great cloud obscured the sun. As it stood right over the steep mass of Cocos and as the clouds were advancing from beyond, it was anybody's guess whether we might expect a rift in them or not. Finally things seemed favourable. Hirschel had made up his mind to dive with us that day so the three of us plunged into the water together. Hodges carried one and I the other of the big cine-cameras.

We dived as quickly as possible under the opaque storm of spray and swam diagonally downwards in the direction of the sheer drop made by the rocky walls. The water was incredibly clear and pellucid. What we lived through during the following five minutes was the most impressive adventure of our whole expedition.

Hardly were we in the shelter of the wall when Jimmy pointed below him. Far beneath us, eighty feet down, was a sloping bottom on to which jutted out a projection of the rocky wall. There appeared a stream of sharks as we had never seen the like. Jimmy darted down to forty-five feet, supported himself against the rock-face and set to work filming. Hirschel stayed well up towards the surface and I took up my position between

The big sharks of Cocos Island. The hammerhead and the tiger shark.

the two of them and filmed Jimmy as he photographed the sharks.

There were at least forty or even fifty white-finned sharks—each one of them some six feet long—and they were gliding like a swarm of trout. They were in little groups of three or four but each group was closely followed by another. The procession appeared to have no end as more sharks kept on coming from behind the projection of rock. From the eager thrashing of their tail-fins it was obvious that they were making for some hidden objective. Woe to any school of fish that stood in the way of this savage pursuit.

Jimmy held up his thumb. That was his sign that a picture was O.K. I pushed up my thumb in answer. We had agreed that he should use his wide-angle lens while I should employ the tele-lens. In this way, we judged, though we might film the same subject our pictures would come out with different perspectives.

Jimmy swam upwards and I went over to him. Far out in the deep water hovered a huge hammerhead. Several imposing mackerel hurried along not far from us. Almost at the very moment Jimmy and I met, I noticed to the right of us a mighty body appear round the rock and follow the line of the wall. It was calmly making right for us. It was a tiger shark fully twelve feet long.

Now—as indeed when we were filming the sperm whales and everything was a matter of seconds—the electrically operated cameras proved their worth. If we had had to wind up a spring neither of us would have been ready for this shot. Also the hundred and twenty metre long spools of film that Jimmy had fixed into the cameras proved practical. They permitted us now to let the film run without interruption for over a minute.

Jimmy, who was about six feet below me, spotted the shark at the same minute as I did. A second later both our cameras were whirring away in the deep water. Never in my life, I think, had I concentrated more than in those next few minutes. Since I was using a tele-lens I had to be very careful about the focus. On the right-side handle was a lever with which I could, while filming, adjust the focus as I wished. You had to move this lever

The twelve-foot tiger shark in the attack.

very slowly and evenly so as not to jolt or jerk the camera during use. At the same time I had to watch the parallax through the viewfinder—and that, with a tele-lens, is quite a ticklish job. The camera had a frame-finder and I had to bring a knob—set somewhat farther back—into line with the median cross. For distances of up to ten metres the knob had to be under the cross and then, as the shark came nearer, to be moved gradually along over the cross. I must therefore execute simultaneously and smoothly three different movements. I had to follow the shark and keep him well in the viewfinder. I must, the nearer he came, press slowly downward with my right hand on the lever. I had to see that the knob of the viewfinder moved along over the median cross—otherwise we should find later on that there would be a bit of the shark in the upper part of the picture, but that his back would be missing.

While I was going through these gyrations more or less un-consciously I was staring fixedly at the eyes of the huge beast as he approached. Anyone who has been opposite a tiger shark, a real tiger shark, and has looked him right in the eye can never forget the experience. This eye is blacker than burnished onyx and is so full of power, so calm, yet so menacing that its glance is impressed on one's memory forever.

Just as the white shark had done some time before, this tiger shark made for us evenly and easily, though since he was coming from a greater distance he was travelling more rapidly. I kept a short distance in front of Jimmy who was rather to one side. Soon the shark filled the whole viewfinder—for I was using the tele-lens. I stopped filming for a moment, grabbed my spear and hurled it at the beast's head. He made a great swift swirl— exactly as the white shark had done—and made off imperturbably towards the open sea.

While all this was going on I could hear whirring coming through the water. I must say that all my admiration went out to Jimmy for he had not stopped filming for one second while I, quite close in front of him, was lunging my spear at the shark. And Jimmy went on filming until the shark had vanished in the distance. The shots showed up eventually as an uninterrupted sequence—the shark making for us, his head monstrously large, the spear coming into the picture, the hit and then the swirl of the beast as it turned to make off into the depths. Moreover he had secured superb definition both for the approach of the shark and for its withdrawal.

We looked at each other and we both jerked up our thumbs. We had taken many pictures during the expedition, but in this moment of climax we had been able to make photographs which were impeccable from the technical point of view.

However, just before the tiger shark had made his appearance, the sun had disappeared, so we filmed without direct sunlight. During the next few days then we were very worried as to whether our shots would come out satisfactorily since, despite the use of the widest aperture, we had according to our exposure-meter under-exposed by two stops. But here the really magnificent Eastman Color Film came to our aid. Although colour films, in themselves, have little latitude of exposure, the pictures show every detail. Both of the photographs of the tiger shark in this book have been enlarged from our colour film.

We were still holding up our thumbs when a warning cry from Hirschel reached us. From the same direction as the first, and in just the same manner, a second tiger shark was coming swimming towards us. He much resembled the first beast and he was of about the same size. Indeed, if we had not seen the original one make off towards the open sea we should have thought he had come back again.

We filmed him but he did not approach so near to us and swam about down below. A few minutes later the first shark came back and then also the second one. Then, shortly after that, there were the two of them again for the third time. So, altogether, we were able to film six views of these creatures which, as far as I know, had never been filmed before. Their behaviour was that of animals quite sure of themselves, but ready for attack, menacing. Just like the sharks in Australia these creatures pushed their heads quite close to us.

By now it had become dark so we swam up to the surface. We had been very lucky. While we had been filming there had been but a thin streak of cloud before the sun, now there was a dark wall of cloud hanging over the island and it soon moved forwards. Grey wisps and tatters clung to the summit. Then the rain began. We really had caught the last glint of sunshine for our shots.

The next day was fine and we went back to the same spot. This time Lotte dived with us, but the tiger sharks did not put in an appearance, though we saw several hammerheads that we photographed from all angles.

After a short rest in the boat we were in such high spirits that we decided to try our luck off the northern point of Nuez. It was not possible to dive right in front of the cape since the water there was very agitated from the clash of two opposing lines of waves which broke, filthy and turbid, in gigantic masses over the crags and rocks. However, to one side, we discovered a sheltered spot where we could get as near as twenty yards to the rocks. This time Eibl had decided to come with us.

Going ashore on the romantic San Blas Islands off the Panama coast.

We had hardly got into the water when we saw the boat driven far off from us. We hovered in water of an abysmal depth and flecked with dirty foam. I hastened to get under the clouds of spray and to reach the rocky wall that was only visible as a vague blur. Jimmy was a short distance behind me, but I had lost sight of Eibl. When I was fortunate enough to get up against the wall—where the sea's strong suction shoved me up and down over a length of fifteen to twenty feet—I saw that Jimmy had lagged behind and was staring around him. He was swaying about in the distance and signalled to me that he would not come farther but return. Also I realized that conditions were much too unfavourable. As the sunlight hardly penetrated at all through the layer of foam it was very dark. Jimmy turned round and vanished from my sight. Pushing my camera before me I hurried back to the boat.

Jimmy was still in the water when I got there and he was staring about in all directions. Something must have happened. In the boat Eibl told me that five large hammerhead sharks had swum very close to him and only when Jimmy had arrived had the animals made off.

'Let's leave this place for the next comers,' said Jimmy in his dry way. 'It would not be fair to take all the credit.'

So we left Nuez when we had conquered only a part of its crags and rocks. The most southerly point of the island must, in better weather conditions, be a very interesting, if also an extremely dangerous, area. Whoever is the first to go under water there must, I think, be prepared for surprises.

That same evening the rain set in and did not let up during the following days. The water in Wafer Bay turned to a dirty yellow. We filled a boat full of coconuts and bade Treasure Island adieu. After ten days' sail we reached the Pearl Islands in the Gulf of Panama where the water was both cold and turbid. So we kept on our course.

After traversing the Panama Canal we got to the fabulously beautiful San Blas Islands which look just like what imagination pictures the South Sea Islands to be. In a charmed chain

The gaily dressed Carib women are amazed by our diving-gear.

they lie off the Caribbean coast of Panama, a shore fringed with virgin forest. The isles are quite flat and covered with thick groves of coconut palms. Some of the islets are so small that only two or three palms and an isolated hut can find place on them. The larger islands, however, were all inhabited by Indians who rowed out in great excitement, seated in their long log-canoes, as *Xarifa* wended her way between the isles.

Both men and women swarmed all over the ship. The men offered for sale parrots and coconuts while the women tempted us with their home-made highly ornamented skirts and blouses. Since these Indians were most friendly and perfectly honest we let them come on board as they liked. Often when we got back from an excursion in the boat, *Xarifa* was filled with multi-coloured figures who made such signs of greeting that you would have thought the ship belonged to them and that we were welcome guests.

We filmed for a whole week, mostly above water, however. The reefs were disappointing and astonishingly poor in fish. The day after we left the islands—we had already done ninety miles—suddenly an appalling grinding noise rumbled through the ship. The motor stopped. Soon the engineer reported that a bearing had broken in the turn-over gear and that the main engine could not be used any more. We hoisted sail and attempted, against wind and current, to beat our way on, and although the weather got steadily worse, we struggled for three days. Straining her cordage *Xarifa* rode over ever heavier seas. We could sail only half against the wind and all our efforts brought us back again and again to the same position. Finally we had to realize that there was no sense in trying to keep on. We had to acknowledge our defeat and sail with the wind back to Panama.

In the meantime, however, Dr. Sommer had managed, through amateur radio-stations to get through an order to Germany for the replacement of the bearing. We had, at first, hoped to get under our own power to Curaçao and have the spare part sent to us there. But now we had to resign ourselves to going back to Cristóbal. It was with very mixed feelings that we sailed once more into the sticky heat of the bay.

Apart from the loss of time there was the question of expense. In the Canal Zone all workshops belong to the Canal Authority and charges for repairs are inordinately high. While we were waiting for the spare part, the turn-over gear was dismantled and in the course of inspection it appeared that other bearings were affected too. For a time we feared that the heat had distorted the main shaft.

All this trouble weighed down the spirits of our people. We had intended to stay out eight months and I now came slowly to realize that the expedition must last nine or maybe even ten months. Most of us had at home a wife or a sweetheart and their letters began to express increasing impatience. Our first officer left on the ground of ill-health and Jimmy, who had come out as commander R.N. of a ship on the West Indies Station, went off provisionally to his job. Finally after we had spent two most uncomfortable weeks everything was repaired and we left Panama once more behind us.

We did not touch at Curaçao but made straight for Bonaire. To complete our film we still needed a good many more scenes which we intended to shoot there. But the weather was bedevilled. Though usually at that time of year it is clear and fine, the sky was overcast all the time and the sun broke through now and then only for a few minutes.

Shivering with the cold we spent many hours on the sea bottom and with nothing else to do but to wait for a fugitive ray of sunlight. The scenes had been fully prepared and indeed rehearsed and each of us squatted in his place and looked up at the boat bobbing about above us. From time to time Xenophon let down an oxygen flask as a sign that a break in the clouds looked imminent. Often the sun shone for so short a space that right in the middle of shooting a scene everything got quite dark again. Then we had to sit by idly once more and stare at the aluminum sheet on which each scene was carefully indicated. We waited until our supply of oxygen was exhausted.

Up in the boat, however, it was still colder for a keen wind whistled around us. Under the little awning of the *Bill I* we huddled together, ate sardines and drank hot tea. Then, as soon as the clouds looked like lifting, we were in the sea again.

I was very disappointed we were not able to continue what we had begun in the Red Sea, that is to say our researches into the vibrations emitted by fish. But we had much too much to do and each day of the expedition's time cost a little fortune. In addition to all this it was by no means easy to anchor *Xarifa* in the spots best suited for the experiment. So, when the Easter holidays came we were all rather exhausted. No one was really satisfied for by this time we ought all to have been at home long since.

We dropped anchor off Punt Vierkant and everyone was given leave over the holidays. In the early morning, however, Jimmy came to me with a proposal:

'How would it be if we two were to take some recordings today? I think everyone wants to get finished as quickly as possible.'

Scheer and Hirschel were quite willing to prepare the equipment. Jimmy explained the working of the oxygen apparatus to a Dutch physician and his friend who were guests on board. Jimmy put on his diving-gear and explained how, before diving, the one most important thing to do is to suck out the breathing-sack so as to be sure that no nitrogen remains in it. Then he took off his tackle.

Half an hour later everything was ready. The Dutchman snapped a few photographs while Jimmy and I clambered down the ladder. At the request of our guests we both removed our mouthpieces and smiled into their cameras. I mention all these details because they may possibly have been in some way responsible for what happened soon afterwards.

Jimmy took the short stick with the microphone that he was to hold in front of harpooned fish; the mike was fitted with a glass float so that it had almost no weight at all. I carried a harpoon-gun. We went under water and swam down to the slanting slope. While Jimmy unrolled the thin cable which he carried in loops, we went on in about sixty feet of water along the declivity, looking for suitable fish.

After a quarter of an hour at last we met a grouper coming sideways towards us. I shot at him, but he tore himself loose and whizzed away down the incline almost as far as the sandy bottom that was over ninety feet below the surface. There the fish hid under a rock. Jimmy laid aside his microphone and made off for the rock in order to get the fish out, for the cook had particularly asked us to bring up something for supper.

I had a very uncomfortable feeling as I watched Jimmy swimming in what was too great a depth for an oxygen apparatus. My experience with this sort of equipment—which we had by that time used for ten years in over two thousand diving operations—had taught me that twenty metres, or say more or less sixty feet, is the safe limit or rather the extreme limit. An inexperienced diver would do well not to venture farther down

than thirteen metres.[1] As far back as 1942 I had carefully
studied on myself the symptoms of oxygen poisoning and went
occasionally deeper for a short space of time for I knew the
symptoms very well. Jimmy, indeed, was just as experienced as
I was; still, when I saw he was not able to get the fish out from
under the rock, I called through the mouthpiece to him, made
signs and then he came upwards again.

He picked up the microphone and we swam on farther. Since
the effects of oxygen poisoning show themselves at once and
then lead quickly to paralysis and unconsciousness, I was, as I
saw him swimming unconcernedly on, quite relieved and reas-
sured. As soon as you are up once more in a safe depth, all danger
is over. I know of no case in which the effects have shown themselves after a lapse of time.

We swam as far as our cable allowed us and about ten minutes after the incident I have just described there came along a
fish which I could shoot in an ideal position just in front of the
microphone Jimmy was holding. I held up my thumb, he held
up his, and we turned back. I swam on ahead and took the fish
off the harpoon. Then I looked around me.

To my astonishment Jimmy was on the surface. It is generally
a bad sign when a diver suddenly swims right up to the top. Still,
he was holding the microphone and he had his head above
water. I took it merely that his supply of oxygen had given out;
so I followed along the cable that had got entangled in several
places in the coral bushes, freed it, and then also swam up to the
surface.

There I was met with excited cries from *Xarifa* some fifty
yards off. The captain was running along the rail and I at once
looked about me to see Jimmy, but I could get no sight of him
either on the surface or under water. Deep below me lay the expanse of the grey bottom and nowhere was any sign of the cable
to whose end he had been holding. I called to the boat that was
anchored nearby and was so frightened that I dived down without my mouthpiece. Water came rushing in. Quickly I was up on
the surface again and took the mouthpiece in my mouth. The

[1]Ten metres is the accepted limit in Britian.

tube was half-full of water, but now every second might be of the utmost importance.

I shot right downwards and tried to drink out the water from the tube. Nothing was to be seen of Jimmy at all. I could hardly breathe any longer. Then I saw a vague blur behind a coral bush. As quickly as I could I swam towards it. Behind the bush lay Jimmy on his back, motionless. His breathing-tube was not in his mouth.

In some way or another I managed to haul him up to the surface. As soon as we were above water I yelled for help but was then at once dragged down again by his weight. I noticed that his manometer still stood at forty atmospheres. I was able to shut the valve on the mouthpiece and to inflate his breathing-bag. Then I held his head above water. In the meantime the captain had arrived with the second boat and we dragged up the lifeless body from the sea. Once on board *Xarifa* Dr. Sommer and the Dutch physician immediately tried artificial respiration. For five long hours we did everything imaginable, but death had already claimed its victim. We were all shocked and confounded at this incredible disaster.

Since I could not imagine there could be delayed action in a case of oxygen poisoning, I concluded that Jimmy, after he had put on and taken off his apparatus and breathing-tube several times, had imagined that he had already emptied the breathing-bag but that he had not done so. Since when he was filming he liked to take short, slight breaths, he had dispensed with half of the weights of his apparatus—which counteract the updrift—and carried always only a relatively small amount of gas in his bag. During the recording of fish vibrations he might further have let even less oxygen into his bag—in this way to keep himself as heavy as possible. All of these circumstances may have well led to his having only nitrogen in his bag. Since the act of breathing in human beings is determined not by lack of oxygen but by the carbon dioxide content in the blood, a diver may not notice, in such circumstances, that he is breathing only nitrogen. The expelled carbon dioxide is continuously absorbed by the chemicals. So there may come about a complete lack of oxygen—called anoxia—which soon produces rapid degenerative changes in the brain and—death.

This danger (which, however, is encountered only in exceptional cases) can be avoided if the hand valve is changed for an automatic-feed valve that maintains a constant intake of a sufficient quantity of oxygen. On the other hand this device opens the possibility for other defects, as with all automatic gadgets. Furthermore, the supply of oxygen with an automatic valve is not very satisfactory since the oxygen consumption depends upon the depth you are at and upon the work you are doing. Taken by itself, an oxygen apparatus has the advantage over a compressed-air apparatus in that with the former it is possible in case of need and by simply pressing a knob to inflate the bag on your back and then quite unaided rise to the surface. The fact that Hodges had not done this shows that when he got to the surface he was already not in full possession of his senses.

We paid our last tribute to our friend and comrade in the little cemetery of Bonaire. None of us could understand how this most expert and experienced diver could have found his death on such an easy operation. We all remembered his cool self-confidence and his humour. We recalled the many happy hours we had spent in his company on the expedition. The sea to which he had dedicated his life had robbed him of it, suddenly, unjustly . . . if only I had looked around me a little later, at the moment that he sank under, I would have been able to bring him aid and assistance.

There was still work to be done. We had to go on with it. On Easter Tuesday we set our teeth and made off for the scene of the tragedy. It lay not a hundred yards away from the place where, on my first expedition, Alfred von Wurzian had met with his accident. In our excitement we had cut the cable of the microphone and that now lay somewhere on the sea's bottom. To search for it, find it and haul it up seemed to us the best way of overcoming our shock.

The water was turbid and seldom can there have been more nervous divers than we were then. But as we overcame our nervousness we also recovered from our shock. Sommer, Eibl, Scheer,

Hirschel, Lotte and I freed the cable from the corals and brought the microphone up.

The next day normal diving work started up again. After a week of intense activity we had made so much progress with our programme that *Xarifa* could begin her voyage home. Lotte and I wanted to take alone some special photographs of fish, so we two stayed behind in Curaçao. However, the batteries of the cine-cameras were at their last gasp and we had neither boat nor help. We felt the lack of our good friend Xenophon. Moreover, our nerves were so frayed that we were able to shoot only a few pictures. We found ourselves, in fact, in the same state that we were at the end of our Red Sea expedition. Finally we handed over all our gear and tackle to a forwarding agency to be sent home by ship while we ourselves flew to New York and then back to Europe.

*Xarifa* made a good trip home. We had signed on as first officer a friendly Dutchman from Curaçao and Captain Diebitsch[1] brought the ship, in fine condition, to Genoa after four weeks' sail—which was very good time. Many of our associates, including Professor Ankel, went to greet her and give her a rousing welcome. Benny, who had valiantly dived in the Caribbean and caught fish that had never seen a penguin, waddled proudly ashore onto Italian soil. Mouche had already been sent home on an airplane from Curaçao. The climate and the sea voyage would have been too much for him. Unfortunately none of the sea-iguanas survived the trip, but the San Blas parrots and the Galapagos tortoises were in splendid condition when *Xarifa* got to port.

The various specimens we had collected were forwarded to their respective destinations. The crew and the members of the expedition went their various ways. Then began the unspectacular activity of sorting out and collating the mass of observations and information we had gathered. *Xarifa* remained under Xenophon's charge in the yachting basin. After her long voyage she needed a thorough overhaul.

[1]Captain Diebitsch later took command of the *Pamir* and met a tragic death.

# We Go Back into the Sea

During the last twenty years the sport of under-water hunting has become popular all round the world. Remote ages ago some fish ventured onto dry land, now Man ventures back into the sea. It needed millions of years for nature's evolution to be accomplished. Man has managed, through his modern technique, to effect his evolution in a few decades.

The difference, of course, resides in this: each link in the chain of natural development must be fully equipped to survive—otherwise that link would snap and the chain of evolution be broken. Furthermore, each new feature of a living organism must be developed from a body and be an integral part of it. In the case of Man—owing to the development of his mental powers—both of these conditions ceased to be imperative.

A crane, an airplane, a gun or a microscope are, biologically speaking, artificial organs which man has created in order to increase his possibilities and power. Within the natural evolutionary processes, as they have been in function up to now, such instruments could not have been produced in thousands of millions of years, since these implements far transcend anything which on a living organism can be formed and maintained. In Man, on the other hand, through the capacities of our brain, nature is able to achieve such results. We devise these tools and then, outside and apart from our bodies, construct them according to plan from parts and materials.

All the same, even such creations of Man's ingenuity are still subject to the laws of nature. They also succumb to natural selection and fight for existence. An invention survives only if it is useful, and a product can only maintain itself if it can face competition and find a market.

New ideas encounter obstacles just as formidable as do new sorts of animals in the natural world. Old ideas and old animals can oppose a stiff resistance to those who would dispossess them. When something is once firmly established in a certain territory —let us say its 'market'—then innovation is combated. For this reason what is novel mostly does not arise from a development or a modification of what is old. Novelties are produced through often devious by-paths and by outsiders.

Such was also the case with the new diving method. This was not invented by scientists or by the technicians of the established diving 'industry' and they also did not arise from a special necessity. Modern skin-diving developed from fun and sport, it derived from a lust for adventure, from a delight in what is novel and from interest in the unknown.

The whole thing began with diving-goggles, such as had been long used by pearl-fishers. In 1932 two Japanese, armed with such glasses, dived off Capri. About the same time Alexander Kramarenko in France took a pair of these goggles and fitted them with small rubber bags to equalize the pressure. Probably others, of whom we know nothing, undertook other or similar experiments. They all experienced the marvel of seeing clear under water. They saw big, rather unsuspecting fish nearby. The idea of using spear or trident to waylay these fish came naturally enough.

The father of under-water hunting must be held to be the American author Guy Gilpatric. As far as I can recall, his imagination was fired by an American naval officer's account of how he had seen, during a voyage to the South Seas, Polynesians, holding a spear, dive into the sea. Gilpatric published in 1938 the first book to be devoted to the new sport. It was called *The Complete Goggler*. I look upon him as my master and he mentions one of my first adventures in his book.

The next contribution to the elaboration of the new method was made by Captain de Corlieu, a French naval officer, when he invented flippers for the feet. Soon the under-water hunters felt the need to perpetuate, for the benefit of others, what they themselves had seen and experienced. So we got under-water photography and under-water films. As a matter of fact, as early as the last century Wilhelm Bauer and Louis Boutain had managed to take under-water photographs, but of their achievement probably none of the young men engaged in the new sport knew anything. Each one, for himself, grappled with the technical difficulties in his own way. My first under-water camera dated from the autumn of 1937. I published my first under-water monochrome photographs in 1939 in my book *Jagd unter Wasser* ('Underwater Hunting') and my first colour photographs in 1942 in *Fotojagd am Meeresgrund* ('Hunting with the Camera on the Sea's Bottom').

Also, inspired by the example of Guy Gilpatric, Jacques Yves Cousteau, Philippe Taillez and Frédéric Dumas formed a group at Toulon. They dived off the French coast and also off the island of Jerba in southern Tunisia. Perhaps it was because we in Vienna were so far off from the sea that we ventured, already before the late war, to plunge into the Caribbean.

However, what was still lacking was 'artificial gills'. In Toulon, as in Vienna, the talk was all about some appropriate breathing apparatus. Cousteau plumped for compressed air and devised, in collaboration with the technician Emile Gagnan, the 'aqualung' which is now used by divers all over the world. We, on the other hand, as I have already mentioned, chose an oxygen apparatus, the first of which was turned out in 1942. As far as I know this was the earliest breathing apparatus (used by skin-divers) whose existence can be proved by published documents.

In much of the present-day diving literature the dangers presented by use of pure oxygen are much stressed. In opposition to this opinion I can say only this—we have experienced no trouble at all with such an apparatus (up to depths of ten fathoms) during more than two thousand under-water adventures. Similar results are also reported from Italy and South Africa. All the same, I recommend sporting divers to make use of compressed air appliances. They are reliable, easy to use and allow one to descend to considerably greater depths.

After the 1939–1945 war a whole industry developed to supply the needs of under-water sportsmen. Dozens of different masks, snorkels, fins and under-water guns came on the market. Diving-gear and under-water cameras advertised the new sport. Comic papers and cabaret shows discovered the world under the sea. Diving clubs were founded. The first international under-water hunting competitions were held.

The weapons employed became more and more effective. With Guy Gilpatric's lance you had to make long and tiresome efforts before you could outwit a fish. Nowadays, with weapons that project a harpoon as far as four yards, shooting a fish has become a relatively easy feat. The oldest under-water arm— the Nautilus of the pioneer diver Commander Le Prieur—used powder. Modern under-water guns utilize $CO_2$ or compressed air. For hunting large fish even explosive harpoon points are employed. Another, but not as yet perfected, device would consist of an electric harpoon much the same as the electric hook used in tuna fishing.

The result of all this was that very soon there were in the shop-windows on the Riviera more harpoons than there were fish in the water. The creeks, inlets and reefs that were once so rich in fish have been all cleaned out. The larger fish have fled before Man's invasion and have taken refuge in the depths. Many under-water hunters have exchanged their weapons for a camera.

Much has been done in recent years to perfect these. There soon appeared covers and cases adapted to all the best known and standard makes and these allow of some or indeed of all adjustments being made under-water. With the Rolleimarin, designed by myself, or with the Fenjohn 16 mm., you can even exchange the filter in the case. The Aquaflex 35 mm. is provided with an automatic pressure equalizer and permits focussing through the lens itself.

Owing to the poor visibility under-water wide-angle lenses

are of great importance. At our suggestion the Schneider optical works in Kreuznach produced for 16 mm. cameras the 'Cinegon' which is very powerful. The tele-effect produced by the refraction of the light on the window of the container can be counteracted. The French physicists Dratz and Ivanoff have devised correction-lenses which can be used with any sort of lens.

In under-water colour photography two methods of artificial lighting are employed, either that of normal flash-bulbs which can be changed under water, or that of an electronic flash with an attached battery. In this connection, the French technician Dimitri Rebikoff has put on the market a whole series of perfected devices among which is the 'Torpille'. Whether, however, the electronic flash is to be preferred to exchangeable flash-bulbs is open to discussion. Louis Marden took, for the *National Geographic Magazine,* with a Rolleimarin and flash-bulbs, photographs whose quality could hardly be surpassed. Each of the two methods has its particular advantage for certain sorts of work.

The first under-water films attracted much public attention to the newly conquered realm below the sea. In *Pirsch unter Wasser* ('Under-water Stalking') we showed, in 1940, life in a coral reef. After the war appeared Cousteau's outstanding films about sunken ships and diving in the Mediterranean. In 1942 with our full-length documentary *Menschen unter Haien* ('Men among Sharks') we were able to break into the evening programme of the cinemas. *Abenteuer im Roten Meer* ('Under the Red Sea') got the first prize at the Venice Biennale and was then shown all over the world. The Italians produced the very successful colour-film *Sesto Continente. Hunters of the Deep,* an American film, was shot in the Pacific. In *Unternehmen Xarifa* ('Under the Caribbean') we showed, for the first time, coral reefs illuminated by projectors. Cousteau's latest film *The Silent World* is an example of perfect camera work and in 1956 won the first prize at the Cannes Film Festival.

Actors also went under the water. For some considerable time struggles between divers and the huge, mechanically operated rubber octopuses (patented by Williamson) were a stock stand-by in horror films. In a very charming way Esther Williams went under water with a revue film. *Beneath the Twelve Mile Reef* showed seascapes in Cinemascope. With *Underwater* Jane Russell brought sex-appeal into a sunken ship. *Frog Men* struck a military note and *20,000 Leagues Under the Sea* a Utopian one. Only a good under-water comedy has yet to be seen.

Much more serious were the matters in which under-water television was utilized. In 1946 at the time of the atom bomb explosion at the Bikini atoll, a submerged television-camera was employed to determine the damage caused to sunken ships while certain weapons were being tried out. In 1951 the British submarine *Affray* which sank in forty-five fathoms in the English Channel was identified by means of a Marconi TV-camera. An under-water TV-camera constructed by Pye was used to locate the remains of the British Comet jet airplane which had come down in the sea. The camera was let down to the sea's bottom and then dragged along with a speed of up to four knots, on a line attached to a ship.

In professional diving and in salvage work the new method is only gradually adopted. Indeed the spheres of activity are quite different. For heavy work the diving-suit will for long be the most suitable equipment. However, the skin-diver can much better explore any given area and repair slight damage to ships for instance. He can ascertain the position of wrecks, take under-water photographs and lay explosive charges.

On many occasions skin-divers and suit-divers could work together to their common benefit.

There had been devised, for the reconnoitring of extensive areas under water, submarine sledges and gliding-boards by means of which a diver is drawn along over the sea bottom. He can steer his way, upwards or downwards, by means of a 'stick' just as an airplane pilot does. For speeds of over four knots a protective shield of plexiglass must be adjusted. Rebikoff has constructed a flashlight apparatus whose batteries also work a propeller which carries the photographer along through the water and his latest invention, 'Pegasus', shows still further improvements. A handy scooter devised by the *Groupe d'Etudes et de Recherches* at Toulon was shown in the film *The Silent World*. Gustav dalla Valle constructed an open underwater torpedo in which two divers can sit one behind the other and which allows them to get out, if they wish, while beneath the sea. It was with a similar vehicle—fitted with a detachable explosive head—that during the Second World War Italian frogmen penetrated into Gibraltar harbour.

In cold water skin-divers must use protective clothing. Two different types have been developed, first, watertight rubber suits under which a knitted woollen combination is worn and, second, so-called 'wet' suits made of sponge-rubber in which a a protective layer is constituted by the enclosed bubbles of air.

Both types allow of diving in winter and even under ice; both have their advantages and their disadvantages. The impermeable suits are the warmer, but in the depths tend to ruck up into painful folds and creases. The 'wet' suits are more comfortable to wear but in deep water lose some of their buoyancy and isolating properties through the contraction of the air-bubbles.

Today, in the United States, it is no unusual sight to catch a glimpse of a black-rubber-clad diver at the steering wheel of his car. A sporting diver will put on his suit at home, drive to where he wants to swim under water and then, without changing, drive home again. You can also see figures, clad in black rubber, flying through the air on manœuvres. In some operations frogmen have been dropped by parachute.

New developments of military significance are kept rigorously secret. Owing to the treacherous formation of bubbles by compressed-air sets, frog-men usually employ oxygen sets with enough gas for two to four hours' working time. Since these men operate mostly at night they are provided with luminous watches, depth gauges and compass. The frog-men are employed for sabotaging bridges and in harbours, for removing mines, for espionage work and to deliver explosives against enemy ships. The greatest problem always remains that of securing a safe return for these divers.

Ships are protected by small water-bombs and electrical appliances against the new dangers. In 1956 Commander Lionel Crabb lost his life, in some mysterious manner, while he was making an under-water visit to examine the installations on the hull of the Soviet cruiser *Ordzhonikidze* anchored in Portsmouth harbour.

It is obvious that skin-divers can be of great service in lifesaving. Also for police work the new method has proved valuable. Already, in a number of cases under-water diving clubs have been able to help in investigations. Bodies of men killed by violence or by accident have been recovered. Revolvers, clothes and other pieces of evidence relating to crimes have been located and brought to light. A regular group of frog-men is being trained by the British police, for the arm of the law must now reach under the water. Not so long ago the Dutch police arrested the members of a gang which specialized in smuggling containers full of coffee through the waters on the frontiers of Belgium and Holland.

Under-water detection promises to be a new profession not only for tracking down criminals but also for the recovery of historical and cultural treasures. In many places off the Mediterranean coasts there have been found Roman amphorae hidden in mud and seaweed—the relics of the cargo on sunken Roman ships. Overnight, as it were, we discovered a new branch of science—under-water archaeology. The French writer Philippe Diolé has been indefatigable in publicizing this latest form of research. No doubt, during the next decades, many interesting archaeological finds will be made under the seas that hold incredibly great stores of precious art objects as well as immense riches in gold and precious stones. With the methods employed up to now many sunken ships—in all the seven seas—either could not be found at all or if they were discovered their cargoes could not be raised to the surface. In this domain the skin-diver has immense possibilities.

Some mention has already been made of prospects in the domain of biological research and these are, indeed, incalculable. In this connection we are not concerned, primarily, with practical considerations but with idealistic ones—the widening of our knowledge of the sea and its inhabitants. In this branch of research zoologists have enough to keep them occupied for a thousand years—and then find themselves still at the beginning of many tasks.

Fisheries also can benefit from the experience of skin-divers. Thus, for instance, skin-divers have, in recent years, been able to watch the operations of nets and other devices used on the sea bottom. From what has been learned in this way a number of improvements have resulted. Jimmy Hodges had himself attached to a trawling-net and then filmed the behaviour of the fishes in front of it.

The aqualung has brought about a revolution in pearl- and sponge-diving. Both in oyster culture and in the recovery of valuable sorts of seaweed the skin-diver has his part to play. After an under-water vacuum-cleaner has been perfected for the cleansing of swimming-baths we shall have the under-water mowing-machine for seaweed, since this is used today in the manufacture of ice-cream, lipsticks, and telephones as well as being employed in brewing, in making styptics and in the photographic and textile industries.

In relation to the animals of the sea Man is still today a nomad. All schemes for 'mariculture' have proved valueless because in the open sea no sort of barrier or fence can be erected. Maybe, however, one day such difficulties may be overcome. Already whales, by means of high frequency emissions, that is to say by invisible fences, are prevented from breaking out from specified areas.

Furthermore, immense subsoil riches lie under the sea. In recent years many teams of divers have been engaged by the big oil companies to collect samples of deposits from the sea-bottom and there to set up gravimeters. Both in Mexico and at Maracaibo oil-wells have for long been sunk under the sea. It is, indeed, assumed that below the oceans there exist immense reserves of oil which have not been touched.

In order to discover something new the next thing to do is to look in new places. What we have been able to observe about the behaviour of sharks may have contributed to make it possible for many areas of the sea, formerly regarded as too dangerous, to become accessible. Anyway, today a whole army of skin-divers, operating both individually and organized into clubs, is at work off the coasts of the five continents.

From Brazil reported Marcel Isy-Schwart, Jack Ackermann from Hawaii, Rodney Jonklaas and the Franco Properi group from Ceylon, Folco Quilici and Jean Foucher-Crettau from Massawa and the Dahlak islands, Don Clark from Tahiti and Hikeru, the zoologist Eugénie Clark from Bimini, Kwajalein from Guam, the Palawi islands and the Carolines; the Bernard Grosky group from the Grenadines, the Marquisas and the Tuamotu archipelago; Don Ollis from the Marshall Islands; Gordon Tumley from South Africa; Jim Oetzel and Tom Trench from the Fijis; Serge de Sazo from the Gulf of Akaba; the Cousteau, Heberlein and Marcante groups from the Persian Gulf; Taillez from Vietnam; Vane Ivanovic from Bali; Henry Tiarks from Jamaica and the Bermudas; Len Staples from Tasmania; the 'Calypso' expedition and William Travis from the Seychelles; R. P. Fraser from New Zealand; Kiko Alcorta from Argentina; Rou McGhee from Alaska; Arthur Clarke from the Torres Straits . . . and the list could be continued over several pages.

Diving for gold nuggets now goes on in North American rivers, in Brazil for diamonds and in Mexico for pre-Columbian treasure. In Nova Scotia John Sweeney has found the remains of the French squadron that was sunk in 1758 before Louisburg. Off Key West the Crile family and Arthur McKee discovered elephant's tusks in a sunken ship while off Abukir Frank Lynch and Captain Lytle located an Egyptian temple under the waves as well as the remains of Napoleon's warships sunk by Nelson at the Battle of the Nile. The exploration of profound submarine grottoes is being actively pursued in France, North America and Australia.

Sport, moreover, encourages new ideas. The under-water clubs are forming a new generation of divers and new methods are being tried out. In North America there are already as many as two hundred and eighty-three under-water clubs. In France you have the *Club Alpin Sousmarin,* the *Club des Chasseurs Sousmarins* and the *Club Méditerrané* which are outstanding. In Great Britain, the *British Sub-aqua Club.* In Italy the *Goggler Club Milano* and many others. In Germany the *Deutsche Unterwasser Klub* with headquarters in Hamburg and many branches. In Australia the *Spearfishing Association of New South Wales.* There are clubs in Oran, Tunis, Tripoli and Istanbul, in Rio de Janeiro, Port of Spain (Trinidad), Panama, Santiago de Chile, Guayamas (Mexico), in Ontario and Vancouver, in Durban and Port Elizabeth, at Dehiwala in Ceylon, at Kanai in Burma, at Kanagawa-Ken in Japan, at Agan in Guam, at Noumea in New Caledonia and at Hobart in Tasmania. There are, moreover, probably a great number of other clubs not known to me while I am writing this.

Specialized publications have been of great service in encouraging the sport. In America *The Skin-Diver* is outstanding and there is the *Deep Sea Digest* which appears in Florida. In Australia there are the *Spearfishing News* and the *Spearfishing Sportlight,* in Italy *Pescasport,* in France *L'Aventure Sousmarine,* in Britain *Triton,* in Germany *Delphin*—and the list is by no means exhausted.

The movement has had some astonishing developments. Two doctors undertook a first under-water operation—on a blinded ray. A wedding has been held under water and at San Fruttuoso on the Italian coast a figure of Christ has been erected under the sea.

We shall probably soon have, for the benefit of tourists, an under-water family coach from which a coral reef can be examined. We may even get under-water *parfums,* submarine masked balls or a submarine State issuing its own stamps.

Deep sea research has also profited by skin-diving, insofar as by this movement public attention was drawn to the sea. By the use of liquid air it may be that compressed-air sets will be made more handy, while skin-divers may reach even greater depths by using helium gas. Possibly also advances in our knowledge of human physiology will enable us to reach greater depths by the means of drugs and other medicaments. Still, probably no skin-diver will ever be able to go farther down than a hundred fathoms deep.

In his bathysphere Beebe reached a depth of over four hundred and sixty fathoms (exactly nine hundred and twenty-three metres). Piccard in his bathyscaph got down to below two thousand fathoms, or four thousand metres. Practically speaking, however, and for research undertaken throughout the immensity of the oceans, such vehicles as the bathysphere and the bathyscaph are both too clumsy and too costly. There is, indeed, no real need for men themselves to descend into the profundity of the seas. The TV-camera—together with other instruments —can record all we want to discover.

In 1948 I published my scheme for a 'Bathyophthalm'—a device consisting of a number of small spheres in which were fixed a TV-camera, searchlight and a photographic appliance guided by remote control. Acoustical devices, as well as devices for attracting and capturing animals were also to be included. However, it must be admitted that such an apparatus would suffer from the necessity of using a cable.

The ideal thing would be a complete automatic apparatus moving independently and guided by remote control. Indeed, technical progress more and more tends not only to make machines work for us but also to direct them, as with a magician's wand, from afar.

Such an apparatus could have a body in the form of a fish and be fitted with a stereoscopic-colour TV-camera whose pictures are transmitted to the surface without any cable. The apparatus would be guided by remote control and could both emit and receive vibrations and smells. It could move along with the fish in the depths. It could observe them, hunt them and lead them into traps.

Oh, yes, I know that all this is as yet a dream, but one day it may be a reality. But, alas, we do know one thing: if such an apparatus ever is constructed then it would not only watch fish but it would also be used for transporting bombs and thermonuclear weapons.

By the seashore little wavelets lap the strand. Small fish are playing about round a variegated shell. A sea-urchin twirls his prickles. . . .

Seen from the sea what Man can do and what he has become appear quite incredible. For us, of course, our lives and our material progress seem quite normal and natural. From the peep-hole of nature, however, we appear to have gone right off the tracks. With almost unbelievable brutality and presumption we grab for ourselves everything in the realm where we had our origins. We modify everything according to our caprice. Whether, in the last analysis, we are really acting wisely—well, that is another question.

Maybe our new sport has another aspect in addition to those we have talked about up to now, for it takes us, naked as nature made us, back into the domain of nature and among living animals, it puts us into a solitude from which a lot of things in the world above look somewhat different. What we are suffering from today is our ever-increasing divorce from nature. When we are surrounded by the fish and the waving tendrils of sea-plants we may regain a little of our lost humility.

# XARIFA EXPEDITION SHIP

RIGGING

*Area of Sails in Square Metres*

| | |
|---|---|
| Mizzen | 98.50 |
| Mainsail 2 | 130.00 |
| Mainsail 1 | 130.00 |
| Foresail | 66.00 |
| Jib | 65.00 |
| Topsail 2 | 32.50 |
| Topsail 1 | 28.00 |
| Storm Foresail | 35.00 |
| Storm Jib | 34.00 |

## Stays

A. Full sail with topsail.
B. Two reefs in lower sails and storm headsails.
C. Mizzen without reef, no mainsail, normal headsail.

# LIST OF FISHES AND BIRDS

Angel fish: *Holacanthus passer* Valen.

Angel fishes: *Pomacanthus* sp.

Auger shell: *Terebra maculata* Linnæus.

Barracuda: Family *Sphyraenidae.*

Basking shark: *Halsydrus maximus* Gunner.

Black shark: *Carcharinus melanopterus* Quoy and Gaimard.

Blue shark: *Prionace Glauca* (Linnæus).

Bonito or Pelamid: *Sarda* sp.

Brown shark: *Carcharinus* sp.

Butterfly fish: Family *Chaetodontidae.*

Calcareous algae: Genera *Melobesia* and *Lithothamnion.*

Canton shark: *Carcharias* sp.

Coelacanth: *Latimeria chalumnae Smith.*

Cone shell: Genus *Conus.*

Coral crab: *Hapalocarcinus marsupialis* Stimpson.

Coral fish: *Pygoplites diacanthus.*

Cowrie shell: Genus *Cypraea.*

Dolphin: *Delphinus delphis* Linnæus.

Eagle ray: Genus *Aetobatis.*

Feather star: Order *Crinoidea.*

Fire coral: Genus *Millepora.*

Fire fish: *Pterois volitans* Linnæus.

Flightless cormorant: *Nannopterum harrisi* Rothsch.

Frigate bird: Genus *Fregata.*

Galapagos fur seal: *Arctocephalus galapagensis* Heller.

Galapagos hawk: *Buteo galapagensis.*

Galapagos penguin: *Sphenisus mendiculus* Sund.

Galapagos sea lion: *Zalophus wollebaeki* Sivertsen.

Galapagos shark: *Carcharias galapagensis.*

Gannet: Genus *Sula.*

Gar fish: *Belone.*

Garpike: Genus *Scomberesox.*

Giant clam: *Tridacna gigas* Lam.

Giant tortoise: *Testudo ephippium* Günther.

Ginger lilies: *Hedychium gardnerianum.*

Globe fish or puffer fish: Genus *Tetraodon.*

Goby: *Elacatinus oceanops* Jordan.

Gorgonid: *See Gorgonien.*

Great white shark: *Carcharodon carcharias* Linnæus.

Green moray: *Thyrsoidea* sp.

Green turtle: *Chelone mydas* Latr.

Grey nurse shark: *Carcharias arenarius* Ogilby.

Ground finch: Genus *Geospiza.*

Groupers or rock cod: Family *Serranidae,* mostly Genus *Epinephelus* Galapagos *Mycteroperca olfax* Jen.

Hammerhead shark: *Sphyrna* sp.

Hog fish: *Bodianus rufus* Linnæus.

Jack or trevally: *Caranx stellatus* Eydoux and Souleyet.

King mackerel: *Scomberomorus commerson* Lacepede.

Mako shark: *Isuropsis mako* Whitley.

Maulputzer: Maulputzer.

Manta or devil fish: *Manta birostris* Walbaum.

Marine iguana: *Amblyrhynchus cristatus.* Bell.

Mocking bird: Genus *Nesominus.*

Nurse shark: *Ginglymostoma cirratum* Gmelin.

Octopus: *Octopus* sp.

Parrot fish: *See Papageienfische.*

Parrot fishes: Family *Callyodontidae.*

Pearl mussel: *Meleagrina margaritifera* Linnæus.

Pilot fish: *Naucrates ductor* Linnæus.

Porgy: *Pseudopristipoma plagiodesmus* Fowler.

Pork fish: *Anisotremus virginicus* Linnæus.

Pteropods: Order *Pteropoda.*

Rainbow fish: *Thalassoma bifasciatum* Bloch.

Red snapper: *Lutianus* sp.

Reef coral: *Montipora* sp.

Remora or Sucking fish: *Echeneis naucrates* Linné.

Rock cod: *Gramma hemichrysos* Mowbray.

Sea fan: Order *Gorgonaria.*

Skippers or sauries: *Scomberesox.*

Small black-tipped shark: *Carcharinus limbatus* Muller and Henle.

Snapper: *Lutianus argentimaculatus* Forskal.

Sperm whale: *Physeter macrocephalus* Linnæus.

Sting ray: *Dasyatis* sp.

Stone coral: Genus *Madrepora*.

Stone fish: *Synanceja verrucosa* Bloch.

Surgeon fish: *Acanthurus* sp.

Swallow-tailed gull: *Creagrus furcatus* Neboux.

Tern: Genus *Sterna*.

Tessellated moray: *Lycodontis tessellata* Richardson.

Thistle coral: *Seriatopora* sp.

Tiger shark: *Galeocerdo cuvier* (Le Sueur).

Trigger fishes: Family *Balistidae*.

Trumpet fish: *Aulostomus maculatus* Val.

Unicorn fish: *Naso unicornis* Forskal.

Wedge-tailed shearwater: *Puffinus pacificus* Gmelin.

Whale shark: *Rhincodon typus* Smith.

Whaler shark: *Galeolamna* sp.

Whitefin shark: *Carcharias platyrhynchus* Gilbert.

White-tipped shark: *Carcharinus* sp.

Wobbegong or carpet shark: *Crossorhinus barbatus* Lacep.

Wrasses: Family *Labridae*.

Yellow-tailed spinefoot: *Xesurus laticlavius* Valen.

# BIBLIOGRAPHY

*A. Books and Sources Quoted.*

BREDER, C. M. *Field Book of Marine Fishes of the Atlantic Coast.* New York, Putnam, 1948.

COOPER, G. *Das Gold der Jahrtausende.* Zürich, Benziger & Co., 1953.

DAKIN, W. J. *Australian Seashores.* Sydney and London, Angus & Robertson, 1952.

DARWIN, CHARLES. *A Naturalist's Voyage Round the World in H.M.S. Beagle.* London, Everyman, Dent & Co.

DOYLE, A. C. *Heaven Has Claws.* London, John Murray, 1952.

GWYTHER, J. *First Voyage.* London, Andrew Melrose, 1954.

HEDGES, F. A. M. *Battles with Giant Fish.* Duckworth, 1925.

NORMAN, J. R. *A History of Fishes.* London, Ernest Benn, 1934.

ROGERS, J. E. *The Shell Book.* Boston, Mass., Branford, 1936.

ROUGHLEY, T. C. *Fish and Fisheries of Australia.* Sydney and London, Angus & Robertson, 1951.

ROUGHLEY, T. C. *Wonders of the Great Barrier Reef.* Sydney and London, Angus & Robertson, 1951.

SMITH, J. L. B. *The Sea Fishes of Southern Africa.* Union of South Africa, Central News Agency, 1953.

YONGE, C. M. *A Year on the Great Barrier Reef.* New York and London, Putnam, 1930.

YOUNG, W. E. *Shark! Shark!* London, Hurst & Blackett, 1933.

*B. Special Books Relating to Diving.*

BARTON, OTIS. *Adventure.* London and New York, Longmans, 1954.

BECK, ALBRECHT. *Tauchkunst der moderne Sport.* Munich, Braun und Schneider, 1952.

BEEBE, CHARLES WILLIAM. *Galapagos, World's End.* Putnam, 1924.

BEEBE, CHARLES WILLIAM. *The Arcturus Adventure.* Putnam, 1926.

BEEBE, CHARLES WILLIAM. *Half Mile Down.* N. Y. Zoological Society, New York, 1934.

BEEBE, CHARLES WILLIAM. *Zaca Venture.* John Lane, 1938.

CARRIER, RICK AND BARBARA. *Dive.* New York, Wilfred Funk, 1955.

CLARK, EUGENIE. *Lady with a Spear.* New York, Harpers, 1951. Heinemann, 1954.

CLARKE, A. C. *The Coast of Coral.* London, Frederick Muller, 1956.

COUSTEAU, J. Y. *The Silent World.* London, Hamish Hamilton, 1953.

COUSTEAU, J. Y., TAILLEZ, P., AND DUMAS, F. *Par Dix-huit Métres de Fond,* Paris, Durel, 1946.

CRILE, JANE AND BARNEY. *Treasure Diving Holidays.* London, Collins, 1954.

CROSS, E. R. *Under-water Photography and Television.* New York, Expositions Press, 1954.

DAVIS, ROBERT H. *Deep Diving and Submarine Operations.* London, St. Catherine's Press, 1935.

DIOLÉ, PHILIPPE. *The Undersea Adventure.* Sedgwick & Jackson, 1953. *L'Aventure Sous-Marine.* Paris, Albin Michel, 1951.

DIOLÉ, PHILIPPE. *Promenades d'Archéologie Sous-Marine.* Paris, Albin Michel, 1952.

DUGAN, JAMES. *Man Explores the Sea.* London, Hamish Hamilton, 1956.

FOUCHER-CRETEAU, R. *L'Aventure est sous la Mer.* Paris, Librairie des Champs-Elysées, 1955.

GILPATRIC, GUY. *The Complete Goggler.* New York, Dodd, 1938. John Lane, 1939.

GORSKY, BERNARD. *Dix Metres sous la Mer.* Paris, Plon, 1946. *Mediterranean Hunter.* Souvenir Press, London, 1954.

GORSKY, BERNARD. *La Jungle du Silence.* Paris, Pensée Moderne, 1947.

GORSKY, BERNARD. *Le Tour du Monde de la Chasse Sous-Marine.* Paris, Pensée Moderne, 1956.

HASS, HANS. *Jagd unter Wasser.* Stuttgart, Franksche Verlagsanstalt, 1939.

HASS, HANS. *Unter Korallen und Haien.* Berlin, Ullstein, 1942.

HASS, HANS. *Photojagd am Meeresgrund.* Seebruck, Heering-Verlag, 1943.

HASS, HANS. *Drei Jäger auf dem Meeresgrund.* Zürich, Orell Füssli, 1947. (English: *Diving to Adventure.* London, Jarrolds, 1952.)

HASS, HANS. *Menschen und Haie.* Zürich, Orell-Füssli, 1949. (English: *Men and Sharks.* London, Jarrolds, 1954.)

HASS, HANS. *Manta.* Berlin, Ullstein, 1952. (English: *Under the Red Sea.* London, Jarrolds, 1952.)

HASS, HANS. *Ich photographierte in den sieben Meeren.* Seebruck, Heering-Verlag, 1954. (English: *I Photographed Under the Seven Seas.* London, Jarrolds, 1956.)

HEBERLEIN, H. *Einsame Inseln.* Zürich, Orell-Füssli, 1956.

ISY-SCHWART, MARCEL. *Hunting Big Fish.* London, Burke, 1954.

IVANOVIC, VANE. *Modern Spearfishing.* London, Nicholas Kaye, 1954.

IVANOVIC, VANE. *Sub-Marine Spearfishing.* London, Nicholas Kaye, 1954.

KENYON, LEY. *Undersea World.* London, Collins, 1956.

LABAT, PIERRE. *The Marvellous Kingdom.* London, Odhams, 1956.

LARSEN, EGON. *Men under the Sea.* London, Phoenix House, 1955.

LATIL, PIERRE DE, and RIVOIRE, JEAN. *Man and the Under-water World.* London, Jarrolds, 1956.

OWEN, D. M. *A Manual for Free-Divers.* London and New York, Pergamon Press, 1955.

PROSPERI, FRANCO. *Matea Mora.* Milan, Garzanti, 1953. *Lord of the Sharks.* Hutchinson, 1955.

QUILICI, FOLCO. *The Blue Continent.* New York, Rinehart & Co., 1954. Weidenfeld & Nicolson, 1954.

REBIKOFF, DIMITRI. *Exploration Sous-Marine.* Paris, Arthaud, 1952. *Free Diving.* Sedgwick & Jackson, 1955.

SCHENCK, H. V., and KENDALL, H. W. *Shallow Water Diving and Spearfishing.* Cambridge, 1950. Cornell Maritime Press.

SCHENCK, H. V., and KENDALL, H. W. *Under-water Photography.* Cambridge, 1954. Cornell Maritime Press.

SMALL, PETER. *Your Guide to Underwater Adventure.* London, Lutterworth Press, 1957.

STELZNER, HERMANN. *Tauchertechnik.* Lübeck, Charles Coleman, 1943.

SWEENEY, J. *Skin-diving and Exploring Under Water.* London, Frederick Muller, 1956.

TAILLEZ, PHILLIPPE. *Plongés sans Cables.* Paris, Arthaud, 1954. *To Hidden Depths.* Wm. Kimber, 1954.

TAZIEFF, HAROUN. *L'Eau et le Feu.* Paris, Arthaud, 1954.

THOMPSON, F. E. *Diving, Cutting and Welding in Under-water Salvage Operations.* New York, Cornell Maritime Press, 1944.

VANDERKOGEL, A., and LARDNER, R. *Under-water Sport.* New York, Henri Holt, 1955.


*C. Articles in Scientific Publications.*

ANKEL, W. E. *Schwimmtauchen als Methode der Zoologie.* Giessener Hochschulblätter, Part 4, 1953.

ANKEL, W. E. *Pottwalfang bei den Azoren.* Orion, Munich, No. 15–16, pp. 604–613, 1955.

COPPLESON, V. M. 'Shark Attacks in Australian Waters.' *Medical Journal of Australia*, 15th April, 1953, p. 449.

COPPLESON, V. M. 'A Review of Shark Attacks in Australian Waters since 1919.' *Medical Journal of Australia*, 4th November, 1950, pp. 680–688.

COUSTEAU, J. Y. 'Exploring Davy Jones' Locker with Calypso.' *National Geographic Magazine*, Vol. 109. No. 2, pp. 149–161, 1956.

EIBL-EIBESFELDT, I. *Über die Galapagos-Expedition 1953–54 des Institutes für Submarine Forschung.* Publications of the Max Planck-Gesellschaft, No. 5, pp. 276–280, 1954.

EIBL-EIBESFELDT, I. *Einige Bemerkungen über den Galapagos-Seelöwen, Zalophus wollebaeki Sivertsen.* 'Säugetierkundliche Mitteilungen', Vol. 3, pp. 101–105, 1955.

EIBL-EIBESFELDT, I. *'Ethologische Studien am Galapagos-Seelöwen, Zalophus wollebaeki Sivertsen.'* Zeitschrift für Tierpsychologie, Vol. 12, No. 2, pp. 286–303, 1955.

EIBL-EIBESFELDT, I. *'Über Symbiosen, Parasitismus und andere besondere zwischenartliche Beziebungen topischer Meeresfische.'* Zeitschrift für Tierpsychologie, Vol. 12, No. 2, pp. 203–219, 1955.

EIBL-EIBESFELDT, I. *'Der Kommentkampf der Meerechse (Amblyrynchus cristatus Bell) nebst einigen Notizen zur Biologie dieser Art.'* Zeitschrift für Tierpsychologie, Vol. 12, No. 1, pp. 49–62, 1955.

EIBL-EIBESFELDT, I. *'Das bedrohte Tierparadies der Galapagos-Inseln. Über die Notwendigkeit wirksamer Schutzmassnahmen.'* Natur und Volk, Vol. 86, No. 5, pp. 145–157, 1956.

FLECKER, H. 'Fatal Sting to North Queensland Bathers.' *Medical Journal of Australia*, 12th January, 1952, p. 35.

FLECKER, H. 'Irukandji Sting to North Queensland Bathers without Production of Weals but with severe General Symptoms.' *Medical Journal of Australia*, 19th July, 1952, p. 89.

GRIFFIN, D. R. 'Hearing and Acoustic Orientation in Marine Mammals.' Papers on Marine Biology and Oceanography, Supplement to Vol. 3 of *Deep Sea Research*, London, pp. 406–416, 1955.

GUDGER, E. W. 'Oviparity—the Mode of Reproduction of the Whale Shark, *Rhinodon typicus.' Copeia*, No. 4, 1952.

HASS, HANS. *'Beiträge zur Kenntnis der Reteporiden mit besonderer Berücksichtigung der Formbildungsgesetze ihrer Zoarien und einem Bericht über die darbei angewandte neue Methode für Untersuchungen auf dem Meeresgrund.'* Zoologica, Stuttgart, Vol. 57, No. 101, pp. 1–138, 1948.

LLANO, G. A. *Airmen against the Sea.* ADTIC Publication (Alabama), G–104.

MANTON, S. M. 'Ecological Surveys of Coral Reefs.' Great Barrier Reef Expedition, 1928–1929, Scientific Reports, Vol. 3, No. 10, 1955.

MARDEN, LOUIS. 'Camera under the Sea.' *National Geographic Magazine,* Vol. 109, No. 2, pp. 162–200, 1956.

MCNEILL, F. A., and POPE, E. C. 'A Venomous Medusa from Australian Water.' *Australian Journal of Science,* Vol. 5, No. 6, pp. 188–191, 1943.

SCHEER, GEORG. '*Galapagos-Expedition des Internationalen Insitutes für Submarine Forschung.*' *Vaduz,* Praktische Schulphysik. Year 31, No. 1–2, 1955.

SCHEER, GEORG. '*Darwin und die Galapagos-Inseln.*' Orion, Munich, Year 10, No. 17–18, pp. 705–713, 1955.

SCHEER, GEORG. '*Über Messungen der Dämmerunghelligkeit auf einigen Inseln im Atlantik und Pazifik.*' *Meteorologische Rundschau,* 8th Year, No. 5–6, pp. 453–460, 1955.

SCHEER, GEORG. '*Die Indianer der San Blas Inseln.*' *Kosmos* 51, No. 10, pp. 453–460, 1955.

TRIEBEL, E. '*Brackwasser-Ostracoden von den Galapagos-Inseln.*' *Senck. Biol.* Vol. 37, No. 5–6, pp. 447–467.

WHITLEY, G. P. 'Shark Attacks in Western Australia.' *Western Australian Naturalist,* Vol. 2, No. 8, pp. 185–194, 1951.


*Periodical Publications devoted to Under-water Sport and Research.*

*Australian Skin Diving and Spear Fishing News.* Under-water Spear-fishermen's Association of N.S.W., 214, Bedford Street, Sydney, Australia.

*Delphin.* Ristau & Co., Heilwigstrasse 118, Hamburg, 20, Germany.

*L'Eau et la Vie Sous-Marine,* 1, rue de la Haye, Tangier.

*L'Aventure Sous-Marine,* 46, rue Bichat, Paris (Xe), France.

*Neptune.* Journal of the British Sub-Aqua Club, 16, Beverley Gardens, London, S.W. 13.

*Pescasport,* Galleria Mazzini, 7–1, Genoa, Italy.

*Spearfishing Sportlight.* Under-water Skin-divers' and Fishermen's Association of Western Australia, 20, Dyson Street, South Perth, Australia.

*The Deep Sea Digest.* Oceanic Research Associates, Box 333, Miami, Florida, U.S.A.

*The Skin-diver.* P.O. Box 128, Lynwood, California, U.S.A.

# Index